Psychoanalysis Online 4

Psychoanalysis Online 4: Teleanalytic Practice, Teaching, and Clinical Research brings a systematic, qualitative research perspective to the question of the effectiveness of teletherapy, teleanalysis, and teleteaching. It suggests that, contrary to some traditional arguments, effective treatment, teaching, and supervision can take place remotely; that affect and imagination are more important than physical presence.

Providing theories of therapeutic action as well as philosophical reflections, the book features examples of online clinical cases, including crisis intervention by email, and aims to stimulate openness to innovation, responsible process and review. Each contributor presents their clinical qualitative research and survey study findings. The Bernardi Three-Level Model, developed for assessing therapeutic change in the traditional analytic setting, is applied to the study of teleanalysis with various patients. It is found that, in videoconference or even in email communication, the sense of closeness in the therapeutic encounter does not depend on physical proximity but on integrity and commitment.

The book concludes with research findings on the effectiveness of videoconference compared to in-the-classroom settings for teaching psychodynamics, supervising psychotherapy, and conducting psychotherapy with Chinese students. It will be of great interest to a variety of professionals and researchers who practise remotely, with particular relevance for those situated in the fields of psychoanalysis and psychotherapy.

Jill Savege Scharff, MD, FABP (USA) is an adult and child psychoanalyst, co-founder of the International Psychotherapy Institute (IPI) and the International Institute for Psychoanalytic Training (IIPT), and author and editor of books on object relations, individual, couple and family therapy, including *The Interpersonal Unconscious and Psychoanalysis Online* Volumes 1, 2 and 3 (Karnac).

Library of Technology and Mental Health
Series Editor: Jill Savege Scharff, M.D.

Psychoanalysis Online 4

Teleanalytic Practice, Teaching, and Clinical Research

Edited by Jill Savege Scharff

Routledge
Taylor & Francis Group

LONDON AND NEW YORK

First published 2019
by Routledge
2 Park Square, Milton Park, Abingdon, Oxon OX14 4RN

and by Routledge
711 Third Avenue, New York, NY 10017

Routledge is an imprint of the Taylor & Francis Group, an informa business

British Library Cataloguing-in-Publication Data
A catalogue record for this book is available from the British Library

Library of Congress Cataloging-in-Publication Data
A catalog record has been requested for this book

ISBN: 978-1-138-31241-8 (hbk)
ISBN: 978-1-138-31242-5 (pbk)
ISBN: 978-0-429-45824-8 (ebk)

Typeset in Times New Roman
by Apex CoVantage, LLC

Dedicated to Coco and Ethan, Emme and Hank

Contents

Permissions and acknowledgements

Chapter 1 "Assessing the scope and practice of teleanalysis: Preliminary research findings", describes the first phase of a project of the International Psychotherapy Institute and Westminster College. The author Janine Wanlass wishes to thank the International Psychoanalytical Association for financial support for the research project and for the opportunity to present an early version of the findings at the IPA Congress in Boston (2015). She expresses her thanks and deep gratitude to research team members Jill Savege Scharff, MD, Caroline M. Sehon, MD, Ellen Behrens, PhD, and Jennifer Simonds, PhD, whose contributions were invaluable and without whom this project would not exist; to Ryan Garcia, PhD, Lea Setton, PhD, and Nancy Pratt, CMHC, who provided translation assistance for the questionnaire; and to participants in the International Teleanalysis Working Group, Becky Bailey, PhD, Ernest Wallwork, PhD, Yolanda de Varela, PhD, Lea Setton, PhD, Nancy Bakalar, MD, and David Scharff, MD, who helped pilot the questionnaire and provided thoughtful clinical reactions to the research effort.

Chapter 3 "Sadomasochistic constellation and distance analysis" consists of an unpublished paper by Jack Novick given during a panel at the FEPAL Congress in Cartagena, September 2016, with a commentary by Carlos Ernesto Barredo, one of the panellists, and translated into English by the editor.

For Chapter 5 "Psychoanalytic process in cyber-technology", Asbed Aryan wants to acknowledge the support of his colleagues Liliana Manguel, Ricardo Carlino and the Clinical Research in Distance Analysis Study Group in Buenos Aires; Jill Scharff who helped with translation, Caroline Sehon and the International Teleanalysis Working Group; Ricardo Bernardi, Marina Altmann and the 3LM Group; and Delia Aryan, his wife.

Chapter 7 "Technology and private practice" is modified from a paper published in *British Journal of Psychotherapy* (2017) by Vincent, C., Barnett, M., Killpack, L., Sehgal, A. and Swinden, P. (2017). "Advancing telecommunication technology and its impact on psychotherapy in private practice" © 2017 Reprinted with permission of Wiley.

Chapter 8 "Research on teaching, supervision and psychotherapy using videoconference technology" is modified from a paper that first appeared in

Psychodynamic Psychiatry (2015) by Gordon, R. M., Wang, X., and Tune, J. "Comparing psychodynamic teaching, supervision and psychotherapy over video-conferencing technology with Chinese students" © 2015. Reprinted with permission of The Guilford Press.

Chapter 9 "The effect of distance training on the development of psychodynamic psychotherapists" is modified from a paper that first appeared in *Psychodynamic Psychiatry* (2017) by Gordon, R. M., and Lan, J. "Assessing distance training: How well does it produce psychoanalytic psychotherapists?" © 2017 Reprinted with permission of The Guilford Press.

Chapters 8 and 9 describe the first and second phases of a research project undertaken with the China American Psychoanalytic Alliance (CAPA). Robert Gordon, the senior author, wishes to acknowledge that the research described therein was approved by the IRB of the Washington Center of Psychoanalysis and was supported by a grant from CAPA. He and his co-authors thank Drs. Elise Snyder, Ira Moses, Cathy Siebold, Ralph Fishkin, Lana Fishkin, and Jill Savege Scharff for their invaluable feedback, and Marieke Jonkman for help with editing.

Chapter 10 "Psychoanalytic teaching by video link and telephone" first appeared in *Journal of the American Psychoanalytic Association* (2015) by David E. Scharff "Psychoanalytic teaching by video link and telephone" © 2015. Reprinted by permission of the managing editor and the *Journal of the American Psychoanalytic Association.*

I want to thank all the contributors, the members of the International Teleanalysis Working Group at the International Psychotherapy Institute; attendees at the various panels and precongress workshops on teleanalysis held at the International Psychoanalytical Association Congresses in Chicago, Mexico City, Boston, and Buenos Aires; and the members of the New Technologies Study Group led by Dan Jacobs at the American Psychoanalytic Association for their interest in and contribution to the pool of ideas. The use of technology to assist therapists and analysts to reach patients and train colleagues who live far from qualified clinicians and teachers is still highly controversial and we desperately need to study its effectiveness compared to traditional tried and tested methods. I am grateful to clinicians who take the risk of exploring innovative methods and who also have the expertise to conduct research.

There are many others to whom I am grateful. Of special mention are Angela Moorman and Maribel Cano, who keep the wheels in motion on the home front; Anna Innes, the indefatigable administrator at the International Psychotherapy Institute, who enables me to continue my teaching and administrative duties while also taking time to write; and my husband David, who supports my efforts in every way and helps me weather the unexpected, as when, while this book was in preparation under the guidance of Oliver Rathbone and Rod Tweedy at Karnac, the publishing house entered a period of transition.

I have been happy to write and edit for Oliver and Rod, and I'm incredibly grateful that Oliver had the vision to establish the series Technology and Mental Health, and personally glad that he asked me to edit it, thus encouraging awareness of and thinking about the impact of technology on development and on the practice of psychotherapy and psychoanalysis in the digital age. Although I don't relish the change, I can't imagine an easier transition than one to Routledge, where the senior editor, Kate Hawes, who has taken over the Karnac list, is well known to me from previous work. I am grateful that she not only honoured the Karnac acceptance of my proposal for *Psychoanalysis 4* and issued a contract, but that she will continue the Library of Technology and Mental Health, the series in which the previous volumes of *Psychoanalysis Online, 1, 2 and 3* have been published along with titles from other international writers of various perspectives. It is with gratitude and affection that I look back on my time as a Karnac author and now look forward to an equally fruitful collaboration with Kate Hawes, Russell George, Charles Bath, and others at Routledge.

About the editor and contributors

Asbed Aryan (Argentina) (sadly deceased Monday July 16, 2018) psychiatrist, full member of Buenos Aires Psychoanalytic Association (APdeBA), International Psychoanalytic Association (IPA) and Latin-American Psychoanalytic Federation (FEPAL); training analyst of APdeBA, FEPAL and IPA for Armenia; and child and adolescent specialist of APdeBA, FEPAL, and IPA.

Mary Barnett (UK) individual and couple psychotherapist registered with the British Psychoanalytic Council (through the Tavistock Institute of Medical Psychology); formerly with the National Health Service and the University of Sussex psychological services; maintains a private practice in Brighton; special interest in psychotherapy research and in the application of an attachment perspective to clinical work and organisational functioning.

Carlos Ernesto Barredo (Argentina) training and supervising analyst and former president of the Psychoanalytic Association of Buenos Aires (2006–2010); former scientific chair of FEPAL (2010–2012); and formerly representative from Latin America on the Board of the International Psychoanalytical Association (2013–2017).

Betty Benaim PhD (Panama, RP) IPA training and supervising analyst, Panama City, Panama RP; supervising analyst, the International Institute for Psychoanalytic Training at the International Psychotherapy Institute in Chevy Chase MD, USA.

Sharon Zalusky Blum PhD (USA) Senior faculty member, New Center for Psychoanalysis in Los Angeles; adjunct supervising analyst, International Institute for Psychoanalytic Training, Chevy Chase MD; psychologist and psychoanalyst in private practice in Los Angeles; prolific author on telephone analysis and the impact of technology on analytic practice.

Robert M. Gordon PhD, ABPP (USA) Diplomate of Clinical Psychology and a Diplomate of Psychoanalysis; formerly on the governing council of the American Psychological Association, president of the Pennsylvania Psychological Association and recipient of its Distinguished Service Award, elected

Honorary Member of the American Psychoanalytic Association; author of many scholarly articles and books in the areas of ethics, the MMPI-2, psychotherapy, relationships, forensic psychology, personality assessment, diagnoses, the Psychodynamic Diagnostic Manual, a PDM-2; editor, researcher, and co-author of the Psychodiagnostic Chart; in consulting practice, Allentown, PA.

Horst Kächele, MD, PhD (Germany) Professor, International Psychoanalytic University Berlin (2010–), formerly Chair, Department of Psychosomatic Medicine and Psychotherapy at the Faculty of Medicine, Ulm University (1997–2009); specialist in psychosomatic medicine; psychoanalyst; researcher in psychoanalytic process and outcome, psychosomatics, clinical and neuro-biological aspects of attachment, and error in psychotherapy; collaborator in the single case archive, Department of Psychology at Ghent University; and co-author with H. Thomä of the three volume *Textbook of Psychoanalytic Therapy*, now in more than fourteen language.

Louisa Killpack (UK) psychoanalytic psychotherapist registered with the United Kingdom Council for Psychotherapy (through her membership of the Association of Group and Individual Psychotherapy); formerly with the National Health Service and now maintains a private practice on the Isle of Wight, Hampshire; special interest in working with borderline personality disorder and patients with chronic physical pain.

Jing Lan, PhD (China) licensed psychotherapist, trained in MFT (Marriage and Family Therapy) programme in Beijing Normal University (Beijing, China) and The Family Institute of Northwestern University; training in psychodynamic psychotherapy through CAPA (China American Psychoanalytic Alliance) since 2011; research interests in couple relationships and therapeutic process.

Liliana Manguel (Argentina) psychoanalyst, full member of Buenos Aires Psychoanalytic Association (APdeBA), International Psychoanalytic Association (IPA) and Latin-American Psychoanalytic Federation (FEPAL); training and supervising analyst, Buenos Aires Psychoanalytic Association; teaching analyst at the University Institute of Mental Health (IUSAM); Professor, Masters programme in Psychopathology and Mental Health; Director of the Extension Department at the University Institute of Mental Health (IUSAM); in private practice of psychoanalysis, psychotherapy, and teleanalysis with adolescents, adults, couples, and families; member of the International Teleanalysis Clinical Research Group.

Jack Novick, PhD (USA) certified child, adolescent and adult psychoanalyst; President, Association for Child Psychoanalysis; APsaA representative to IPA Board; training and supervising analyst, International Psychoanalytical Association; supervising analyst, Michigan Psychoanalytic Institute; adjunct supervising analyst, Combined Programme in Child Analysis and Child

Psychotherapy at the International Psychotherapy Institute; in private practice of child and adult analysis in Ann Arbor, Michigan; special interest in work with parents.

David E. Scharff, MD, FABP (USA) Chair of the Board, Co-Founder and Former Director, International Psychotherapy Institute; Chair, The International Psychoanalytic Association's Committee on Family and Couple Psychoanalysis; Clinical Professor of Psychiatry, Uniformed Services University of the Health Sciences and Georgetown University; Supervising Analyst, International Institute for Psychoanalytic Training; Teaching Analyst, Washington Psychoanalytic Institute; Author and editor of more than 30 books and numerous articles; Director of distance learning courses in China and Russia. He is a child and adult analyst in private practice in Chevy Chase, Maryland.

Jill Savege Scharff, MD, FABP (USA) adult and child psychiatrist, fellow of the American Board of Psychoanalysis, certified adult and child analyst of the American Psychoanalytic Association (APsaA) and of the International Psychoanalytic Association (IPA), co-founder of the International Psychotherapy Institute (IPI), founder and supervising analyst of the International Institute for Psychoanalytic Training (IIPT), author and editor of books on object relations individual, couple and family therapy including *The Interpersonal Unconscious,* and *Psychoanalysis Online, volumes 1, 2 and 3* (Karnac).

Amita Sehgal MA, PhD (UK) couple psychoanalytic psychotherapist registered with the British Psychoanalytic Council (through the Tavistock Institute of Medical Psychology); Visiting Lecturer at Tavistock Relationships; Consultant Psychotherapist at The Balint Consultancy; maintains a private practice in London; special interests in the neurobiology of contemporary attachment perspectives in couple psychotherapy, collaborative separation and divorce, consultation to family lawyers; author in the field of couple psychotherapy.

Caroline M. Sehon, MD, FABP (USA) Chair and supervising analyst, International Institute for Psychoanalytic Training (IIPT) at IPI; Chair, IIPT Tele-analysis Clinical Research Group; psychoanalyst, adult and child psychiatrist; member of the American Psychoanalytic Association (APsaA) and the International Psychoanalytical Association (IPA); and author of publications on object relations individual, couple and family therapy including chapters in *Psychoanalysis Online, volumes 1, 2 and 3* (Karnac).

Penni Swinden (UK) psychoanalytic psychotherapist registered with the British Psychoanalytic Council (through the Psychotherapy Foundation for her work with individuals and the Tavistock Society of Psychotherapist for her work with couples); formerly with the National Health Service; background in teaching and counselling administration; supervisor and a Visiting Lecturer at the Tavistock Centre in London; maintains a private practice in Hampshire and London.

Jane Tune, MS (China) clinical psychologist with a Masters in Psychology, working at the Green House Clinic in ShenZhen; in psychotherapy training at CiDu psychotherapy training company of China.

Christopher Vincent (UK) psychoanalytic couple psychotherapist registered with the British Psychoanalytic Council (through the Tavistock Institute of Medical Psychology); Consultant Visiting Lecturer at the Tavistock Relationships, London; member, the Mental Health Research Group in the Faculty of Health Sciences at The University of Southampton; maintains a private practice in Hayling Island, Hampshire; special interest in the interface between psycho-social research methods and psychoanalysis, regarding the support and treatment of couples where one partner has a chronic illness.

Xiubing (Summer) Wang, MS (China) candidate in analytic training, Chicago Institute for Psychoanalysis; in private practice of adult psychotherapy in ShenZhen, Guangdong province, China; researcher on psychotherapy and psychoanalysis in China.

Janine Wanlass, PhD (USA) Director, International Psychotherapy Institute (IPI), Chevy Chase MD; Professor and founding chair, Department of Counseling, Westminster College, Salt Lake City, Utah USA; faculty member, IPI psychoanalytic couple therapy videoconference course; faculty member, the continuous course in couple, child and family therapy in Beijing, China and Moscow, Russia; psychoanalyst and psychologist in private practice, treating children, adults, couples, and families; researcher on technology in psychotherapy and psychoanalysis, clinical applications of object relations theory, and treatment of trauma.

Introduction

Psychoanalysis Online 4 begins with a research study into the use of technology in clinical treatment and moves on to examples of clinical teleanalytic treatment in various settings, most of which include a clinical research focus. The book concludes with chapters on research into the use of technology in supervision and seminar teaching of psychoanalytic theory and practice nationally and internationally.

Janine Wanlass presents the results of a questionnaire to explore the nature and scope of teleanalytic practice and its comparison to traditional in-the-office psychoanalysis in the experience of analysts' world-wide, part one of a longer project. Internationally respected researcher Horst Kächele gives his commentary on this questionnaire survey and is particularly appreciative of the rich descriptions in the narrative content. After Betty Benaim illustrates with extensive process notes the use of teleanalysis as a temporary setting to maintain continuity of care for a young woman injured while in long-term treatment, she and Jill Savege Scharff discuss the interaction of technology and unconscious dynamics. The clinical discussion moves from the situation of this young adult woman to that of a young adult man, as Jack Novick presents his thoughts on distance analysis of an 18 year old with a sadomasochistic constellation, followed by commentaries from South and North America by Carlos Ernesto Barredo and Caroline M. Sehon, dealing with the role of the internal father and the negative transference, the impact of the anal stage of development, and attacks on the frame that enact the transference. Asbed Aryan presents process notes from the teleanalysis of a an obsessive and yet reckless male patient with remnants of childhood psychosis, and then examines this teleanalytic material using the Bernardi Three-Level Model, developed for assessing therapeutic change in the traditional analytic setting. Applying the same 3 L-M model in her clinical research, Liliana Manguel takes a second look at her work with a secretive woman patient who cuts her ties to place and person but connects to Liliana on her own terms, namely by insisting on distance analysis. For these two authors, the sense of closeness does not depend on physical proximity but on an encounter of integrity and commitment. That value is demonstrated in the chapter by Horst Kächele, and in the commentary by Sharon Zalusky Blum, on case study research into the effectiveness of a therapeutic alliance initiated on email communication. In the next chapter, Christopher Vincent, Mary Barnett, Louisa Killpack, Amita Sehgal, and Penni Swinden portray the effects of new videoconference technology on private practice, to which David Scharff adds his commentary, developing their remarks on the relationship between the technology-assisted frame and content. In the penultimate pair of chapters, Robert Gordon, Xiubing Wang, Jane Tune, and Jing Lan present their findings on the effectiveness of videoconference compared to in-the-room settings for teaching psychodynamics, supervising psychotherapy and conducting psychotherapy with Chinese students, followed by Janine Wanlass's commentaries, reflecting on their hypotheses about the effectiveness of supervision, teaching and treatment conducted remotely and about how psychoanalytically oriented distance training transfers to subsequent clinical work. Lastly, David E. Scharff explores and illustrates the particular teaching technique, opportunity, and group dynamics he experienced in videoconference settings for teaching psychoanalytic theory and application.

In *Psychoanalysis Online 1, 2, and 3* contributors focused their lens on close examination of clinical process to address the impact of technology on development and mental health, describe the teleanalytic setting, and illustrate the technique of technology-mediated psychotherapy and psychoanalysis whether by telephone, Skype, or secure videoconference. *Psychoanalysis Online 4* brings a systematic qualitative research perspective to further inquiry into the effectiveness of teletherapy and teleanalysis. Providing philosophical reflections, theories of therapeutic action, and clinical examples for discussion of actual clinical work online including crisis intervention on email, this volume hopes to stimulate controversy, openness to innovation, responsible process and review, and forward thinking.

Some argue that if the body of the patient and the body of the therapist are not present in the same room, any so-called therapy taking place in cyberspace cannot be real. But for those who have done it – and described the experience as Anderson, Benaim, and Varela did in the first *Psychoanalysis Online* – it certainly feels real, and their treatment was assisted by no more than competent and secure audiovisual connection. Already we have the possibility of virtual reality, which refers to an artificial environment which is experienced through sensory stimuli picked up by two of the five senses, sights and sounds provided by computer software, and gloves and helmet. In everyday life, virtual reality is accepted as a major step forward in shrinking distance and expanding awareness of other types of being, civilization, culture, and habitat. Our resulting actions are determined by, and determine, what happens in the environment. But in psychoanalysis and psychotherapy the reaction has been mixed. So what if images sent by drone to your office can now transport you to the desert, and with a turn of your office chair you can look all around as if you were there? Some colleagues would argue that if your body is not there you won't actually be hot. Others will counter that you may well feel hot because of associations to various cues that signal heat. And your pulse may quicken at the sight of an oasis. We do not yet have *customized* virtual reality, available from an office computer, but when it arrives we will be as accustomed to communicating in virtual reality as we are now with audiovisual technology. Still some will say that therapy using virtual reality is not the real thing. Certainly you and your patient are not there physically, but you are very much there in terms of affect and imagination, as you are in an analysis of the traditional variety.

Virtual reality and psychoanalysis share a common root: both have to do with the process of becoming something beyond yourself as currently configured. Indeed both are truly virtual.

Chapter 1

Assessing the scope and practice of teleanalysis
Preliminary research findings

Janine Wanlass

Technological advances, the increasing mobility of the work force, financial constraints, and use of social networking media to traverse geographically distant spaces are changing the worlds of the analysands we treat. In concert with these rapid sociocultural changes, greater numbers of psychoanalysts are utilizing technology to maintain contact with their analysands, providing sessions by telephone, Skype, or video connection systems to sustain the frequency, depth, and continuity of psychoanalytic treatment. Additionally, technology provides potential access to analytic treatment for analysands who reside in areas where analytic training and experienced analysts are absent, opening a world of possibility and greater choice in treatment options. While some construe the incorporation of technology in analytic treatment as progress, others voice criticism that technology compromises analytic process and interferes with the development of transference dynamics. These are interesting speculations; however, little is known about the practice and experience of "teleanalysis", or conducting psychoanalysis through the assistance of the telephone or other high quality video connection system. For the purposes of this research project, teleanalysis refers to a psychoanalyst engaging a patient in analytic treatment at a minimum of three times weekly with at least some portion of their analytic sessions occurring through the use of technology.

Although some anecdotal reports exist about teleanalysis practice (Leffert, 2003; Lindon, 2000; Scharff, 2010, 2011, 2012, 2013a, 2013b), empirical studies are relatively scarce in the psychoanalytic literature (Gordon, Wang, & Tune, 2015). With this deficit in mind, a research group composed of psychoanalysts and academic researchers designed a three-stage research project to assess the scope and practice of teleanalysis, funded in part by a research grant from the International Psychoanalytical Association (IPA) and approved by the Institutional Review Board (IRB) at Westminster College. In gathering research team members, care was taken to include psychoanalysts familiar with psychoanalytic theory and technique and researchers with established expertise in clinical research methodology.

In this chapter, I will present the preliminary findings from stage one of this research effort, involving analysis of questionnaire data from IPA analysts and candidates about their use of technology in clinical practice. Additionally, I will outline our plan for stage two of this research, where we will gather interview data from a subset of the responders to stage one. This qualitative research component will expand our understanding of the quantitative findings. The last stage of our intended research effort incorporates outcome data from analysands, a much more complex enterprise still in the planning stage at this point in time. Drawing from the data gleaned in stage one, this chapter concludes with a discussion of the study limitations and implications for further research and clinical training in the teleanalysis field.

Research question

What is the nature and scope of teleanalysis practice? Describing the characteristics of current teleanalysis practice represented the first step in our research process. To address this question, we gathered descriptive data about how, where, and by whom teleanalysis is currently practised. Specific areas of interest in our investigation were drawn from discussions in an ongoing Teleanalysis Study Group, hosted by the International Institute for Psychoanalytic Training (IIPT) and originally an international working group of the IPA (Scharff, 2011).

In our research, we expected to find that technology was frequently used to conduct analysis, with combined in-office and remote sessions appearing more commonly than remote-only analysis. We speculated that the most common reasons for use would be analyst or analysand travel, a preference for an analyst in a different geographic location, or limited options for analysis in the analysand's geographic area. We presumed that technical difficulties, challenges in understanding nonverbal communications, and issues with emotional containment would present the strongest obstacles in practising teleanalysis. In the United States, concerns about licensure and HIPAA compliance might rank high among the list of deterrents.

Overall, we predicted that most users of teleanalysis would rate it as non-equivalent to in-office sessions but find it a good alternative when in-office sessions were not feasible. We hypothesized that users of teleanalysis would rate it as efficacious, while non-users would see it as a break in the frame, ineffectual, and too compromised to substitute for in-person work.

Measures

To assess our research questions, we developed a 15–20 minute, 23-item questionnaire composed of multiple choice, Likert-scaled and open-ended questions. Items were based on input from a combined team of psychoanalysts with the clinical expertise to identify relevant content areas and measurement experts with the necessary methodological expertise to construct effective questionnaire items and analyse empirical findings. The questionnaire was piloted on a small group of English-speaking psychoanalysts and revised to correct problems in wording, scaling, and understanding. The questionnaire was translated into Spanish and French to gather the largest possible participant sample and to reflect different training and practice paradigms represented in the membership of the IPA.

Questionnaire items included demographic information about the analyst or candidate, such as age, years in practice, and geographic location of their practice, to help us describe our participant pool and assess the potential impact of cohort effects on opinions about and use of technology. For example, are younger analysts who have grown up with technology more comfortable with employing technology in their practice? Another section of the questionnaire examined types of technology used, frequency of use, and factors influencing decisions to use technology. A sample question was, "In your opinion, what is the most compelling reason to offer analytic sessions through technology? Please describe." Responders were asked to indicate whether they used telephone or videoconferencing and whether they conducted analysis entirely via technology or in combination with in-office work. The final section of the questionnaire assessed the perceived impact of technology on analytic process, challenges encountered in using technology such as difficulties managing crisis situations or technological malfunctions, and estimates of the treatment efficacy of teleanalysis compared to in-office work.

We gathered questionnaire data from both practitioners and non-practitioners of teleanalysis. Practitioners answered all items, while non-practitioners responded to the demographic questions and offered opinions about the efficacy of tele-analysis practice.

Participants

Research participants were recruited from IPA member analysts and candidates via an email communication distributed by the IPA, describing the purpose of the study, requiring completion of an informed consent agreement, and providing a link to the online survey in the language of their choice. Descriptive statistics were used to capture the sample characteristics. Our response rate was lower than anticipated, comprising 341 responses or only 6 per cent of the population surveyed. Respondents represented 50 different countries, with Europe, South America, and North America each accounting for approximately one third of the sample. The United States, Brazil, Argentina, and Italy were the countries with the highest number of responders, irrespective of population. Seventy-three per cent of the participants responded in English, 30 per cent in Spanish, and 7 per cent in French.

The average age of study participants was 60.5 years, with 68 per cent of the sample falling between the ages of 49 and 71. The average age of IPA members is 63.27 (J. Beavis, personal communication). Regarding gender, 59 per cent identified as female, 39 per cent as male, and 1 per cent as other. Psychologists (53 per cent) and physicians (36 per cent) dominated the clinical disciplines represented. Seventy-eight per cent of participants were practising psychoanalysts, while 22 per cent described themselves as candidates in training. The group of

Table 1.1 Participant characteristics (N=341)

Age	Mean 60.5; Standard Deviation 11.4
Gender	Female 59.3%; Male 39.4%; Other 1.2%
Country of residence	United States (n = 83); Brazil (n = 33); Argentina (n = 28); Italy (n = 21); Germany (n = 16); Canada (n = 13); Other (n = 147, representing 44 other countries)
Clinical discipline	Psychologist 53%; Physician 36%; Social Worker 5%; Mental Health Counsellor 4%; Other 2%
Professional status	Psychoanalyst 78%; Candidate in Training 22%
Years of practice as a psychoanalyst	None 13.225; 1–4 years 13.79%; 5–9 years 14.37%; 10–14 years 13.79%; 15–19 years 6.90%; 20–24 years 14.94%; 25–29 years 8.62%; 30–34 years 6.32%; 35 years or more 8.05%

psychoanalysts displayed a wide range of years in practice, suggesting that this sample captured opinions from newly graduated analysts to those practising over 35 years. These participant characteristics are summarized below in Table 1.1.

Results

Use of technology

Sixty-five per cent of our participant sample reported using technology to conduct an analytic session at least once, while 35 per cent reported no technology use. For those who used technology, Table 1.2 presents the types of technology employed, with use of the telephone dominating over other methods.

For most respondents who used technology, it represented a small portion of their analytic practice and typically was combined with in-office work in treating their analysands. Their degree of reliance on technology to conduct analysis is displayed in Figure 1.1.

Respondents were asked to rate the reasons for using technology in their analytic practice. Mean scores and standard deviations are displayed in Table 1.3.

In this forced choice response set, the primary reasons for use included travel and relocation of analyst or analysand after starting the analysis. An open-ended question about the most compelling reason to use technology was content coded. Dominant themes among the English-speaking responders (73% of the sample)

Table 1.2 Types of technology used

Type	Percentage
Telephone	63.2%
Skype with visual	41.8%
Skype with audio only	25.4%
FaceTime	08.5%
Videoconferencing technology with business associate agreement (for HIPAA compliance)	02.0%
Videoconferencing technology without business contract	01.0%

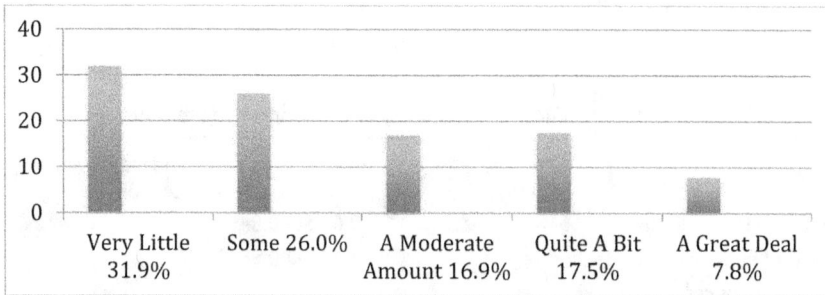

Figure 1.1 Degree of reliance on technology

Table 1.3 Reasons for technology use

Reason	Mean Score and Standard Deviations (1 not at all – 5 quite a bit)
Convenience	2.27 SD 1.49
Travel of analyst or analysand	3.56 SD 1.56
Crisis	2.78 SD 1.49
Analyst and analysand reside in different locales (known prior to starting analysis)	2.54 SD 1.75
Analyst and analysand reside in different locales (one or both moved geographic locations during treatment)	3.30 SD 1.67
Requested by analysand	2.74 SD 1.52
No options for in-person analysis where analysand resides	2.43 SD 1.61

were the geographic relocation of either analyst or analysand, the provision of analytic treatment in a geographic area where none was available, an illness or a personal crisis that made in-office meetings impossible, and the only option for continuity of care and sustaining analytic process in an existing analysis. This last theme category is quite broad and may overlap with other responses, such as travel, illness, or geographic relocation.

Challenges of technology use

We were also interested in the challenges and difficulties faced in using technology to conduct psychoanalysis. Respondents were asked to rate a list of common difficulties encountered with technology use, and their mean scores and standard deviations are presented in Table 1.4. Overall, the group of respondents using technology reported few difficulties, with trouble interpreting nonverbal cues leading the ratings as "somewhat frequent".

Table 1.4 Mean scores on difficulties encountered with conducting teleanalysis

Difficulty	Mean Score and Standard Deviations (1 not at all – 5 quite a bit)
Technical disruptions	2.06 SD 0.84
Lack of familiarity with technology	1.62 SD 0.88
Security concerns	1.76 SD 1.01
Worry about HIPAA compliance	1.56 SD 0.95
Trouble with emotional containment	2.06 SD 1.05
Trouble establishing a working alliance	1.73 SD 0.95
Trouble managing crises	1.83 SD 1.04
Trouble interpreting nonverbal cues	2.93 SD 1.35
Deterioration in analysand functioning	1.63 SD 1.07

Table 1.5 Dominant themes in primary challenges using technology

Dominant Themes	Narrative Examples of Themes
Absence of physical or bodily presence, limiting nonverbal cues	"Part of information is missing, everything based on non-verbal communication. Not being sure in what condition and where the patient is."
	"Loss of nonverbal material, which modulates, and sometimes alters or contradicts, verbal communications. I don't feel at ease, as if something fundamental is missing."

Dominant Themes	Narrative Examples of Themes
Reliability of technology	"The most immediate is the reliability of the technology."
	"Slow internet causing buffering or delayed picture or sound."
	"Sometimes the sound or the picture is not clear; the actual work is not different in my opinion."
	"Other than ruling out teleanalysis with some patients like malignant hysterics, the occasional phone disconnection or poor reception while bothersome is rather easily accepted even relatively unnoticed by patients."
Concentration and focus	"It is hard to maintain attention."
	"Keeping focused, to avoid being distracted by other things while on the phone."
Effects on relationship and transference dynamics	"There is a sense of coldness in the contact between the members of the dyad."
	"It affects the transference: too much like a masturbatory phantasy."
	"The way that the technology inherently obstructs having paramount elements of the transference available."
	"The sense of extra 'intimacy' created by the face-to-face nature of the method."
Adaptations to setting and analytic frame	"Harder to maintain the frame of a scheduled session with boundaries – some patients use the alteration in the frame to make the session a convenience, not a commitment."
	"A major challenge is that I have to rely on the patient to create a setting of integrity and must give up control over the environmental management. IT is all analysable!"
	"Need to find a private location while travelling."
	"Patient must be familiar with technology."
Resistance by analysand, analyst, or institution	"The 'as-if' quality of the analysis is significantly heightened, especially when there is ambivalence about meeting in person, which I think is part of the request to meet by phone at least in some instances. This can become a way to keep the 'threat' of analysis at arm's length."
	"My own obstacles; as I prefer working in person and always have to overcome some resistances in case of a telephone/Skype session. I feel it is more difficult to feel the best/right time for interventions."
	"Institutional resistance in a conservative profession."

Table 1.6 Minor themes in primary challenges using technology

Minor Themes	Narrative Examples
Security	"Using Skype I worry a lot about security, and have moved to a costly secure system."
Licencing	"As a psychologist I cannot do Skype analyses with people in different states in the United States because I am not licensed in those states."
Changes in technique	"Learning not to talk too much."
Working with silence	"Understanding the silences."
	"Silences have to be communicated as listening."

An open-ended question asking about the primary challenge in technology use was content coded for dominant and minor themes. Minor themes, or the inclusion of atypical outliers, are presented here because they help to illuminate the full range of responses within the English-speaking sample.

Relative effectiveness and impact on analytic process

The entire group of participants, both users and non-users of technology, were asked to express their opinions on the perceived overall effectiveness of using technology to conduct psychoanalytic sessions. Each respondent was asked to select the descriptor most consistent with her/his viewpoint. The range of views endorsed highlights the lack of consensus on this issue. Most agreed that tele-analysis was not equivalent to in-person analysis yet they differed on their perception of its acceptability. One participant critiqued our choices, noting that we did not offer the option of technology-assisted analysis being superior to in-person, suggesting negative bias in the way we asked the question. The percentage of responders endorsing each descriptor is presented in Table 1.7 below.

A linear regression was calculated to examine the relationship between ratings of the relative effectiveness of teleanalysis and various predictors. Specifically, the regression model explored the degree to which analysts' rating of efficacy was predicted by age, professional status, and the degree of reliance on technology in analytic practice. We found a significant regression equation (F $(5,93)$ = 10.58, p< .000), with an R^2 of .362, a small to moderate effect size. Of the predictors in the model, only the analyst's degree of reliance on technology predicted the analyst's beliefs about treatment efficacy. Age and professional status did not contribute to the model. Therefore, it appears that regardless of age or professional status, those who use analysis and rely on it in their practice are more likely to rate it as effective.

We were curious about the perceived impact of technology on *analytic process*, viewed as a defining characteristic of psychoanalysis and essential to its effectiveness, yet difficult to define operationally. Our observations in this area draw from the English language sample only, as we are still analysing the Spanish and French samples. Open-ended responses were content coded for themes. Dominant themes drawn from narrative responses about the impact of technology on analytic process are captured in Tables 1.8 through 1.14 and discussed in the paragraphs that follow.

In examining these dominant themes, the range and intensity of opinions voiced about the impact of technology on analytic process was striking. For example, while participants repeatedly referenced the absence of in-office bodily presence associated with the use of technology, some participants believed it compromised the process entirely. One person wrote, "I have found that any use of technology has a profound negative impact on the analytic treatment and process. From

Table 1.7 Relative effectiveness of technology use

Statement Characterizing Effectiveness	Percentage Endorsed
Equivalent to in-person	09.5%
Not equivalent to in-person, but a good alternative	22.0%
Not equivalent to in-person, but an adequate alternative	20.3%
Not equivalent to in-person, but a marginally acceptable alternative	29.0%
Not an acceptable alternative to in-person	19.1%

Table 1.8 The impact on analytic process 1

Theme: Missing a physical or bodily presence

"Since I only use the telephone, the verbal closeness is quite different – the patient is in my ear, and I am in the patient's. At the same time, the physical presence is missing or at best much reduced. I am not confident that the unconscious, body-to-body communication is as effective."

"I find the lack of the two body experience to be challenging though not insurmountable. The advantages far outweigh the disadvantages, however."

Table 1.9 Impact on analytic process 2

Theme: Distractibility, focus, and connection

"[I] feel somewhat less connected with more distractions."

"I find that sessions can be just as focused and sometimes more so on the phone or phone with Skype."

"It's detrimental to contact and psychoanalytic listening, puts focus more on manifest and conscious processes."

Table 1.10 Impact on analytic process 3

Theme: Effects on disclosure and resistance

"The use of technology has facilitated the analytic treatment in several instances, by allowing the patient to reveal aspects of his/her experience that she/he did not feel sufficiently comfortable revealing in the office. In those instances, dream material actually increased."

"[It affects analytic process] surprisingly little. The first 1–2 sessions there has been some reservation and increased defensiveness. Sometimes, however, the patient has been more open and free in her/his associations and valuable new progressive material and insights have taken place."

"The lack of eye and body contact helps in analysand's free thinking."

"By and large, it is less satisfactory due to the absence of the nonverbal and attendant difficulties with attunement. Occasionally, material related to trauma and physical abuse has been more accessible initially with the physical safety of phone sessions."

Table 1.11 Impact on analytic process 4

Theme: Therapeutic relationship and transference

"The patients have been able to work in the transference, examining aspects of the therapeutic relationship (positive/negative) that were illuminated by the use of the medium itself."

"I'm still uncertain about this. With my patient we have a well-established in person relationship, which I think is a foundational experience and carries over to the Skype experience. I think Skype adds another element of complexity that may emerge in the transference–countertransference relationship."

"The process clearly is different. Sometimes, the distance allows the client to engage deeper or more anxiety-producing material. But the development of the analytic relationship is more limited, and it is easier for both patient and analyst to give in to the temptation to avoid direct engagement."

"A great sense of intimacy conducive to treatment alliance."

Table 1.12 Impact on analytic process 5

Theme: Analytic frame and setting

"... the beginning and ending of sessions is altered, such that arrivals, departures, and waiting room interactions, for example, are also absent."

"It requires re-thinking the parameters of the setting; this takes time and I used my supervision group to help me to identify those areas that needed acknowledgement."

"the screen is like a protection for the patient and for the analyst."

"First of all, and in my opinion, analytic work may only be conducted via Skype when the frame has been very firmly established and time-tested. I wouldn't accept working via Skype with a new or fairly new patient. The working alliance must be, in my opinion, very firmly established prior to technology-assisted treatment. From my experience, Skype can mask a variety of difficulties in the patient."

Table 1.13 Impact on analytic process 6

Theme: Continuity of care

"Remote sessions aided by technology have worked well and have enabled analyses to continue that would have previously become forced terminations."

"It is not the best but better then missing sessions."

"Makes continuity possible where [it] would not otherwise be."

Table 1.14 Impact on analytic process 7

Theme: Overall effectiveness

"I find it unsatisfactory for the most part. The time delays in speech, and the loss of visual cues and emotional 'feel' from being in the same room, make the analysis feel limited and partial."

"It is a parameter, but about 90% of in-office experience is the same. Must be worked with, interpreted, and include some face-to-face experience."

"In a couple of situations of analytic therapy, the patients significantly preferred the in-office setting but they were still able to use the opportunity via technology to deepen the analytic process."

"I have come to feel that the analytic process is fully active even when it is conducted 100% through the phone or Skype. There is a difference in each other's perception which has allowed the analysis to explore the areas of physical presence without mental responsiveness and mental presence and reception without physical presence."

"It helps in special circumstances, but in my experience it is not the same as attending my patients at my office or even at a hospital."

my perspective, it is truly only analysis when there are 2 BODIES in the room together." Others spoke of increased sensitivity to facial expressions on Skype (if conducted face-to-face) or a closeness emerging over the telephone by being "in the patient's ear", which felt more intimate than in-office meetings. Similarly, in comments about overall effectiveness, one respondent concluded, "[Technology affects the analytic process] Very severely. A true analytic experience is not possible." Another participant noted, "With the relationship already established, it has little or no impact [on analytic process]."

Some respondents highlighted special considerations when technology was incorporated into the analytic situation. For instance, in discussing the analytic frame, one analyst remarked:

The use of technology requires a bit more time for set up before sessions. Because of the risk of losing the internet connection, we have had to establish protocols for when we lose the connection. We also had to establish other new protocols, such as who initiates the session (who calls whom) and how to establish an environment on the patient's side that is confidential and non-intrusive.

Another participant commented, "It [technology] creates different issues than when in person. For example, patients often have feelings about you being able to see into their home."

Discussion of findings

What is the nature and scope of teleanalysis practice? Some of the findings from this research project matched what we expected to discover, while others contradicted ideas drawn from our anecdotal experiences with teleanalysis. As predicted, about two thirds of participants acknowledged using some form of technology in at least some analytic sessions. Most used telephone or Skype, with very little reliance on more sophisticated telemedicine videoconferencing platforms. We found this surprising, particularly in the United States, where HIPAA requires a level of security inconsistent with Skype use. Perhaps practitioners are reluctant to incur the expense of a HIPAA-compliant telemedicine platform when their use of technology is infrequent or perhaps practitioners and patients are uninformed about the available options. This finding may relate to comfort and convenience, as most people have used Skype and smartphones for regular everyday communications.

As anticipated, most practitioners of teleanalysis combined this method with in-office sessions. Typical reasons for use mostly concurred with our projected findings, as travel and analyst and analysand residing in different geographic locations were endorsed as reasons. What these findings suggest, however, is that the use of teleanalysis may be a necessary adaptation that occurs as the analysis progresses rather than a planned approach to beginning an analysis. In other words, an analytic dyad uses teleanalysis when the analysand discovers he/she may have to travel for business more frequently than originally anticipated. When the analysand or analyst has to relocate to a distant geographic location, the in-office analysis may shift to a teleanalysis format. Thus, the analytic dyad shifts to this method to preserve the analysis.

In contrast with our predictions, a preference for an analyst in a different geographic location from the outset of analysis or the lack of available analytic treatment in the patient's locale were not strongly endorsed as reasons. What might account for these findings? Perhaps they are less compelling than we imagined, or perhaps the majority of our participants came from areas where analysis was plentiful. For example, a respondent from Buenos Aires or New York City would have ready access to analysis, while one from Butte, Montana, might struggle. The number of respondents from major metropolitan areas must certainly outweigh those from rural or underdeveloped areas. Thus, these reasons for employing teleanalysis, a preference for an analyst in a different geographic location or an absence of available analytic treatment, may be specific to a minor subset of our participants. For this subset, these reasons are highly relevant, while for those with greater access to a variety of analysts and analytic treatments, these reasons to use technology drop in priority.

Reports on specific challenges associated with technology use were somewhat surprising. Mean scores on potential problems such as technology disruptions, security or licensure concerns, crisis management, and establishing a working alliance suggest they are infrequently experienced. Since technology glitches and problems frequently appear in anecdotal reports (Leffert, 2003; Lindon, 2000; Scharff, 2010, 2011, 2012, 2013a, 2013b), often with a commentary about effects on the transference dynamics, we thought more technology users would identify this as a common problem. Of the choices provided about potential problems, only difficulties interpreting nonverbal cues received a "somewhat frequent" mean rating.

These reports of few or minor problems can be understood in a number of different ways. Perhaps there is a defensiveness among those advocating technology use that prevents us from acknowledging the frequency of technological problems. For example, maybe we minimize the number of dropped connections, which we do not track without a specific directive to do so. Most of us do not count or record the number of technology drops, rather we focus on sustaining the stream of associations or attend to the transference dynamics generated when these drops occur. We may adjust to technology drops as just ordinary occurrences in the same way that we accept occasional traffic delays with patients seen in the office setting. In this way, our technology disruptions may not register as problematic, even though they have an impact on our analytic sessions. A competing explanation might be that there are fewer technology glitches resulting from better internet connections, dramatic developments in technology products, and increased familiarity with technology, all of which have occurred in the past few years. This explanation suggests that we have better technology options and user training, creating a more comfortable technology environment for our analytic practices.

Data drawn from the open-ended question on challenges with technology use seemed contradictory to the quantitative data on first glance. The most highly endorsed challenge was the reliability of the technology itself. Considering both qualitative and quantitative data, we might conclude that if pressed to identify a challenge with technology use, participants will speak to technology-induced disruptions, even though they happen infrequently.

Lack of concern about security, licensure issues, or HIPAA regulations also generates a range of competing potential explanations. Since this sample is international and reliance on technology is infrequent relative to in-office work, perhaps security, licensure issues, and HIPAA compliance do not register as priorities for concern or deterrents for use. Without further research, it is impossible to know if those who rely exclusively on teleanalysis for their practice or for work with a particular patient have identified and resolved these concerns. Perhaps they use a telemedicine platform with a business associate agreement, practice in an area where licencing laws do not regulate teleanalysis practice, or feel convenience trumps security considerations. Practitioners in the United States may not know which videoconferencing systems are HIPAA compliant or assume that use of the telephone resolves security concerns.

Consistent with our predictions and the anecdotal literature (Leffert, 2003; Lindon, 2000; Scharff, 2010, 2011, 2012, 2013a, 2013b), challenges in reading and interpreting nonverbal cues was the highest endorsed category of problems. This issue is particularly relevant for those practitioners relying on audio only technology; however, the distortion of some nonverbal communications through videoconferencing, such as tone of voice or blurred facial expressions, may create similar interpretive difficulties. We rely on the analysand to put more into words, which must change the analytic experience in some ways. For example, the patient whom you cannot see visually tells you he is changing bodily positions, making it more conscious than unconscious in expression. Additionally, some nonverbal cues such as olfactory ones are completely absent when using distance technology, eliminating an important aspect of the analytic experience for the analytic dyad. For instance, we do not smell the analysand's perfume or particular body odour, which typically influences our countertransference.

What does our research suggest about the perceived effectiveness of teleanalysis? Opinions vary widely on this question. We predicted a difference between users and non-users of teleanalysis, which was supported by the data. Users tend to rate teleanalysis as more effective than non-users. However, we expected that most psychoanalysts would see teleanalysis as a non-equivalent but good alternative to in-office sessions. This was not confirmed by our findings. Nineteen per cent rated it as an "unacceptable" alternative, 29 per cent viewed it as a "marginally acceptable" alternative, and 20 per cent rated it as an "adequate" alternative. Only 20 per cent considered teleanalysis a "good" alternative, with 9.5 percent rating it equivalent to "in person". This suggests that almost 50 per cent of the sample view teleanalysis as a problematic alternative to analysis conducted with patient and analyst in the same room.

How can we understand this finding? What does it mean for treatment and training? One option is to conclude that technology-assisted psychoanalysis should not be considered as a serious treatment option. However, there are other possible explanations. Historically, psychoanalysis has resisted change. This is evident in our collective resistance to conducting empirical research, a standard in the psychotherapy industry but less commonly produced in psychoanalytic circles. Although once in the forefront of psychotherapy outcome research (Bergin, 1971; Strupp, 1963, 1964), psychoanalytic and psychodynamic approaches have lagged behind other theoretical orientations in establishing empirically based conclusions about therapeutic effectiveness, particularly in regards to long-term treatment (Lambert, 2013).

As a therapeutic community, we have been less active than our non-analytic peers in exploring issues of diversity, a standard focus in most graduate clinical training programmes. In some analytic institutes and professional organizations, we have persisted with a training analyst system that potentially undermines our growth and may contribute to deteriorating morale (Kernberg, 2000, 2007, 2015). So, perhaps this more negative view of technology expresses our collective resistance to change.

Additionally, the average age of respondent was 60. This is not a group of digital natives who have grown up with technology. We have to wonder if recruitment and inclusion of a younger sample of analysts would produce the same conclusions about perceived treatment efficacy. Our regression analysis suggested age was not a predictor, but would a younger sample change this finding? Would we see that age and comfort with technology predict opinions about effectiveness? Furthermore, we do not have empirical data to tell us what our analysands think about the effectiveness of teleanalysis practice. What would our analysands say about outcomes from this form of treatment?

And what about the effects of technology on analytic process? Reponses to this open-ended question were perhaps the most varied of any topic. First, respondents clearly defined analytic process in many different ways, with some focusing on the frame, others on the transference dynamics, still others on treatment effectiveness. We could speculate that these are each different aspects of analytic process, which has yet to be defined empirically by our profession and may differ somewhat from analytic dyad to analytic dyad. It would be interesting to consider both the identified components of analytic process embedded in the respondents' narratives and the opinions expressed about technology as a vehicle for analytic process. The way we asked the question may have unintentionally confounded our understanding of the findings. For instance, we might have first asked respondents to define what they view as analytic process, and then requested their opinion about how technology influences it.

Limitations and implications

Limitations

Stage one of this study has serious limitations which impinge on the validity and generalizability of the findings. While the questionnaire was carefully developed and constructed by experts in psychoanalysis and measurement, some questions emerged as problematic. For example, some questions about respondent demographics were more appropriate for an American than international audience, such as questions about ethnicity. Similarly, questions in the technology challenges section that referred to HIPAA regulations had little relevance for European or South American participants. The French version of the survey had some minor translation errors, which were not discovered until after distribution.

The primary limitation, however, was not the questionnaire itself but our response rate and sample size. A 6 per cent response rate is simply abysmal from a design standpoint, limiting our choice of statistics and calling into question the validity and generalizability of our findings. Why the low response rate? How can we understand this? This survey was one of several distributed to the same population in the same time period on teleanalysis (Werbin et al., 2014). People may have tired of answering questions on this topic or assumed the surveys were one and the same. The survey took 15–20 minutes, and this length may have prohibited some from responding. The survey was distributed in an email, which many people ignored or opened but did not click on the link to the survey itself. Multiple methods of distribution, an introductory email directing people to watch for the survey and outlining its importance, several follow-up emails, or addition of a snowball sample might have increased our response rate.

In our research, we will move to stage two of our research project, a qualitative study focusing on psychoanalysts' perceptions and experience of teleanalysis to best capture and interpret the clinical complexities of analytic work. Drawing from participants in stage one who agreed to further contact, we will adopt a stratified sampling strategy identifying a small group of practising analysts to be interviewed in more depth. These analysts will practise in different geographic locations with varying levels of experience, training, backgrounds, and patterns of teleanalysis practice to convey the commonalities and diversities of practitioners in the field.

Researchers have argued strongly for the blending of qualitative and quantitative methodologies, hopeful that such a strategy will enable us to create a more comprehensive picture of therapeutic interventions that rely heavily on interpersonal components and subjective experience (Chiesa & Fonagy, 1999; Lund, 2012; Lutz & Hill, 2009; Williams & Hill, 2001). Qualitative approaches offer a richness of data in narrative form that parallels analytic practice, much like a process transcript illuminates the specifics of a dyadic analytic exchange. Qualitative researchers have countered arguments challenging its objectivity, contending that qualitative research is theory- based and the trustworthiness of qualitative data can be established (Lincoln & Guba, 1985; Morrow, 2007; Williams & Morrow, 2009). We hope to complete stage two of this research within the next year and to further analyse data gleaned in stage one.

Certainly, our research efforts are not enough. We need more empirical data and much larger samples to understand what teleanalysis shares with in-office analysis, where points of difference emerge, and the impact of technology on the analytic dyad. We need additional information about indications for and against teleanalytic treatment, which may help us better select patients and analysts who can work effectively with this medium. We need to know more about what drives opinion about teleanalysis, both from its supporters and its opponents. Additionally, we need empirical data from analysands to hear their views about the benefits, challenges, and efficacy of technology-assisted treatments. Such questions can only be explored with a sustained research programme embraced by multiple diverse research teams in varied settings.

Research questions often emerge from our anecdotal experiences, and research findings typically generate implications for clinical training and practice. This study is no exception. Findings from stage one raise important possibilities. For instance, since the majority of analysts use technology for some aspect of their practice, could we help them become more efficacious with targeted training in teleanalysis? Additionally, if more training and clinical discussion emerged within our institutes and professional organizations about teleanalysis practice, would our collective resistance shift? Since many graduate programmes now require coursework on telemental health, we could use this opportunity to generate programming to help us thoughtfully consider its dynamic implications. Psychodynamic practitioners are the group of choice to discuss transference/countertransference expressions within this treatment modality. Following the model of the teleanalysis study group at IIPT, we could promote clinical discussion groups with cases featuring teleanalysis, increasing our clinical understanding of its impact and assisting newer users in considerations such as necessary adaptations to the analytic frame.

If we consider this research project as exploratory, even this small sample raises issues about teleanalysis practice, with important implications for research and training. Smartphones, Skype, texting, and FaceTime are part of our everyday world. Whether we like it or hate it, technology and ongoing technological advances are here to stay. We cannot expect that such an important aspect of our social culture will be absent from analytic practice. In fact, our findings confirm that most analytic practitioners are using some form of teleanalysis. Denial does not serve us as an analytic community. Rather, it is important that we study the phenomena, we think about its meaning, and we engage in discussion about the implications of its use in analytic settings, including providing adequate training and consultation to teleanalysis practitioners.

References

Beavis, J. (2015). Personal communication.

Bergin, A. E. (1971). The evaluation of therapeutic outcomes. In: A. E. Bergin & S. L. Garfield (Eds.), *Handbook of Psychotherapy and Behavior Change: An Empirical Analysis* (pp. 217–270). New York: Wiley.

Chiesa, M., & Fonagy, P. (1999). From the efficacy to the effectiveness model in psychotherapy research: The APP multi-centre project. *Psychoanalytic Psychotherapy*, 13, 259–272.

Gordon, R. M., Wang, X., & Tune, J. (2015). Comparing psychodynamic teaching, supervision, and psychotherapy over video-conferencing technology with Chinese students. *Psychodynamic Psychiatry*, 43(4), 585–599.

Kernberg, O. (2000). A concerned critique of psychoanalytic education. *International Journal of Psychoanalysis*, 81, 97–120.

Kernberg, O. (2007). The coming changes in psychoanalytic education, part II. *International Journal of Psychoanalysis*, 88, 183–202.

Kernberg, O. (2015). Resistances and progress in developing a research framework in psychoanalytic institutes. *Psychoanalytic Inquiry*, 35S, 98–114.

Lambert, M. J. (2013). Outcome in psychotherapy: The past and important advances. *Psychotherapy*, 50, 42–51.

Leffert, M. (2003). Analysis and psychotherapy by telephone. *Journal of the American Psychoanalytic Association*, 51, 101–130.

Lincoln, Y., & Guba, E. (1985). *Naturalistic Inquiry.* New York: Sage.

Lindon, J. (2000). Psychoanalysis by telephone. In: J. Aronson (Ed.), *The Use of the Telephone in Psychotherapy* (pp. 3–13). Northvale, NJ: Aronson.

Lund, T. (2012). Combining qualitative and quantitative approaches: Some arguments for mixed methods research. *Scandinavian Journal of Educational Research*, 56, 155–165.

Lutz, W., & Hill, C. E. (2009). Quantitative and qualitative methods for psychotherapy research: Introduction to special section. *Psychotherapy Research*, 19, 369–373.

Morrow, S. L. (2007). Qualitative assessment in counseling psychology: Conceptual foundations. *The Counseling Psychologist*, 35, 209–235.

Scharff, J. S. (2010). Report of panel on telephone analysis. International Psychoanalytic Association Congress, Chicago, August 2009. *International Journal of Psychoanalysis*, 91, 989–992.

Scharff, J. S. (2011). Findings of the International Working Group on teleanalysis. Precongress, International Psychoanalytic Association meeting, Mexico, August 2011. *Bulletin of the International Psychotherapy Institute*, 15, 2.

Scharff, J. S. (2012). Clinical issues in analyses over the telephone and the internet. *The International Journal of Psychoanalysis*, 93, 81–95.

Scharff, J. S. (Ed.) (2013a). *Psychoanalysis Online: Mental Health, Teletherapies, Teletraining.* London: Karnac Books.

Scharff, J. S. (2013b). Technology-assisted psychoanalysis. *Journal of the American Psychoanalytic Association.*

Strupp, H. H. (1963). The outcome problem in psychotherapy revisited. *Psychotherapy: Theory, Research, & Practice*, 1, 1–13.

Strupp, H. H. (1964). The outcome problem in psychotherapy: A rejoinder. *Psychotherapy: Theory, Research, & Practice*, 2, 100.

Werbin, A., Burdet, M., Giménez Noble, F., Sahovaler Litvinoff, D., Hirsch Hardy, J., & Ambort, G. (2014). Remote therapy research: A research on distance psychoanalysis sponsored by the International Psychoanalytic Association. www.remotetherapy.net/home.html.

Williams, E. N., & Hill, C. E. (2001). Evolving connections: Research that is relevant to clinical practice. *American Journal of Psychotherapy*, 55, 336–342.

Williams, E. N., & Morrow, S. I. (2009). Achieving trustworthiness in qualitative research: A pan-paradigmatic perspective. *Psychotherapy research*, 19, 576–582.

Commentary

Horst Kächele

One German proverb warns us that every beginning is difficult, but a famous quotation by Hermann Hesse, the Nobel laureate, praises the charm of the beginning. Janine Wanlass's research reflects both aspects. The author rightly points out that there are "interesting speculations; however little is known about the practice and experience of 'teleanalysis' or conducting psychoanalysis through the assistance of the telephone or other high-quality video connection system". As the project has been funded by a grant from the International Psychoanalytical Association (IPA), the study limits its object of scrutiny to psychoanalytic treatment at a minimum of three times weekly with at least some portion of the analytic sessions occurring through the use of technology. This focus on psychoanalysis only incurs an unfortunate limitation to the task of mapping out the use of technology in present-day psychoanalytic and psychotherapy practice.

For stage one of the research, the first approach of the study group was to design a questionnaire and mail it out to members and candidates of the three regions of the IPA. This seems feasible to me, but the response rate was lower than anticipated. Only 6% of the population surveyed responded. It is not surprising to me that 73% percent of the responses came from Anglo-American members. The divergence in response from English-speaking respondents in Britain and Europe and those in the United States deserves more attention. The age of the respondents matches the advanced age of IPA members, which in itself raises the question whether the silver-haired, over sixty age group is the one to advance the inquiry into technology in psychoanalysis.

When the questionnaire reduced the criteria for the use of technology to having conducted an analytic session at least once there was a fairly sharp division in the sample: one third of responders declined the use of technology and two thirds endorsed it, but only a third of the endorsers employed technology quite a bit or a great deal.

The primary reasons for using technology were travel of one of both partners, followed by relocation during treatment and, easy to understand, intervening crises. The situation of analyst and patient each residing in a different location when initiating treatment was not as prominent as expected. One could conclude that the aid of technology does not pre-empt local analytic practice as usual to a significant degree. The challenge to traditional analytic practice resides in the provocative use of technology as a tool to initiate and facilitate an analytic encounter. So to me it would be important to sharpen the distinction between use of technology within established, usual analytic work for the purpose of bridging temporary distance or unusual interruption and its use as an option for providing psychoanalysis to those not in a position to gain analytic treatment except in new electronic environments.

Early in psychoanalysis, the exchange of letters written for therapeutic reasons was not uncommon. Koopmann (2002), a literary scientist, re-evaluated the therapeutic impact of the 1800 letters that Goethe wrote with only a few responses from Mrs von Stein. Kurt Eissler (1963) even called that basically unilateral, primarily letter-mediated exchange a "protopsychoanalysis".

Before using technology in psychoanalysis, analysts need to develop a coherent understanding of the new media. Certain basic principles must be understood.

All communications are bi-directional and more or less symmetrical. However, therapeutic discourse is more or less asymmetrical (Labov & Fanshel, 1977). The media of the exchange is secondary, but the rules of communicative coherence must be respected. Therefore communications need an agreed-upon frame concerning the place of the session, the time at which the session occurs, and the length of the session. The frame defines the rules of exchange.

Letters may be written from any place to another. This is true for written communications such as e-mails and text messages, for voice communications such as telephone and Skype, and for audiovisual technology as well. And letters may be written at any time! But there is no agreed-upon rule when to read a letter. And whether one should respond or not! E-mails and text messages, at least, specify the exact time of sending but not the place from which it was sent, and they leave open the place and time at which the recipient takes notice of them! Letters may be very short or very long! E-mails as therapeutic tools also may vary (Gabbard, 2001). Text messages as a therapeutic medium of exchange are usually very short (Buchholz & Kächele, 2015). Telephone and Skype calls as therapeutic tools have a pre-agreed time and length but not necessarily agreed places from which to access cyberspace.

Having made these points about media briefly, I will take up the challenges of the use of technology conveyed in the report. The report documents well the concerns about technical issues that arise. The more interesting details are found in the narrative examples provided, such as regret over the "loss of nonverbal material which modulates, and sometimes alters or contradicts, verbal communications". The gold of the search for an understanding is to be found in the narrative content. Therefore the proposed next research phase of conducting in-depth interviews is really promising.

Then the author takes up the question of the relative effectiveness of teleanalysis and its impact on psychoanalytic process. Here it is relevant to note that there is such a variety of opinions as to what constitutes "psychoanalytic process" that agreement on the definition and assessment of analytic process is not available to us at this time (Vaughan et al., 1997). As I have noted elsewhere,

> Multiple unresolved methodological problems concerning traditional psychoanalytic theory, including the lack of a consensually-agreed definition of 'psychoanalytic process', are among the principal factors responsible for the relative paucity and limited findings of empirical studies of 'psychoanalytic process'. Further, an encompassing formulation of an approach to the study of traditional 'psychoanalytic process' is so complex and multi-dimensional that its use in empirical assessment is unlikely to be fruitful.
>
> (Schachter & Kächele, 2016, p. 78)

I would prefer to stay with the rich descriptions provided by the paper in Table 8–14, and leave aside the issue of whether or not there is "psychoanalytic process". Using new tools for studying therapeutic exchanges like conversational analysis are at hand to help researchers understand the nature of these communicative processes (Buchholz & Kächele, 2013).

In this vein, it is not surprising that "the range and intensity of opinions voiced about the impact of technology was striking". It is no wonder that different analysts will express different notions as to the conditions under which they will feel comfortable conducting analysis. The various points in the discussion section underline the necessity of being even more curious as to how the worldwide analytic community will accommodate to the challenges and demands of the new media. The research is a more than timely effort to continue this line of inquiry.

References

Buchholz, M., & Kächele, H. (2013). Conversation analysis – A powerful tool for psychoanalytic practice and research. *Language and Psychoanalysis*, 22, 228–243.

Buchholz, M. B., & Kächele, H. (2015). Emergency Short Message Text Intervention in chronic suicidality studied by conversation analysis. In: J. Scharff (Ed.), *Psychoanalysis Online 2 Distant Communication in Development and Therapy* (pp. 145–160). London: Karnac.

Eissler, K. R. (1963). *Goethe. A Psychoanalytic Study, 1755–1786*. Detroit: Wayne State University Press.

Gabbard, G. O. (2001). Cyperpassion: E-Rotic transference on the internet. *Psychoanalytic Quarterly*, 70, 719–737.

Koopmann, H. (2002). *Goethe und Frau von Stein: Geschichte einer Liebe* (Goete and Mrs von Stein: Story of a love). München: Beck.

Labov, W., & Fanshel, D. (1977). *Therapeutic Discourse: Psychotherapy as Conversation*. New York: Academic Press.

Schachter, J., & Kächele, H. (2016). The traditional concept of "Psychoanalytic Process": Ready for retirement. In: J. Schachter & H. Kächele (Eds.), *Nodal Points: Critical Issues in Contemporary Psychoanalytic Therapy* (pp. 78–95). New York: IPBooks.

Vaughan, S. C., Spitzer, R., Davies, M., & Roose, S. P. (1997). The definition and assessment of analytic process: Can analysts agree? *International Journal of Psychoanalysis*, 78(3), 959–973.

Chapter 2

Teleanalytic sessions for sudden immobility

Betty Benaim with Jill Savege Scharff

In this chapter we will consider and illustrate teleanalysis as an adaptation to sudden immobility. In this case, teleanalysis was not the preferred modality. It was a second choice because of inability to get to the analyst's office, beneath which lay unconscious reasons driving the necessity for sessions on the telephone.

Introducing the patient

Elena is now a 35-year-old woman who has been in psychotherapy twice and is now in analysis on the couch for loss of memory, depression, and relationship difficulty for 17 years since adolescence. At the age of 19, she was treated twice weekly by Dr Betty Benaim for three years for dissociative memory loss following a car accident, and again at 25 for four years for depression. At age 33 she entered treatment, this time in three times weekly analysis on the couch, all at Dr Benaim's office, for depression, school difficulty, and conflict with her mother Lupe and her father, Eduardo; her brother, Daniel, and his child, Pedrito; and her boyfriend, Alfredo. Her analyst, who is comfortable working in the office or on the phone, had always been willing to be available by telephone to accommodate a crisis or an immobilizing depression. Even though Elena did not leave the house and slept all day, she made it to her sessions and had never used the telephone. Then she had another car accident. She could move only with great difficulty immediately after the accident, and Dr Benaim felt that telephone sessions were clearly indicated. Elena declined her offer in favour of an appointment in the office. But once Dr Benaim had witnessed the physical damage Elena had done to herself, and worked on it with her, Elena could admit that she was unable to drive and move around, and then she accepted telephone sessions.

We will prepare the way with summaries of her two previous therapies, and of the beginning of her analysis. We will then give process notes of the appointment in the office after the accident as a basis for comparison with teleanalytic work. We will then study two telephone sessions after the analysand was unable to get herself to Dr Benaim's office. To understand the accident, and the call for telephone sessions 17 years later, we need to go back to the beginning of treatment when Elena was 19 and first consulted Dr Benaim.

The first treatment – psychotherapy

The consultation was about Elena's loss of memory following a car accident when she was driving and lost control of the car. She could not remember her friends at the university or her professors, and only slightly remembered her father and mother but not very clearly. Medical tests showed that she had no physical or neurological damage. So Elena agreed on individual psychotherapy sessions with Dr Benaim twice a week.

After about a year of psychotherapy she reported her first and only dream. She remembered the dream in two photographs. There was no movement in the dream. One photo was, as she recalled, in a big place full of people. It had a high ceiling. When she described the place she raised her arms making a movement that described an arch. She didn't remember anything else about this photo. The second photo was in a dark passage, with some people in it. She remembered she was sad. There was no association to the photos. Dr Benaim asked her what she did the day of the dream. She said she had gone to study with a friend that lived near Obarrio, a Panama City neighbourhood. Dr Benaim had been in a church there two or three times, attending funerals of friends. The movement Elena made with her hands seemed to describe that church and its very high ceiling with many arches. Dr Benaim said, "The photo reminds me of the church in Obarrio."

Elena didn't seem to react to the comment, but two days later she seemed transformed. When Dr Benaim said, "You look different," Elena replied, "Something painful happened, I recovered my memory," explaining that she realized that the church in the dream referred to the funeral of a dear friend who died of cancer, and then to her own averted death in the accident, and all the details came back to her mind.

They continued to work for two more years on her painful family relationships. Elena's parents had never lived together. Her mother, Lupe, worked in Panama City as a dental assistant, while her father, Eduardo, worked and lived in the interior of Panama as a director of a chain of stores. When Elena was about 4 years old, her mother had a relationship with another man. Her mother Lupe and her lover put Elena out of her mother's room where she used to sleep, and some months later the man abandoned them. It was from this relationship that her brother Daniel was born. Elena's father adopted him and continued to support them all responsibly, sending enough money for food and school and a house in a low middle class area, visiting every weekend and maintaining contact by phone. During his daily phone-calls, he asked Elena to tell him about her brother and mother as if she were his informant. Elena had a terrible relationship with her mother, who never prepared her food. Elena was a very sad, fat, lonely child who felt unloved by her mother for whom she seemed never good enough. Elena processed her pain about her difficult relationship with her mother, how she missed the presence of her father and of having a home with warmth and love, and how painful it was that Lupe's favourite child was Daniel, whom Elena also loved very much. Elena recovered sufficiently to go away to college and treatment ended. Dr Benaim did not consider teletherapy at that time.

Discussion

We are struck by Elena's fragile ego and its hysterical organization. We wonder if her capacity for such total dissociation in response to the single-shock trauma of the car accident has a pre-history in terms of earlier trauma in the disorganized and neglectful family setting. Elena finds in Dr Benaim a steady, kind figure to whom she can convey her victimhood and elicit concern. More than that she is eventually able to dream and allow her unconscious to come in contact with Dr Benaim's unconscious. Through the dream and the physical movement of Elena's arms, her painful, repressed memory was conveyed and released from repression.

The second treatment – psychotherapy

After three years Elena came back to therapy tremendously depressed after an abortion that she arranged because she didn't want to be a bad mother like hers had been and because her boyfriend had other plans that did not include her. She was so extremely depressed that she didn't leave her bed, or her room, except to come to therapy.

Working with Dr Benaim, Elena worked on her losses, and acknowledged that she repeatedly chose a man that could not commit to be in the relationship. Her then boyfriend had a mother who could give Elena love. Elena suffered very much in having to return to her own house, where she couldn't stand being with her mother.

After about a year, she enrolled in university in Panama and tried to study for the same career her father had. But she failed to complete her work, and felt guilty that she couldn't finish. After about four years of psychotherapy, she was back in school in a subject unrelated to her father, and she was doing better. She still felt ambivalent about him, however; she was angry at him but she needed his financial support. She felt in debt to him, and wanted to try life on her own.

Discussion

Despite gains in the first treatment, Elena remains a vulnerable young woman. Dealing with her requires great sensitivity and careful technique. Depressed by her total dependency on her father, there is no room for a viable relationship with a young man. We learn that for the second time Elena leaves therapy as soon as she is feeling better. She claims that she cannot bear to be beholden to her father for her relationship to Dr Benaim. It seems that the narcissistic aspects of her personality structure take over and so she does not realize how much treatment she needs. We begin to wonder whether her relationship to Dr Benaim is becoming a threat. Does Dr Benaim begin to take on the colouring of the problematic objects, instead of being merely the kind, steady listener that Elena keeps on returning to? Is that why Elena quits at a certain point in the development of the therapeutic relationship?

The third treatment – analysis

Elena came for help again, this time for yet another failed relationship with a man. She wanted to get prepared for losing the man in her life because he was committed to another woman. Physically she was transformed – thin, very attractive, stylish, working in real estate. By this time, Dr Benaim was an analyst. Elena accepted her offer of three times a week analysis on the couch. About six months into analysis Elena started having problems with her woman manager, who directed her to be seductive with clients. This seemed to be a repetition of her mother's use of her father to take the family out to shops and restaurants on the weekend. Elena felt humiliated, not validated, uncared for. Feeling unprotected, Elena terminated her employment.

When Elena left her job, she didn't go out of the house, except to come to analysis. She was lonely and terrified of getting depressed again. She didn't exercise, and cut the relationship with a couple of friends she had at work, and with her brother Daniel and his Venezuelan wife and son. She was very angry at Daniel for stealing money from her father and mother to buy drugs. He lost his job, and his wife left for Venezuela with their child Pedrito, and Daniel would join them later.

Elena's father continued to visit her during the weekends. She felt very angry with him as an intrusion in her life. She reported a sensation of nausea when her father slept in the room next to her because she couldn't stand his smell. This theme of nausea was repeated during several sessions. During the work in analysis, Elena associated the nausea with the closeness of her father, and recovered an infantile memory when he was in bed with her, very close, touching her. She didn't recall penetration but cried very much at this memory and was furious at her father. After this piece of work she created a boundary with him. She also separated from her mother to live in her own house alone, forbidding either parent to invade her space. But she is still repeating the same pattern as her mother: She chooses men who cannot commit to a relationship in the conventional way of marrying and having a home. She has had about five relationships, all with men who have other relationships while with her, who mistreat her as her mother does, and who finally leave her.

At this point Dr Benaim had to leave her for two weeks' scheduled vacation at a time when all of Panama, including Elena, takes vacation. Towards the end of the break, Elena called to say she had something to talk about and wanted to confirm when her next appointment would be. Dr Benaim found this unusual, and sensed some urgency. So she suggested an emergency telephone appointment before their sessions resumed, but Elena declined the offer.

Discussion

Elena increases her vulnerability by losing her external structure of a job to go to. Her physical display of sexuality has become a troublesome asset liable to be exploited and she retreats to her bed. Now we learn of the earlier trauma that we suspected – an episode of incestuous behaviour during the window in development of the ego when dissociation is an option. We feel concern about the occurrence of a scheduled break right after the emergence of this early trauma.

The analytic session in the office after an accident

Elena entered the session with great difficulty walking and wearing an orthopaedic collar around her neck. I offered her the chair to sit in, since I noticed it was difficult for her to bend and lay down on the sofa. She refused the chair, just as she had declined the telephone session. Painfully she put herself in the sofa and began to speak.

ANALYST: What happened to you?

ELENA: I was in a car accident. I will tell you about it, but first I want to tell you about my weekend at the beach coming up to it. Alfredo invited me to his house for a party on Saturday night with his closest friends, his sister and brother, some friends, and his parents. I felt good that he included me with his intimate friends. We were all drinking and his close friends started speaking about how someone's older cousin had penetrated them. I started to feel very sad. I began to drink more and more.

ANALYST: Their sexual abuse connected you with your abuse.

ELENA: Yes, I didn't realize it, but now as I am talking I feel nausea, and it was very difficult for me. Why did they have to speak about it in front of me? I began to understand many things about Alfredo. Things began to connect.

ANALYST: What did you feel?

ELENA: I felt very ashamed. And I drank so much that I got drunk. And Alfredo carried me and put me in my car and Alfredo drove my car and put me to bed alone in my house. When I woke up, a couple of hours later, I felt so ashamed. What will the family think about me? I made a fool of myself. I felt so sad, like a piece of garbage. How could I get drunk in front of all his family? I felt humiliated.

ANALYST: You felt humiliated and not worthy of intimacy, since you relived your abuse.

ELENA: Yes, so I felt I didn't want to stay at the beach. I couldn't take the humiliation. So I dressed and took my car at 3 a.m. and drove back to Panama. The road was very dark, and there was a part with many curves, I didn't see them. I just lost control of the wheel. There was a precipice. I didn't have the seat belt on. The car turned over three times and rode down the precipice.

It landed upside down. Suddenly I heard a blast. The car was going to explode. I don't know how I pushed myself out of the window. All my body was hurt, and I crawled and pushed myself up the hill. I was half way up, and someone in the dark gave me a hand and pulled me up the rest of the way. I got bruises all over my body, but nothing broke. My back was hit. It is difficult for me to lift my arms up, and everything hurts. But nothing is broken. It will take time, and I will be ok. It is difficult for me to walk, but I can do it.

ANALYST: So you pushed yourself up the hill. You wanted to live.

ELENA: Yes. The car burned totally. If I would have been unconscious, or have stayed down, I would be dead.

ANALYST: You also wanted to kill yourself. To drive drunk in the darkness, in that dangerous road, it must be that a part of you wanted to die, and a part of you wanted to live.

ELENA: Yes, I wanted to die. I was so ashamed and hurt. To get drunk in his house, in front of his family – how low! What will they think about me? I felt worthless, humiliated. And I wanted to run away.

ANALYST: To run away from life, to die. The first time you came here, you had a car accident, you lost control of the car, and you lost your memory. Now you've had another car accident. You nearly lost your life.

ELENA: Yes, I didn't think about it that way. But I have to recognize it is true. But I want to live. More than ever.

The session was over. Elena rose from the couch slowly and in great pain. She rejected my offer to meet by telephone. However, after this session, Elena sent a text to request sessions by phone until she felt able to move around.

Discussion

What an extraordinary and terrifying story. We get the impression that Elena really wants Dr Benaim to see the full impact of her self-destructiveness. Why now? Elena is vulnerable because of giving up the dissociation defence against emergence of the abuse history. By chance her friends were talking about sexual abuse, which brings the topic up, makes her anxious and ashamed, and disorganizes her. To hear that others were abused takes away the specialness of her victim identity. All the aggression she feels at how she was and is treated turns on herself disastrously. We note that Dr Benaim is well aware of the repetition of trauma, the action of the death constellation, and the conflict inside the self over living or dying. But she does not tie the events around the accident to the break from analysis. What might Elena be feeling towards the analyst as a transference object that could not prevent her abuse and that abandoned her as soon as it was revealed? In this case, it seems that analyst's visual perception of Elena's damage and her pain of lying on the analyst's couch is an essential communication pulling for a good object response but obscuring the negative transference. As Elena lies on the couch in pain, she seems to be saying, "Look what you and your vacations have done to me. Look what you allowed to happen." Does she want to punish the good Dr Benaim she has taken in over the years for abandoning her during the vacation? We see some danger in the lack of attention to the negative transference as Dr Benaim works to rehabilitate Elena's hold on life. From this session we might assume that it is more difficult to interpret the negative transference in teleanalysis, but it is more likely a feature of this analyst's style with this patient she has known for many years.

The first session on the telephone

ELENA: Hello. I am sorry I cannot come to the clinic to see you, because I have a lot of pain. Eduardo (her father) had the bright idea of taking me to the interior to have x-rays and tests taken. His girlfriend is a Dr, so the price would be much cheaper. But it is a very long trip, and I couldn't take it. My back got worse, and we were in a small car, not even in the big jeep. I felt every stone in the road. So halfway there, I told him I just can't take it, and he drove back to Panama. It was unbearably painful for me.

ANALYST: You allowed him to abuse you again, since in your condition it was uncomfortable to travel that far.

ELENA: Yes, I don't understand. I know he cares for me, but this is too much. What could I do? I depend on him financially. But I couldn't take it. So I stopped the plan. But now, I can't even hold a glass of water in my hands, they are so weak. My room is in the second floor, and I can't get down the stairs to the kitchen. So I depend on Lupe and Eduardo to take care of me, to feed me. I need their help. And I must say, Lupe is spending time with me; she feeds me, helps me out. And Eduardo. But now they both have the keys to my house! I had to give them the keys, since I can't go down the stairs to let them in. I am totally dependent on them, but I hope it is temporary. I need to be independent. As soon as I get stronger I will take the keys back. I cannot stand them coming into my home without my permission.

ANALYST: You are in a state of dependence that is very scary for you.

ELENA: Yes, I am always thinking how uncomfortable I feel because I don't want my space interfered with. I have to recognize that now I need them and they are there for me. They dedicate their time to me, and I can feel how they care. I could appreciate their good parenting – but only until I get better.

I cannot complain about my father as a provider. He gives me all the material support I need. I have a good car. Well, it was totally destroyed but he has given me good cars, an education, clothes, food, a good house. Lupe has been a hard worker. Now she is retired and spends her time doing puzzles. But they have not given us the emotional support we need, neither Daniel nor me. But I have to accept the way they are.

Now I am in my room most of the time, because I cannot move around. I am counting the days and the hours to when I get better and can get out of the room. I am not sad or depressed as before. Some years ago, I was in my room, and I didn't want to get out of it. I could walk, and I didn't move, didn't go out. I stayed in bed depressed all day sleeping, not wanting to speak to anyone but you.

Now things are so different. I am in my room because I have to be here for medical reasons, but I am thinking all the time I want to get well and go out, and do something with my life. I want to have a life. I have an idea of what I want to do – projects, how to build them, advertise them. I want to work on my own, have my own projects.

ANALYST: So you see a difference. Before, you were in bed, you were depressed, and you didn't have a connection with life. Now you are in bed because you injured yourself. Because of your emotional feelings, you took too many risks while driving. And you wish you could recover so you could go out and have a life.

ELENA: Yes, exactly. And I know how important it has been for me to have a friend. Most of my friends just sent me a chat message. Ana Ester is different; she is my real and only friend. She calls, comes to visit. She cares. I like to chat with Alfredo, and he visits me sometimes. I need to have the relationship.

ANALYST: I see a parallel with our relationship. Maybe you would like to come and see me, but it is not possible, so you will use the phone meanwhile. But maybe it is not good enough for you.

ELENA: Well, I like to come to the clinic. It makes me get out of bed, and out of the house. Also I like seeing you. But now, this is ok for me, since it is too painful to move. I was thinking of Christmas; my mother is travelling to see her son and her grandson. I understand; I would have loved to go and see Daniel and Pedrito. I miss my nephew. He is a nice, sweet boy. Christmas is coming soon. I want to decorate a tree and feel the difference in the house. Even if I will be alone.

Discussion

We note that her shame and humiliation about her drunkenness and involvement in a car accident have been replaced by a return to complaint about her abusive object, her father, and yet she has made gains towards acceptance of the way he is, separate from her. The death constellation seems to be closed, rather than being seen as happening all the time. When Elena complains about friends sending her chats instead of visiting, Dr Benaim picks up the negative transference. She refers to phone sessions as a second best offer, like the experience of having an electronic chat not a visit with friends. Elena feels understood. She definitely prefers to actually see Dr Benaim in the flesh and be in proximity to her, but under the circumstances the phone will do. Or will it? Not all patients can tolerate the distance of online psychoanalysis. Not all analysts can tolerate it either. Dr Benaim is comfortable with it for other patients, but is she feeling it as a necessary evil in this case? Acceptance of teleanalysis depends on the subjectivity of the patient.

Comparing this session to the previous one, Elena's ability to talk spontaneously is not affected by being on the phone. But she does not convey her physical distress as effectively as she did when there in the analyst's office.

Analytic session on the phone after a three-week Christmas break

ELENA: I feel ashamed that I couldn't get to the appointment. I would have liked to get more organized but I couldn't. There have been too many things going on. Concerning the accident I am feeling much better, but I have to accept that I have to take it easy and work on recovering my mobility. I am quite calm even though sometimes it is hard. I have to accept that now I have to depend on someone else and I don't have anyone to depend on except for the most necessary things.

ELENA: My grandmother died.

ANALYST: Tell me about it.

ELENA: She died on the 22nd of December. I was very angry at first because we would have no Christmas, no New Year's celebration. As it turns out, it is not that I didn't have Christmas: I had it in a very different way. I could be with my aunts and spend time with my father in a different kind of closeness, and at the end that is what Christmas is about. In fact I felt her death like a gift because this Christmas is the first time I felt welcomed in the family. I felt needed, loved, united. It was the sensation of family that I was missing for a long time. Travelling to the interior was not easy for me, but I did it, I took care, and I am back to Panama. If I could not have been there, I would have had no Christmas, nothing. Instead, there was a little light under the door. I felt better.

There are many things coming together. The accident has been very dramatic and also my grandmother's death. The accident has been a radical change in my life. There exists a before and an after the accident in my life. It has made me more appreciative of every instant. What happened with my grandmother has made me closer to my father. I have renewed that relationship. So much had been lost. I understood that my relationship with my father is one of love and hate. At moments it hurts me very much, because of the abuse and now I know also because of the abandonment. But I could now appreciate the positive side; that he was beside me taking care of me the way he could, and I was well taken care of in the moment of the accident. But after the death of my grandmother, he disappeared. Now I have to handle myself alone, whatever way I can, and that is the way it is, and it doesn't stop me from loving him as a father.

After that Daniel came. Lupe had been to spend Christmas with Daniel, Pedrito and the Venezuelan girl and they came back here to stay for two months. And Lupe is having problems with them. I told her: so you don't feel bad with Daniel, you could come to my house and live in a room there while he lives at your house. I did what I had to do. But she stays with them at her apartment, and calls me to complain every day.

ANALYST: You had the capacity to see the positive part in your father, and were able to offer Lupe a place in your house. That is something new and different.

ELENA: I think that Lupe needs drama, and that is how she connects to Eduardo. There was a time when she used me for her drama. I am the reflection of my mother, of all her frustrations, and sadness. I mean I am the person that *could* have brought her a lot of happiness into her life, but she needs drama, misery. Sometimes I feel that it is much better that I wasn't her favourite daughter, or I would have ended up like Daniel. Yes, it really hurts, but I feel better. It doesn't sting like before.

ANALYST: It hurts you that you have never been her favourite child.

ELENA: It does hurt, but it is an old pain. She is in purgatory, suffering so much that she can't even feel the pain.

ANALYST: And it hurts you. Speak to me about the pain.

ELENA: It is a basic pain that comes too naturally to me. For me it is new to see that pain in another perspective. It was too dominant in my life. It has taken too much space. For the first time I could see it in a different way. It does not need to occupy all your life. Lupe's hatred has impregnated all the stages in my life. As a child it made me a very sad child. During adolescence also I was very sad, and it has been very difficult for me to be a woman. And if I add Eduardo's abandonment, well, not financial but emotional, there is much resentment. Now I look at Lupe and Eduardo, and I recognize their limitations. I could see that the loneliness that is so heavy for me is very much like Eduardo's, and the heaviness of my depression is Lupe's heaviness, but I don't identify with it in either case. I could see now that it is not a part of me. I accept that I don't have a family – neither functional nor dysfunctional. I feel at peace. I do have roots. I have them and they are mine, and they come from my grandmother. There is much of my grandmother in me, very much of what I lived in the interior is in me, and I have it, and I have it in my blood. Lupe passed me a lot of anger, and I am cleaning it out. I am going to take the good part and fight for the good part.

ANALYST: So you feel you have a Lupe part.

ELENA: Physically I look very much like Lupe, even my gestures. She failed me in many aspects, but I was always in school. I feel even proud of having been able to manage everything.

ANALYST: Being in contact with your grandmother and with your father's family you realized that you have roots, and you are rescuing the good parts and giving your parents back their burden.

ELENA: It is difficult. My grandmother died, and now Lupe is with Daniel and Pedrito, and everybody forgot that I had an accident. What used to take me 15 minutes now takes me an hour. But I do it. It hurts me not to have family, but I will not stop. I have a very lonely life because I haven't known how to do it differently. But now I want to make myself a different life.

Hello! I don't know if the line is cut off . . .

ANALYST: I am here.

ELENA: And all this, I want to mention that the accident has marked my life very much. After the accident many things were put into place. I always say I feel lonely, that I don't have friends, but it fills me up to know that I have two friends in my life that are true friends. Ana Ester has been a very good friend even though she is at a very difficult moment in her life; she has been there for me. And Alfredo has been there in some way. Since the accident our relationship is one of real friendship, and I am enjoying it very much, but I don't want to become emotionally dependent on Alfredo at this moment when I feel so vulnerable.

ANALYST: Maybe you feel I abandoned you during the time your grandmother died and you had the accident.

ELENA: Not abandoned. This is home plate. I could always come back when I need it.

Discussion

There seems to be a lack of mourning for her grandmother (her father's mother) to whom she had felt close until she lost her mind to Alzheimer's disease. The grandmother's death brought the family together in ways that were gratifying to Elena. We begin to wonder if there has been a grandmother transference to Dr Benaim as one who brings the parts of Elena together. While her analysis proceeds in ongoing phone sessions, Elena has come a long way in a short time towards acceptance of the reality of her external objects. She experiences corresponding relief in her internal world.

Just as she speaks of making a new life for herself, Elena wonders if the telephone connection has dropped. In teleanalysis there are reality factors to consider. The phone line really can cut off, and then there are emotional and unconscious reactions to the technical realities of the teleanalytic setting. But in this case, there is no technical interference. Elena has a moment of feeling that Dr Benaim has disappeared. Dr Benaim simply gives the reassurance that she is there, listening as usual. This is enough to restore Elena's spontaneous flow of thoughts. But an opportunity is missed. Dr Benaim could have used the moment to show how Elena might attack herself by losing her good object as soon as she contemplates a new life for herself.

Analytic session on the phone a week later

ELENA: I have been stuck inside the house for three months. I feel vulnerable at this moment and dependent on other people, and that stresses me. Like with my father – I cannot keep on depending on him, and I cannot let myself get too fond of Alfredo, since I already know what is going to happen. But I can't avoid it, because he is the only friend that is there for me and takes me for a ride to get some fresh air.

ANALYST: Now that you are vulnerable, you feel so lonely, and more than ever you need someone to help you and be with you. You are very angry.

ELENA: I don't know if I am angry. I feel comfortable being independent. So, why is it I get so damaged emotionally? My father is in mourning, and he upsets me so much. He wants to help me and at the same time he doesn't want to help me. I should have found a person to be in a relationship with a long time ago. That would have relieved my father of the function of taking care of me. Eduardo's answer is: I give you the money and do with it whatever you can. I answer him, thank you very much. What will I do with that?

ANALYST: I feel you are very angry at him.

ELENA: I am irritated. I don't want to have their half-life. I want my life to be complete. In these moments that I am like this, solitude hits harder. And I go back to Alfredo. It is just a matter of time until he gets involved in his soap opera, and another woman appears, and he throws me away.

ANALYST: You need a relationship that is more permanent. But you are stuck with Eduardo and with Alfredo. They cannot give you that.

ELENA: I am stuck in the neediness. I have been hooked up with them for too long. I try not to be desperate and to have patience instead.

ANALYST: I have been thinking that each time you come back to me you are impelled by a drama. And now it is the same.

ELENA: Yes. The treatment always comes to an end eventually because of Eduardo's pressure. I do not want to deal anymore with Eduardo. What bothers me most is that he takes away therapy. I feel like punching him in the face, may God forgive me. He tells me he doesn't see any results from the therapy. How do I explain to this person who wouldn't understand ever in his lifetime what therapy is? I can't. I am tired of explaining my life to Eduardo because he is not in my life. But he is, because I have to ask him for money. For me it is very hard to do this fight with him. It is hard for me to beg for love. That is what I am angry about. I don't understand that he cannot understand what I need. And it is not him that has to take care of me. My relationship with Lupe is so bitter. With Eduardo, he has me worn out, and with Daniel it is almost nil. And with Alfredo I get stuck in that soap opera. They are people who don't love me.

ANALYST: You need Eduardo to be there like a mother. He has done what he could. He has his own life, and you resent it.

ELENA: I would like to be with him and go to his place, but I cannot be in that mess. Now, since his woman goes there to stay some days, the room she occupies is the one that has a big bed, the one that I occupied. And she sleeps there with my father. When I go there I have to sleep in a room that is like a closet.

ANALYST: She has taken your room and the place where you would like to be. There is no space for you in his life as a couple. You are filled with resentment of him because you feel abandoned by him and by your family.

ELENA: Yes that is the word – abandonment. It is a key word. I try to do the thera-
    peutic work alone, in my bed. The abandonment term has marked all my life.
ANALYST: You feel lonely. And that abandonment has marked you. You feel
    abandoned, and so you would abandon me and the analysis. This is a pattern
    that has repeated itself during our long relationship over these last 17 years.
    When you came to me the first time, it was very dramatic. You had lost your
    memory. We worked for a few years and you recovered your memory and
    became less depressed. As soon as you felt stronger, you fled treatment for
    Colombia. Then a few years passed; you came back from Colombia destroyed
    and depressed, with a big drama in your life. Your boyfriend had left you,
    you had had an abortion. You came back to your parents and to therapy for a
    couple of years. Later, when you felt less depressed you abandoned therapy
    again. Many years went by and again, when drama was approaching, when
    you felt you were about to lose your job and you were in a relationship with
    a boy who is not yours but belongs to another girl, you came back with your
    drama to therapy, and I offered you analysis, which you accepted. We have
    worked for a couple of years and we are deepening the work on your rela-
    tionships. So you have another drama, the accident, your crisis with Eduardo,
    and now you want to leave analysis. It seems to me that you need the drama
    in your life to put together your parents as a couple and make them take care
    of you. Once you are able to do it, you cannot tolerate it. You cannot toler-
    ate being with them, and you have to separate from them. Then you separate
    from me, from your analysis. The repeating of this pattern is not a solution for
    your life. It does not help you become independent. And it is possible that in
    one of those dramas you will kill yourself and never come back.
ELENA: I do not lose the hope in analysis. I would like to trust my father and
    believe he wouldn't do a thing like that.
ANALYST: For you analysis is vital. It is the difference between life and death.

Discussion

Elena has been stuck inside the house for three months. Is she making the most
of being an invalid? Is she exaggerating for secondary gain? Is being stuck inside
the house a metaphor for being stuck inside her neurosis? Does part of her want to
stay dependent in opposition to her analyst wanting her to grow? Does she want
to change and pay the price? Is she enjoying the convenience of having telephone
sessions or is she avoiding working with Dr Benaim on how hard it is to tolerate
the loss of her physical presence? At first, Elena denies that she is angry at Eduardo and Alfredo for failing her. She says she is just irritated, and even though
Alfredo cannot offer a permanent commitment, she is grateful that he takes her for
a ride for fresh air. It must be so enjoyable to be driven safely instead of facing the
anxiety of driving alone, having driven a car off the road. Eventually Dr Benaim's
comments reach Elena, who admits to wanting to punch her father in the face,

adding that she feels displaced by the woman in his life. Elena addresses her Oedipal anxieties more directly than before, and is more in touch with her rage. Dr Benaim interprets Elena's turning aggression against her analysis, at potentially great cost to her life. We see the analyst confronting the patient and proactively fighting for the relationship.

There we leave Elena and Dr Benaim. We see that Elena's improvement creates a crisis for the treatment. But we cannot say that this arises because of frustration of teleanalysis compared to analysis in the office. In either setting we think that the patient's dynamics will drive the outcome. We are left to wonder, will she quit again, while she is ahead?

Chapter 3

Sadomasochistic constellation and distance analysis

Jack Novick

I will describe the parallels between a young man's self-destructive, sadomasochistic presentation and his use of distance modalities.

Eighteen-year-old Kevin said that he had come for assessment only because of pressure from his mum. He was on academic probation, rejected by his circle of friends, filled with rage at everyone, and obsessed with thoughts of being laughed at and denigrated by all. He was seen four times a week in person during the academic year. During the long school breaks analysis was maintained by phone and online contact using videoconference technology (VTC). Four years later he graduated with the highest academic honours from the most difficult undergraduate programme, had a girlfriend, was respected by many for his leadership abilities, and was recruited by the most prestigious company in his field of specialization.

Beginning phase

Very quickly we got into Kevin's belief that I was an agent of his parents and that I was there to judge him. He spent much energy detailing the misdeeds of his parents, especially his father. Since I routinely work with parents of all children and adolescents, I had talked with the father and could confirm that he was indeed a controlling, demeaning parent. This validation of an external reality allowed Kevin and me to define our work together as discovering how his inner self had responded to his father's sadism, how his mind works to protect him from real and imagined danger, and how he could increase his options so that he could discover more effective and less costly means of self-protection.

We talked about an immediate goal of helping him gain control of his rage. I introduced the idea of "emotional muscle", saying that it takes more muscle to maintain a car at the appropriate speed than to slam the gas pedal to the floor and be out of control. He drove home repeating "emotional muscle" to himself and returned eager to work on self-regulation and mastery. This led to differentiating between anger as a crucial signal and anger as a state that he uses as a weapon, as an attack on himself and others, a way of protecting his father, and a way of attaching to me and his parents.

His behaviour now oscillated between extreme masochistic attacks and successes that he experienced as sadistic attacks on others. He approached each exam with terror that he would fail; when he did well he was certain that everyone envied and hated him. At the end of four months we had a two-week break and our first opportunity to continue analysis by VTC and phone.

At our first distant session I couldn't make out Kevin's words because of a roaring sound over the phone. It was a cold, blustery day and he was standing outside, freezing and unprotected from the high wind. This first distance period of work made his sadomasochistic presentation more clear, and we began to work with it. In person he often slumped in a posture of guilt, self-directed rage and incompetence. The way he used the phone made his sadomasochism even more evident, especially in my counter-reaction. I had thoughts of saying demeaning things, and I could feel how Kevin provoked the vicious sadistic attacks from his father. In the two weeks of phone analysis we began to unpack the dynamics of his sadomasochism. We looked at his provoking attack, and how this defended against his anger, and protected both me and his father as he gave us reason to attack him. It became clear that this was his way of attaching to his parents and me. We could contrast the reality that he had left me on vacation, but this activated his overwhelming guilt and linked with the trauma in infancy when he had been abandoned by his parents.

Middle phase

Gradually Kevin began to internalize my focus on his strengths and accept that he had and could enjoy his growing competence and success. This allowed for a conflict between what we call the "closed system" of sadomasochistic, omnipotent self-regulation and the "open-system" of reality-based modes of self-regulation, including positive sources of self-esteem. He no longer insisted that academic or social success was a "fluke", a chance occurrence outside his control.

At the next school vacation we not only continued work on these themes but also included the way he used or misused distance analytic work as related to conflict between open-system competent and creative functioning and closed-system failure to make the phone or VTC work. It should be noted that his field of expertise included computer science, yet he often could not get the equipment to work. We could then link these failures to prior instances of *successful* distance work, as if he had to apologize for doing well.

As he allowed himself more extended periods of success, his fear of the envy of others became more prominent. When he did extremely well on an exam he would not tell others his grade for fear they would envy and hate him. The second spring of work together approached; this time I would be away for several weeks. It was warm enough for Kevin to be outside and he would talk to me while walking through the school quadrangle. If someone came within shouting distance his voice would drop and I could barely hear him. Was he ashamed of being in therapy? Yes, but more central was that he felt that he had something special, something his parents, siblings and classmates didn't have, and that he would therefore be envied and hated.

The fear of being seen and overheard continued. The next time we had distance sessions he tried to soundproof his room and turned the radio so high that we couldn't hear each other. The fear of being overheard was part of what he termed his "paranoia" and related to a longstanding fear of being seen, being heard, and, most self-denigrating, his fear that he smelled. Interestingly, we made most headway with his fear of being overheard on VTC. There was little reality to his concern about being overheard in sessions on VTC, and he began to realize that his paranoia was an internal problem.

We had six weeks of phone and VTC sessions; during this time he recovered memories of holding in his poop as a child and really stinking. His encopresis was confirmed in my talks with Kevin's mother, who added that his father was embarrassed and angry and probably told Kevin that he stinks. After numerous repetitions during times of distance analysis he began to find practical solutions to his fear. He bought a top of the line headset and taught me to use VTC as a more reliable form of distance communication. He became adept at using phone, iPad or computer, and when there was a failure he quickly saw his role as, for example, in not charging his phone.

Termination and post-termination

Distance analysis became a smooth extension of in-person analysis during the termination phase. He continued to work through and face the conflicts of ending our work together. Despite his significant improvement in all areas of his life, we both recognized that there was still important work to be done. Father had been against the analysis from the beginning, and he made it clear that analysis would end when Kevin graduated. In a letter to his parents Kevin said that he wanted to continue his work with me via VTC and asked if they would support the therapy. If not, he would find a way to pay for it himself.

Related to distance analysis is the use of email between sessions for self-analytic work. After Kevin graduated he decided that he wanted to do VTC once per week with email work between. In a major step for him he decided to pay for it out of his earnings and not tell his parents. Here is an email he sent to me after a month of weekly VTC work.

> I don't know if I mentioned this in the previous email but I found a certain comment made yesterday by the doctor (a proctologist he had consulted) to be very interesting. I told him that my feelings and sensation have been different ever since the haemorrhoid surgery in high school. He responded by saying that it was surgically repaired, and it won't ever feel the same. It's been altered and will be different forever; it won't go back to what it was before. And it got me thinking that maybe that was the hope I was having. That maybe it felt so weird to me because I was hoping one day it would go

back to normal or to the way that it was. It's along the same lines with the hope I have for my father changing or with getting back together with R (his former girl-friend). They both have to do with rejection. I have a very difficult time with rejection, whether it be personal, romantic or professional. Perhaps it stems from the feeling of rejection I had as a child, when my parents weren't there to give me the love and support I needed. And maybe I thought that if I were to be miserable, I would get that love and attention. But it never works out that way. I always push people away and get negative attention. I've continued that same solution through rejection today but I need to find more positive solutions to dealing with a breakup, understanding my dad won't change, and getting a business proposal rejected. It all affects me so personally and so deeply because I circle it back to when I was a kid, and made the connection that rejection equals lack of love and support. However, when a person breaks up with you it could be because of distance or lifestyle choices or timing. When a business proposal gets rejected it could be because it's modified and combined with a better one, or not on top of the list for business priorities. And when my dad doesn't treat me like I need or like a father should, it's not because I'm not smart, handsome, lovable or a good kid, it's because the faults, insecurities and shortcomings in his own life currently trump his parenting abilities.

Supplementary email communication

A major goal of analysis is to establish the capacity for self-analysis. Here is an email sent by Kevin a few weeks later:

> I was thinking, we really have two things to work on regarding my social anxiety.
>
> 1.) My concern that everyone's interested in me, that I'm so important to the point that everyone's focused on me. People are always more interested in themselves to begin with (even if I'm up on stage giving them a presentation). They're more likely concerned about what they're eating for lunch, or picking up their kids after work, etc.
> 2.) If people are focused in on me, and interested in me, it doesn't imply that something's wrong. I automatically assume that if someone's looking at me, it must be because I'm doing something weird or I look weird. What if they're looking at me and thinking 'boy, that kid must be lifting weights'. Or 'he reminds me of my son/nephew'. I need to get over the connection I make between attention and negativity.

Despite the decrease in frequency and the fact that we met only on VTC, the work we had done for years together allowed us to look at all levels of exchange including the transference of feelings that I had rejected him, that I envied him, and that I would only accept him as a damaged smelly child.

Conclusion

I know that there are major controversies about distance analysis, ranging from questions of legality to whether such work can be called analysis. However, reality has moved on and, whether we like it or not, distance analysis by phone, VTC and email has been done by many for years – and the number is increasing daily. Patients, especially younger ones, take for granted that we live in a wired, connected world. They assume that this is a useful, expected modality of interaction.

I have shared some material from the analysis of a late adolescent to illustrate that pathology will impact whatever procedures we use. Equally, I have tried to illustrate the value of work in varied media and demonstrate that such work furthers the treatment and offers concrete measures of progress. We can retreat from this reality or use it to the benefit of the patient and further the relevance of psychoanalysis in the 21st century.

Commentary

Carlos Ernesto Barredo

This clinical case report shows Jack Novick's sincerity and generosity, which make it possible for us to have a useful dialogue about his experience with his patient he calls Kevin.

Dr Novick begins with a discussion of the negative transference, which of necessity put him in a place where he was seen as the parents' agent. In my opinion, the matter of the father in particular is the reason for the consultation. The complicated vicissitudes of Kevin's relationship to his internal father image are at the root of his symptoms and the difficulties in his life.

To approach this issue from a reality perspective, validating the young man's opinions about his parents and the arguments that sustain his attitude, even though it was possible to secure a positive transference and promote many favourable changes, a sequence of events nevertheless influenced the course of the analysis and its later denouement.

The sadomasochistic constellation in which Kevin takes pleasure in submission and rebellion, challenging others and inflicting punishment on himself, lost some of its impact when Kevin was encouraged to develop what Novick interestingly calls "emotional muscle".

The anxiety that was reported about exams appears to refer also to what happened in each session. As for what I think, the difficulties encountered the first time that the analytic couple engaged in a distance analytic session provided an opportunity to show vividly elements of resistance that were already there in the sessions held in person – and then to work with them in the transference.

I believe that the key to understanding this case is to recognize the interweaving of actual memories from the phase of development of sphincter control (and verified by the mother) and phantasies of being the creator of a wonderful product: himself (see Freud's 1910 paper on a particular type of object choice in men). Being both creature and creator himself is a strategy that, in failing to acknowledge his parents' procreativity, aims to avoid the castration complex.

The concept of the father's pleasure in both its subjective and objective senses becomes the nucleus around which Kevin maintains the ties to his parents, the emotions that go with them, the symptomatic satisfactions that Kevin obtains from them, and the conflicts that take shape in that context.

That is why I think that the father's resistance to Kevin's continuing analysis after graduation, despite the obvious benefits already accrued, also reflects the resistance of the young man, who thus obtains a compromise solution shown also in maintaining a remote analytic contact that allows him to take refuge in the texts of e-mails, where, once again, the products of his solo elaboration substitute for the collaborative work with the analyst.

I regard analysis fundamentally as an experience of alterity, and for that reason I share with others the view that self-analysis is impossible. In this case self-analysis by email becomes the field in which the young man plays at creating his own theories. His theories, however, tend to resonate with the analyst's interpretations. For instance, Kevin explains the rejection that he felt as a child as a result of his parents' failure to provide him with the love that he needed, and his imperfections as being due to his parents' limitations and difficulties. The belief at stake is that, based on the ideal father imago with which he is identified, he should have been created without any failings. The infantile sexual theory that underpins the sorrows of late adolescence is expressed in the feeling that the previous generation did not do its job well and now will do better.

The presence of this theory accounts for the block against elaborating that grief and taking responsibility for one's own failings, giving rise to depressive feelings of gratitude for the power necessarily received as coming from the Other.

I think that this marks the point at which this analysis gets stuck. This does not escape Jack's awareness. He makes it manifest when he affirms that both he and his patient recognized, despite the significant improvements achieved in several areas of Kevin's life, that much work remained to be done. We also see it in Jack's decision to include in his account the e-mail in which the young man mentions his exchange with the surgeon. This is a good example of acting out, where Kevin makes an interpretation outside the treatment situation, telling the surgeon what he has introjected in his analysis, without recognizing it. Nothing will be the same after having gone through that experience. The physician, a displaced figure of the analyst, introduces a limit here, acting as an agent of castration, as Lacan (1956–1957) points out in his reading of Freud's (1909) Little Hans paper. The ghost of self-gestation has been shaken in its omnipotence. From now on the self will have to depend on another for its creation, something that although glimpsed is still not accepted. Kevin does not want to know about that, even though he presents his intellectual ideas about it.

Finally, I agree with Dr Novick that the practice of analytic treatment at a distance is an area of exponential growth in our work as analysts. Looking beyond the current controversies concerning distance analysis, especially as to whether it is a legitimate way of training candidates, we see a burgeoning field of research into the conditions necessary for the practice of technology-assisted analysis, the effects of technology on analytic process, and the clinical results of distance analysis.

References

Freud, S. (1909). Analysis of a phobia in a five-year-old boy. In: *Two Case Histories ('Little Hans' and the 'Rat Man'). Standard Edition*, 10, 1–150.

Freud, S. (1910). A special type of choice of object made by man. (Contributions to the Psychology of Love I). In: *Five Lectures on Psycho-Analysis, Leonardo da Vinci and Other Works. Standard Edition*, 11, 163–176.

Lacan, J. (1956–1957). *The Seminar Book IV: La relation d'objet* (pp. 199–408). Paris: Éditions du Seuil, 1994.

Commentary

Caroline M. Sehon

The theory and practice of teletherapy and teleanalysis among children and adolescents is rarely discussed or rigorously studied. Fortunately, Dr Novick has offered us the possibility to examine transformative moments along a four year, four times weekly analysis traversed by a child analysis expert and an 18-year-old college student. While the treatment was conducted predominantly in the office, distance-mediated sessions were introduced after four months and continued periodically during vacations taken by patient or analyst. After graduating from college, Kevin relocated and transitioned during the termination phase from four times weekly analysis to weekly videoteleconference (VTC) sessions accompanied by once weekly emails.

I will discuss the amplified potential for the teleanalytic setting to reveal hidden areas of the patient's mind, to challenge the analyst's capacity to hold a secure internal setting in the midst of the patient's attacks upon the frame, and to unleash especially fertile material within the transference–countertransference field. Sometimes the practice of teleanalysis is devalued as being inferior to in-office work; some critiques claim that the distance-mediated setting makes it impossible to analyse the negative transference, or question the depth of the treatment when the analyst is "blinded" to ordinary sights, smells and sounds. I will examine those elements of the teleanalysis that both catapult the treatment and stand up to the critique that teleanalysis cannot achieve comparable or enhanced outcomes.

Leveraging challenges to the frame

Teletherapy and teleanalysis is not for the faint of heart, as the analyst must rely upon a secure internal setting in the face of varying external settings. The sessions between Dr Novick and Kevin occurred often in the midst of many apparently unstable external settings. It is unclear whether an agreement had been established between patient and analyst about where the patient would be situated. Did Kevin make such decisions unilaterally? Did Dr Novick give Kevin a wide berth to situate himself where he would find himself most comfortable (akin to those situations in child analysis when the analyst sometimes goes out to the street or parking lot to meet the child if fearful or resistant to come inside)?

Dr Novick shares poignant elements of Kevin's history of abandonment and early trauma. We do not know much about his parents' relationship to each other and to Kevin except that his father seemed to be a formidably frightening and traumatizing figure. I sensed a terrible experience of neglect and trauma at the hands of Kevin's parents, which contributed to his developing a very disorganized attachment to them in which the *tie to the bad object* became his primary organizing experience.

Therefore, it is no wonder that ghosts from the nursery would descend upon the analytic stage in the "here and now" with Dr Novick. Of course, in the in-office setting we would expect nonverbal archaic characters to enter the transference–countertransference field. When the analytic couple is willing and able to introduce a modification to the traditional frame by including some dimension of distance-mediated work, we can expect these characters to be expressed vividly in relation to the teleanalytic setting itself, where they are easily detected and amenable to interpretation.

Suddenly, the analytic couple is contending with new characters in the field when Kevin moves outdoors to bring in a new character – the "roaring wind". We are transported from the in-office setting, where Kevin relies upon his analyst to provide a quiet and private frame, to a threatening environment, where we encounter the omniscient presence of the winds that dominate the analytic scene and drown out any audible discourse between analyst and patient. Was Kevin consciously attacking the frame in a fierce defiance of the analyst, or was he in the throes of his rejecting internal objects and needing desperately for Dr Novick to capture these nasty voices in ways that had gone unheard within the office setting? What can we make of the fact that Kevin and his analyst persisted in that setting despite the analyst's compromised capacity to hear the patient's spoken voice? Was Dr Novick in the grip of an enactment and held hostage to the sadistic character at play in Kevin?

Like a dream, we are offered a complex condensation of images to which we can associate. Kevin's dependent and helpless infant self is present in this image of the 18-year-old tethered to his analyst by phone as if by a symbolic umbilical cord, all the while feeling overpowered by a rejecting (sadistic) internal object, represented by the menacing winds. It would be convenient for Kevin to blame the raging winds rather than to own his aggression and take stock of his unconsciously determined attack on the analyst. Similarly, Kevin consciously "sound-proofed" his room by turning up the radio volume so that his peers could not hear him, but unconsciously filled his analyst's mind with toxic surround sound.

Despite all these threats to the integrity of the frame, Kevin did not fully overpower the analyst's listening resources. We learn of Dr Novick's "counter-reaction" feelings of condescension and rage towards the patient, echoing the sadistic attitude of Kevin's father towards him. Analysands who are more impacted by what is not verbalized within their families than by what is actually communicated find a nonverbal way to communicate their experience; for instance, in relation to the setting. In teleanalysis, the disruption to the setting can provide valuable clues to the underlying messages that the patients need our help to decode and understand. Perhaps Kevin was terribly unsure that his analyst could ever truly help him if he were to merely hear his litany of complaints against his parents, and so desperately needed Dr Novick to have an embodied experience of his primitive characters before he could feel understood.

The teleanalytic setting as a vehicle into the patient's mind

Divergent analytic settings – in-office versus telephone/VTC – provide fertile ground for the manifestation of a split transference, as well as a valuable opportunity to encounter the patient's separate selves in ways that may otherwise go unnoticed. In Kevin's case, Dr Novick reflects that the "first distance period of work made his sadomasochistic presentation more clear" . . . In person, Kevin in a masochistic surrender often "slumped in a posture of guilt, self-directed rage and incompetence", whereas in remote sessions, he expressed his sadistic, controlling and demeaning part against his analyst. In my experience practising, studying and researching teleanalysis, it is particularly common for the analyst to discover how parts of a patient's personality become fractioned between in-office or remote sessions. We gather the impression that the remote setting seems to allow Kevin to unleash more forcefully his attacks on the setting itself, and thereby on his analyst and himself, in identification with his sadistic father.

From another perspective, Dr Novick bears witness to the shifts between the patient's good and poor use of the distance-mediated sessions. When he is engaged in "open-system competent and creative functioning", he can take full advantage of these sessions. Yet, despite Kevin's sophisticated computer know-how as a digital native and computer science specialist, he also misuses the remote sessions when embroiled in the "closed system of sadomasochistic, omnipotent self-regulation". Such a thoughtful perspective sheds new light on the ways in which patients may reveal unique aspects of their personality functioning, depending on how they choose (unconsciously or not) to relate to the teleanalytic setting.

It was only in the context of distance-mediated sessions that Kevin recalled his struggles with stool retention and encopresis as a young child, and showed how his developmental challenges were apparently exacerbated by his parents. Even though we are given only the verbal rendition of Kevin's anal stage development and encopresis, and the body of the soiling child is not in the office with us, we may find our olfactory senses responding. While Kevin may well have remembered these experiences even if the entire treatment had taken place in the office, we might wonder whether he felt less inhibited to reveal such stories to Dr Novick within the relatively greater safety some patients experience in the remote setting.

Conclusion

There are heightened demands upon the analytic couple when they move between in-office and virtual settings. Teleanalytic work requires a careful attention to the ways in which the frame is discussed, established and maintained in the face of various challenges to it. Kevin's transformation from a frightened and enraged adolescent to a self-reflective and self-determined young man is a powerful testament to the usefulness of teleanalysis for this particular analytic couple. Despite the prominence of the negative transference, Kevin worked steadily with Dr Novick and stayed the course of treatment towards a reportedly successful termination.

This case study inspires many questions and hypotheses about the relative advantages and disadvantages of the in-office setting versus the remote setting, the efficacy of distance treatment for fostering authentic analytic process, and the mode of therapeutic action. I think it is important to maintain an ethical stance of negative capability at the outset and along the way as to whether distance-mediated sessions can usefully occur and then whether they should continue or not. We need to expand our literature to include those forays into distance tele-analysis that were unsuccessful or foreclosed due to pressures to conduct only in-office work. We also need more reports like this one from Dr Novick, showing the challenges and benefits of teleanalytic treatment.

References

Fraiberg, S., Adelson, E., & Shapiro, V. (1975). Ghosts in the nursery: A psychoanalytic approach to the problem of impaired infant-mother relationships. *Journal of the American Academy Child Psychiatry*, 14: 387–422.

Fairbairn, W. R. D. (1940). Schizoid factors in the personality. In: *Psychoanalytic Studies of the Personality* (pp. 3–27). London: Routledge & Kegan Paul, 1952.

Ferro, A. (2009). Transformations in dreaming and characters in the psychoanalytic field. *International Journal of Psycho-Analysis*, 90(2): 209–230.

Chapter 4

Case study research

A psychotherapeutic relationship established by email

Horst Kächele

The importance of establishing a therapeutic alliance is widely recognized as fundamental to successful psychotherapy, not only for psychodynamic therapies but for all treatment modalities (Horvath, Del Re, Fluckiger, & Symonds, 2010; Luborsky, 1976, 2000; Safran, 2003). But if the patient stops at the therapist's door no alliance can occur. For various reasons many potential patients do not succeed in taking the necessary steps to make contact. This is where technology can help us to reach them. Email communication can facilitate the establishment of an alliance that supports a therapeutic relationship.

There are very few detailed accounts of what actually goes on in the world of email exchanges between patient and therapist. With colleagues at the University of Ulm, I started the Ulm Textbank in the 1980s – an information system integrating techniques of linguistic data and text processing in the creation of texts from traditional psychotherapy process notes that can thus be accessed, created and analysed by a wide range of psychotherapy researchers using a uniform interface (Mergenthaler & Kächele, 1993). Now we need to be collecting data from written online communication in psychotherapy. We need primary data, not just opinions (Luborsky & Spence, 1971) so that we can examine the process of online communication in psychotherapy. So in the case example that follows, I have selected seven emails from the patient to the therapist and four responses from the therapist to the patient out of a total cache of 200,000 patient words and 30,000 therapist words written on email over a three-year period. First, I will set the example in context by a brief mention of relevant research on the therapeutic alliance and its clinical application.

The therapeutic alliance

The therapeutic alliance is a multi-dimensional construct defined by four aspects (Horvath & Greenberg, 1994):

a)   the patient's ability to work purposefully in therapy
b)   the affective link between patient and therapist

c)   empathic understanding and involvement of the therapist
d)   agreement between patient and therapist regarding treatment tasks and goals

The helping alliance

In his research on the importance of the therapeutic alliance to the success of psychotherapy, Luborksy (1976), one of the founders of scientific research into the process of psychotherapy, introduced the term *the helping alliance* and spent years perfecting a research instrument called *the helping alliance scale*. The helping alliance is a term for a number of obviously related phenomena converging on the degree to which the patient's relationship with the therapist is deemed helpful for the achievement of treatment goals. This is consistent with Freud's (1912b) recommendation that the mild positive transference should be considered a bearer of success.

After many years of alliance research Luborsky (2000) drew the following conclusions:

1)   The quality of the alliance in the early hours of therapy is a predictor of treatment success, regardless of psychotherapeutic methods of diagnosis and patient characteristics.
2)   A good alliance is fundamental to success, even though it may seem that success in therapy has made the treatment alliance possible. For instance a patient may say, "I feel better, so I can be more engaged in the therapeutic relationship".
3)   Therapist and patient do not always agree on the assessment of the quality and importance of the alliance.

Applying his research findings to the clinical arena, Luborsky (1984) made the following recommendations for clinical technique in therapeutic relationships:

1)   Use language and behavioural support to achieve the patient's treatment goals.
2)   Help the patient towards understanding and acceptance.
3)   Develop empathy, respect and appreciation for the patient.
4)   Help the patient maintain useful defences and empowering action patterns.
5)   Maintain a realistic yet confident attitude that treatment goals can be achieved.
6)   Acknowledge progress in achieving goals and confirm readiness to end treatment.
7)   Help the patient express thoughts and feelings related to various topics.
8)   Encourage a "we-alliance".
9)   Reflect together on what patient and therapist have made together.

The development of a positive therapeutic alliance requires the participation of both parties to the interaction. Therapy is a bi-personal model. If no positive alliance has come about, the treatment is unlikely to be successful. If there are disruptions to the therapeutic relationship, the most effective technique is to focus on the here and now rather than the repetition of a particular aspect of behaviour. With immediate and careful processing, disruptions can be addressed and the therapeutic alliance thereby strengthened.

But what if ambivalence dominates the field? Bleuler eloquently addressed the topic of affective ambivalence for the first time in a lecture at Burghölzli in 1910, later printed in English.

> Even the normal individual feels, as it were, two souls in his breast, he fears an event and wishes it to come, as in the case of an operation, or the acceptance of a new position. Such a double feeling tone exists most frequently and is particularly drastic when it concerns persons, whom one hates or fears and at the same time loves. This is especially the case when sex is involved which in itself contains a powerful positive and almost equally powerful negative factor.
>
> (Bleuler, 1934, p. 125)

Contemplating treatment, the patient may be unable to reconcile his wish for help with his dread of revealing his powerful feelings of love and hate, sexual desire, guilt, and shame, especially when these attach to the person of the therapist. When this unresolved ambivalence dominates the field, the decision to engage with the therapist can be overwhelmingly difficult. In this case a preliminary communication that occurs without the physical presence of the therapist can be helpful in bridging the gap between desire for help and successful treatment. In some cases, the gap may be so large that a sustained period of communication may be necessary to the establishment of a treatment relationship. In the case I will present, a lengthy email correspondence led to an ongoing treatment relationship.

Clinical illustration

The following report describes the initial contact and initiation of treatment via email correspondence. It began in response to an online "box" I created for people who were experiencing grief and into which they could post their suggestions and responses to a few brief questions and answers. Then came the following email:

Email # 1. From Susan X to Horst Kächele: 18 March, 2002

Dear Horst Kächele

I appreciate the offer of an "online grief box". It costs less to overcome grief that way. It is easier to make a statement via email than to speak about one's difficulties face-to-face.

For quite some time, I have carried around the idea of contacting a "professional". But the problem with me is that I want to get in touch when I feel very bad. Then I want to talk to someone "immediately". I want the contact. But when I feel good, I want nothing to do with any help. I feel strong and, so to speak, "not in need of help". Between times, I think more and more often about it, and am more aware of the need for assistance. But I have no idea what my problem really is, or whether and how and who can help me.

I see my fellow students very clearly. I perceive their problems, and I am able to help them. But I perceive myself very vaguely. I do know who I am. So my first difficulty is, What should I say? What is relevant? What is important? I doubt I could understand my deeper problems.

I am 25 years old, studying psychology, now in my 4th year. I have completed training as a social worker, and in order to finance my psychology studies I hold a part-time job on a rehab. care ward. I have my social life "fully under control". I am social. I am known as a stable, helpful person who can get a lot done and endure hardship. About a year ago my mother died of cancer. I had a very intimate relationship with her. I cared for her at home. Last summer I got a questionable diagnosis of multiple sclerosis (MS).

For some time, since the death of my mother one year ago, I haven't felt stable for any decent length of time. Depressive moods came over me. I felt passive, lacking in motivation and capacity, but above all there were times of high inner tension. Massive suicidal thoughts or death wishes always occur very suddenly and seem to me so overwhelming that I'm afraid I will lose control of myself. I have great fear of being adrift in a dark world, because it is getting worse. It is more difficult to control each time. The way to climb out of this is getting steeper.

I was perhaps always a bit weighed down with concerns, but I am generally positive, cheerful, welcoming and appreciating life. I feel incredibly far away from this woman. I feel I have been screwed up and I'm emotionally flat. I have a feeling that whatever might happen, I would not mind. I do not care.

Of course, I'm outwardly usually the strong Susan that has everything under control. It is incredibly hard for me to open at all. I will not deny that, of course, I hope to get an answer.

Thank you very much,

Susan X

Such an email, such an electronic appeal, triggers a variety of emotions. It makes me realize that for some people – and probably this is not rare – it is less difficult to describe their problems via email than face-to-face. The anonymity of the participants generally allows a greater degree of openness, sincerity, and intimacy (Walther, 1996).

The writer does not see me, I do not see her, but I read in her lines that danger is imminent. Remarkably, she discusses her ambivalence about wanting help when she feels bad and not wanting it when she feels good, but then she points to a triggering moment for the current escalation. She describes a strong person and a weak person. I realize that I will have to name her strength in the reply I will send out the next day.

Response # 1 by Horst Kächele to Susan X's email # 1: 19 March, 2002

Dear Susan X.

Your letter tells me that you have a wonderful way of expressing yourself, contrary to your self-assessment. After reading your letter, I think you should dare to risk and seek a conversation with a psychotherapist. I am thinking of different women therapists that I could refer you to. Why a woman? Intuition tells me that. But let's arrange to meet, and then we can consider together what could be useful. So, I hope to hear from you again.

Sincerely,

Horst Kächele

I refer to Susan's expressive ability in written form, and I want to encourage the writing person to come one step closer. Why did I recommend a female therapist? I can only say that I sensed it. Maybe my decision had to do with her mentioning the death of her mother. Specifically, I express my hope that she maintains contact with me. On the same day I receive an answer, a few hours later. And I get a little critique. She's right. I have dodged the task of giving her a substantive reply.

Email # 2. Susan X to Horst Kächele: 19 March, 2002

Dear Horst Kächele

I am very pleased with the quick response that I had hoped for. However, I had hoped you [would] take more of a position about what I have written. If it would be so easy to arrange a meeting, then I would certainly have done it! But you certainly have your reasons, and from the perspective of a therapist, asking to meet to interview me is certainly the most obvious response.

Right now I feel the urge to express myself in writing. For me, that is certainly better than talking. Everything is spinning, everything is in question. I'm searching, searching. For now, I want to stay holed up.

Nevertheless, thanks for your comments. Maybe I can take the next step.

What does your intuition say? And isn't it sometimes better not to lift the lid to see if the water has stopped boiling? I am scared to empty the pot and take a look what is in there. I am afraid that only a loose shell remains, and that the idea of any content is a farce.

Thank you and best regards,

Susan X

Susan is able to take the point of view of the therapist. She is not naïve about therapy, although she presents herself as reluctant to engage in a therapeutic relationship. She must have had previous treatment experience. Explicitly she emphasizes her "desire" to express herself in writing, probably in fear that she would be even more confused in an interview. From her reference to my "intuition" I read another subtly ironic twist, and it leaves me with doubts about my skills. Because I believe her reflective ability is high, I give an interpretation in the next email – and I offer to continue the email exchange.

Response # 2 by Horst Kächele to Susan X's email # 2: 20 March, 2002

Dear Susan X!

Alright, we can continue with writing. Here is my response. The disparity between the negativity of your self-assessment and the appealing quality of your self-portrayal seem significant. I am impressed by your clear ability to understand others, to respond to them, and to recognize that your view of yourself is blurred in comparison.

The ability to be autonomous is a great protection but it also restricts your reaching out for help. So that's a dilemma.

That's it for now.

Greetings Horst Kächele

PS How do you know my first name? For a student you are pretty free of the formalities of respect, and I am okay with that.

Email # 3. Susan X to Horst Kächele: 20 March, 2002

Dear Horst Kächele!

I really do appreciate your efforts. I'm not without respect, on the contrary. However I dislike an artificial form of address in a contact like ours, and it pleases me that you let me know that you were surprised. I didn't do too much thinking about the way to address you, and you didn't feel harmed by it.

I am in great distress. I feel I have few reserves. I am very afraid of losing control. I can no longer cope. My mood is so incredibly unstable.

I wonder why I have managed so far quite well with my life, and now I have the feeling that I cannot master it anymore. I'm afraid I'll go crazy, lose all my abilities, and give up strategies never to be found again. That's it! That is me! That is what gives me the sudden urge to write things. It is a feeling of having to express it more quickly to an addressee, not only for myself.

It's not like a distance from the top to the bottom. No, it is an abyss with sharp edges impinging on my senses, a way in into the dark with no opportunity for return. This is what I am feeling nowadays.

The dull, dark, passive feeling in recent months has lifted. The feeling has become a little lighter. At the same time I am temporarily under a huge strain, a fear, a feeling of panic I haven't known before. As I said, the atmosphere inside me is unstable, and I yearn for peace.

I read these lines and judge myself incomprehensible and inadequate. I am guilty of abusing you, using you as a trash bin, I do it anyway and feel better. Of course I hope for a response, an inspiration, a direction.

I beg your pardon, and thank you.

Susan X

Again and again she puts forward her distress. I approach it very carefully. I experience a great contrast between her measured, expressive writing and the emergency situation she writes about. I keep responding but with a mere container function.

Response # 3 by Horst Kächele to Susan X's email # 3: 21 March, 2002

Dear Susan X

You do not annoy me, not at all. I don't have plenty of time today because I still have to prepare for a Congress in addition to meeting family responsibilities. Nevertheless, I have read your long letter. The great change in you gives me the impression that there is a strong desire for another Susan to come to light, a Susan who wants to live differently. But it's not an easy thing to abandon old strengths. Leaning on someone is hardly allowed but with me you can do it.

So we'll stay in touch,

Horst Kächele

I point out that her distress – whatever this may be – may indicate a process of change. Since I still know little about the psychosocial situation of the writer – except that she is a student – I remain cautious. I continue to offer to stay in contact.

Email # 4. Susan X to Horst Kächele: 21 March, 2002

Dear Horst Kächele

I'll take your offer with thanks. I am in a dangerous situation – the lid is lifted, and I cannot cool the boiling water. I am still able to close the lid again. Possibly the water must boil until it has evaporated, nothing left. There is a real physical pain that torments me and does not allow me any rest.

In contact with you I feel weak. I have to admit to myself that's kind of a pleasant sensation, taking some of the pressure off.

I appreciate your efforts,

Susan X

This letter makes me feel that the strategy of keeping in touch is on the right track. Susan can express a certain acceptance of the new feeling of being allowed to be weak, even though feeling vulnerable is hard for her to bear. My concern that her distress may indicate underlying psychiatric illness or even psychosis leads me to further inquiry.

Response # 4 by Horst Kächele to Susan X's email # 4: 24 March, 2002

Dear Susan X

I am thinking about your sharp mood changes and the feeling of being on the precipice of an abyss. I sense your great need, and sometimes it sounds as if you think you may need psychiatric assistance, which I cannot do in the epistolary way.

So what is it that makes the way to an interview so hard?

Greetings,

Horst Kächele

The renewed attempt to clarify what stands in the way of a verbal conversation moves our dialogue along a little further.

Email # 5. Susan X to Horst Kächele: 25 March, 2002

Dear Horst Kächele

Thank you for your answer. You're right, what is the problem? Why do not I just go to a therapist? I'm suspicious, vulnerable, afraid of being mis-understood, laid bare, having to stand still and remember, and then finding that this human being cannot help me, does not understand me. And it is this lability that holds me back time and again. Still, I sometimes feel strong and growing more so. Then I think again, I do not have the right to help. I should get over this by myself.

Yet in dealing with innermost problems I feel somehow underdeveloped, unable to express myself, unable to interact – and this bothers me more and more. I have always been very hard on myself. I put myself last. What I really want now is to bring everything together. I now realize that thinking about myself alone or writing about it in this form does me no good. And I see the danger in my trying to help others when everything is so chaotic in me. What has been closed off for a long time is now opened up. My feelings are raw and I am overwhelmed. I do not have the equipment to deal with the opening up and to find a new, perhaps more honest balance.

Sometimes I think maybe I'm so close to it, I would need only a tap of the index finger to move me in the right direction. Well, that is how I feel right now, at twelve o'clock on March 25. I am getting the feeling that this is the beginning of the discovery of myself. Inside the high walls, there's nothing there, nothing is growing. I have not existed. I just acted.

Maybe you still have time for me. Thanks for your effort. How do you happen to actually write to me? I appreciate it.

Many greetings, Susan

I am relieved that the previous epistolary work has now led to a conversation. I respond to email # 5 by offering an appointment via email.

Email # 6. Susan X to Horst Kächele: 26 March, 2002

Dear Horst Kächele

I will come to the appointment at your office. 3 o'clock is fine. Where are you? I hope you won't be disappointed. I won't be able to express myself in direct conversation as well as in the written kind of non-binding contact. But I have already given you some hints about myself. Maybe they can point the way for me.

Many thanks,

Susan X

First appointment in my office, Wednesday 27 March, 2002

The patient in black clothing takes up little eye contact. Susan is very silent. I remember that for years she has been taking care of her mother suffering from cancer and that her mother died recently.

Susan says, "I made sure to have done everything humanly possible for her." This formulation surprises me. Susan conveys a strange feeling of guilt, but for what?

Susan reports among other things that she had made two previous attempts at getting help. In December 2001, she approached the Student Counselling Centre and received a date for an initial interview but could not accept it; later she visited a female psychiatrist.

Susan says, "So I tried it twice. I hated myself and my decision to seek help. And the chemistry didn't work. I am also sure that I recounted my problems in a poor way. I only knew that drugs would not help."

I acknowledge that she is obviously still looking to find the right kind of help and that she now knows where I am to be found. The same evening I get a long email.

Email # 7. Susan X to Horst Kächele: 27 March, 2002

Dear Horst Kächele

I felt very well at today's meeting with you. I felt well taken care of. But I'm afraid of a new contact I don't have the strength for it. I am resigned to the way I feel at the moment: I do not know if I am worth your effort. I long for peace and relief of my pain. I can put the lid back on the kettle, but will I continue to live soulless? Will I continue to live soulless and die of cancer by the time I am sixty? (How polemic – sorry). If so, will I try to kill myself (also polemic), but seriously, will I be able to complete it? Or is there a third option? I would have never done it to my mother, but she is gone now. And everyone else in this world will go on living without me, even if they wouldn't think so.

I do not know how things will develop, if they will develop, and if so, how. Secretly I want to find a viable way. I want to see the light.

I would be happy to get feedback from you, perhaps even another appointment to meet sometime. (Of course, "happy" to put it mildly, is really modest. I really hope for a reply, but of course I do not expect it. I'm strong enough to withstand everything and need no one!) I will not bother you. I will not presume on you. I will stop contacting you if you send the appropriate signal.

Thank you, and best wishes to your sunny room,

Susan

With this email, I am ending my example, but this was far from the final email. On the contrary, with this exchange in 2002, a long-lasting, helpful relationship began and persisted until 2005. Therapy was conducted sometimes in my office and in email exchange. The email communication was the primary component of the treatment because for long periods of time the patient was not able to talk in the sessions she attended at my office from time to time.

Conclusion

A therapeutic alliance is not always easy to develop. Technique for preparing the patient for therapy has to be adjusted for each individual case. In earlier times the exchange of letters probably assumed this function. Today email exchanges provide a speedier version of that function. However, there is a broad consensus among online researchers (Knaevelsrud, Jager, & Maerker, 2004) that online communication provides inadequate support and fails to help patients who have borderline symptoms or are prone to dissociative states of consciousness, suffering from loss of reality, suicidality, or psychosis. This may be a valid criticism in the case of brief email interventions. Certainly, if these types of email exchanges are to be useful for paving the way into intensive therapeutic work, they need to be explored and discussed and subjected to research. For this disturbed patient, however, the provision of a continuous long term email correspondence over many years led to a gradual intensification of therapeutic work in the face-to-face setting.

References

Bleuler, E. (1934). *Textbook of Psychiatry: II General Psychopathology* (Chapter 7. Disturbances of Affectivity, Affective Ambivalence). New York: Macmillan. https://archive.org/download/textbookofpsychi00bleu/textbookofpsychi00bleu.pdf

Freud, S. (1912b). The dynamics of transference. *Standard Edition*, 12: 97–108.

Horvath, A. O., Del Re, A. C., Fluckiger, C., & Symonds, D. (2010). Alliance in individual psychotherapy. *Psychotherapy*, 48: 9–16.

Horvath, A., & Greenberg, L. (Eds.) (1994). *The Working Alliance: Theory, Research and Practice*. New York: Wiley.

Knaevelsrud, C., Jager, J., & Maerker, A. (2004). Internet-Psychotherapie: Wirksamkeit und Besonderheiten der therapeutischen Beziehung. *Verhaltenstherapie*, 14: 174–183.

Luborsky, L. (1976). Helping alliance in psychotherapy: The ground work for a study of their relationship to its outcome. In: J. L. Claghorn (Ed.), *Successful Psychotherapy* (pp. 92–116). New York: Brunner/Mazel.

Luborsky, L. (1984). *Principles of Psychoanalytic Psychotherapy: A Manual for Support-ive-Expressive (SE) Treatment*. New York: Basic Books.

Luborsky, L. (2000). A pattern-setting therapeutic alliance study revisited. *Psychotherapy Research*, 10: 17–29.

Luborsky, L., & Spence, D. (1971). Quantitative research on psychoanalytic therapy. In A. E. Bergin & S. L. Garfield (Eds.), *Handbook of Psychotherapy and Behavior Change* (1st edn, pp. 408–438). New York: Wiley & Sons.

Mergenthaler, E., & Kächele, H. (1993). The Ulm Textbank Management System. In: L. E. Beutler & M. Crago (Eds), *Psychotherapy Research: An International Review of Programmatic Studies* (pp. 219–225). Washington, DC: American Psychological Association.

Safran, J. S. (2003). The relational turn, the therapeutic alliance and psychotherapy research: Strange bedfellows or post-modern marriage? *Contemporary Psychoanalysis*, 39: 449–475.

Walther, J. (1996). Computer-mediated communication: Impersonal, interpersonal and hyperpersonal interaction. *Communication Research*, 23: 3–43.

Commentary

Sharon Zalusky Blum

It was bound to happen. Twenty-five years ago telephone analysis was a subject deemed unfit to be debated in psychoanalytic journals. No practitioner dared bring up the idea except with friends and colleagues. Over two decades later, after many journal articles, books and discussions at national and international meetings (Scharff, 2013, 2015; Zalusky, 1998), psychoanalysis by telephone has gained wide and open acceptance. It may still be debated, but the topic has by and large been destigmatized. It is now fitting that our psychoanalytic attention move from the telephone and turn to the role of email in the psychotherapeutic process.

I am honoured to discuss Horst Kächele's moving account of a young, grieving psychology student who reached out for help via email. Kächele in this brief chapter has made another significant contribution to the growing literature on email communication and psychotherapy (Buchholz & Kächele, 2015). Spanning decades, Dr Horst Kächele is known internationally for his distinguished psychoanalytic research. He is aligned with the spirit of Freud the researcher, who continued to forge new ground, revising assumptions when new information came to light. In writing this email case presentation, Kächele represents an openness and a willingness to move forward with the times.

It is a welcome change. Until recently, North American and European analysts taught psychoanalytic theory as if it were written in stone, impervious to the radical changes and advancements happening throughout modern society. Our colleagues seemed to have forgotten Freud's recommendation to physicians practising psychoanalysis:

> I must however make it clear that what I am asserting is that this technique is the only one suited to my individuality; I do not venture to deny that a physician quite differently constituted might find himself driven to adopt a different attitude to his patients and to the task before him
>
> (Freud, 1912, p. 110).

Since the beginning of psychoanalysis there have always been clinicians who quietly set aside many traditional psychoanalytic theories and techniques in order to help their patients have better lives. They have done so, however, in a vacuum.

Our traditions and prejudices created an atmosphere in which clinicians were reticent to put into print what they were actually doing to help their patients (Renik, 2006). Fortunately for us, Kächele has never been one to practise in private.

Email

While there are few detailed accounts of what actually goes on in email exchanges between patient and therapist, there are many email communications in everyday practice, and it is useful to differentiate among the various types.

First, there are those emails coming from prospective patients who are more comfortable using email to inquire about therapy (Blum, 2013). Through email these future patients are easily able to give details about why they might be seeking help. Some others reach out via email because it is more convenient. They are able to give the therapist considerable information in a short time. Many patients are accustomed to communicating through email at their work. Some others are afraid they would inconvenience the therapist if they attempted to make a spoken communication, which they fear might interrupt work with other patients. Then there are those who are simply ambivalent about direct contact with another.

There is a different kind of email communication that exists between the patient and the therapist in an ongoing therapy. Some patients may communicate with their therapist by email when they feel the subject matter at hand is too exciting or too dangerous to be discussed face-to-face (Gabbard, 2001). In such a case, no immediate response by the therapist is needed. The topic of the email will be discussed at the next session. In a similar vein there are those patients who email the therapist when they remember something after a session and are afraid they will forget it before the next appointment; they send an email so the therapist can hold the information.

In this chapter, Kächele has presented another type of email, one very different from those mentioned above: it is email used as a lifeline. It is a type of therapy that occurs mostly through the written word over an extended period. It can be characterized as ongoing crisis intervention. For those like myself who have had an ambivalent relationship with email, studying Kächele's transcript of the email exchanges between himself and the student can be an enriching and transformational experience. The clinical work between the two is captivating. I found myself reading it over and over again. Susan, the psychology student, came alive to me. She was able to poignantly articulate her struggle – her wish for and fear of contact. I was, however, disappointed that we were presented with only the first nine days of this compelling email communication.

As a therapist I empathized with Kächele. Susan's suffering was felt in every line. The delicate balance that he achieved was breathtaking. I valued Kächele's clinical acumen, but more importantly I appreciated his deep humanity.

This case was unusual for many reasons. It had a perhaps unique beginning. The initial intervention began before the email communication was even initiated. It could be inferred that Kächele was the one who reached out to Susan by creating an online "box" for people experiencing grief. The respondents were asked to post their suggestions and answer a few brief questions. So when Susan responded with her initial email she already knew that Kächele was interested in issues surrounding her grief.

Though Susan was anonymous to Kächele, he probably was known to her, a fourth-year psychology student. Through her study it is likely Susan had heard of Dr Kächele and read parts of his work. I would venture to say that before she wrote the first email she already had a positive transference to this scholar. Immediately she opened up not only to herself but to Kächele. Susan explained her urge to express her raw and overwhelming feelings *in writing*. To her it was important that there would be someone interested at the other end of the email connection; a journal entry would not suffice. Gabbard (2001) articulates this paradox:

> The person sending an e-mail message is alone, but not alone. The apparent privacy allows for freer expression, but the awareness of the other receiving the e-mail allows for passionate attachment and highly emotional expressiveness. The Internet has led to new definitions of privacy as well as of intimacy.
>
> (p. 734)

Susan's well-developed ability to express her internal complexity facilitated the work with Kächele. He responded immediately to her. He was warm. He complimented her ability to communicate her thoughts and feelings. He suggested Susan come in and together they could decide what would be helpful. I imagine most therapists under a similar condition would have responded with such an invitation. Susan answered by saying it was not that easy – if she could have, she would have. She stated her fear:

> I'm suspicious, vulnerable, afraid of being misunderstood, laid bare, having to stand still and remember, and then finding that this human being cannot help me, does not understand me. And it is this liability that holds me back time and again. Still, I sometimes feel strong and growing more so. Then I think again, I do not have the right to help. I should get over this by myself.

After expressing her deep-seated fear, Susan attempted a visit, but the contact evoked more fear.

The transcript is instructional. In it are some important clues about how to conduct an email treatment.

1) Be authentic. Kächele succeeded with Susan because in addition to having strong clinical skills he was authentic with her.
2) Keep in mind when starting email communication the importance of forming a therapeutic alliance.

3) Own your own limitation. Kächele let Susan know about his availability. When he was busy with his congress and other obligations, he told Susan.

4) Set ground rules. It is important to let the patient know how available you are willing to be. Will you check email daily or twice a day? If you are unable to respond immediately, it is important to acknowledge having received the email and estimate when you will respond. It can be anxiety-provoking for either member of the dyad when there is uncertainty. As therapists we need to bear the unknown. For our ambivalent patients we need to repeatedly demonstrate our reliability.

5) Payment. Therapists must decide for themselves whether or not to charge for email communication. Here again the therapist needs to be explicit, either way. That is part of setting this unusual frame.

Conclusion

Email is a very complicated medium in which to do therapy. It is challenging because you do not see the other. You do not hear a voice. You cannot witness the initial reaction to your words. Those on the other side of the exchange cannot see the warmth in your eyes or feel your patience. Misinterpretations of what is written (on both ends) may go unchallenged. It is made even more difficult when you do not have a prior therapeutic relationship. Though without visual or auditory cues the patient may be freer to create in fantasy the "you" that he or she needs, wants, or fears, unfortunately for us it becomes harder to appreciate who we are in fantasy to the patient. Interpretation is thus more complicated.

However, with all of email therapy's drawbacks, there still is much to gain.

We have an opportunity for learning new information that we ordinarily do not know about our patients. We discover how they write, how they formulate their problem unencumbered by our presence. We discover how they organize their thoughts. Some like Susan are able to provide us with a compelling narrative. They can express their problems more fully without interruption or concern about our reactions. We find out how the person benefits from our interventions, or ignores them. Email therapy also gives us time to reflect in a deeper way on what we have just been told. And, relative to spoken communication, we are – and probably should be – more careful about what we write.

If our objective is to be helpful to the suffering of others, we must accept that at times we need to extend ourselves beyond our own comfort zones. We must realize that there are people who cannot in person sustain contact for extended periods. With email therapy there is hope that one day they will be able to risk a fuller experience in person with another human being. From email to the telephone to our office and back again and again, we will work to create therapeutic alliances that can endure the pain of ambivalence.

The world is changing. We must change with it. What is next? Analysis by text?

References

Blum, S. Z. (2013). Musings on therapy and technology. In: J. S. Scharff (Ed.), *Psycho-analysis Online* (pp. 49–57). London: Karnac.

Buchholz, M., & Kächele, H. (2015). Emergency SMS-based intervention in chronic sui-cidality: A research project using conversation analysis. In: J. S. Scharff (Ed.), *Psycho-analysis Online 2* (pp. *145–159*). London: Karnac.

Freud, S. (1912). Recommendations to physicians practising psycho-analysis. *The Stan-dard Edition*, 12: 111–120.

Gabbard, G. O. (2001). Cyberpassion: E-rotic transference on the internet. *Psychoanalytic Quarterly*, 70: 719–737.

Renik, O. (2006). *Practical Psychoanalysis for Therapists and Patients*. iBooks. https://itun.es/us/ub9IA.l.

Scharff, J. S. (2013). *Psychoanalysis Online: Mental Health, Teletherapy and Training*. London: Karnac.

Scharff, J. S. (2015). *Psychoanalysis Online 2*. London: Karnac.

Zalusky, S. (1998). Telephone analysis: Out of sight, but not out of mind. *Journal of the American Psychoanalytic Association*, 46: 1221–1242.

Chapter 5

Psychoanalytic process
in cyber-technology

Asbed Aryan

Presentation

Psychoanalytic treatments, conducted online or on the telephone, need our sustained attention to building a theory base if we are to continue refining best practice. This is especially true and urgent, given that nowadays many analysts around the world are doing teleanalysis to meet the conditions of modern life in a global economy. Considering the topic of teleanalysis, I ask: Who is it for, why is it needed, how is it done, and how does it affect the psychoanalytic process? My purpose is not to deal with the nuts and bolts, the "how to" aspect, but rather to conceptualize the analyst–patient encounter in the virtual setting.

Since 1988 I have functioned as a training analyst in APdeBA, the Buenos Aires Psychoanalytic Association. Since 2005 I have conducted three-times-a-week training analysis and once-a-week supervision in our mother tongue, Armenian. I meet the requirements of the International Psychoanalytical Association (IPA) for remote analytic training, in that I conduct the sessions in my office in Armenia or in Buenos Aires for two months a year (100 hours), and for the rest of the year, I conduct the sessions online using Skype or Oovoo, with or without a video image. Early on in this clinical experience, I concluded that the sense of presence is not exclusively physical. But surely we have known this for years, over 3500 years ago. In a recent article, there is a quote from a Mesopotamian letter of the 17th Century BC from a writer in the mountain of Fagros to a reader in the village of Shemshara: "While reading your words I had the impression that you and I had found each other and embraced, however far apart we were" (Manguel, 2015, p. 3). As my clinical experience extended over time, I further concluded that psychoanalytic process occurs in virtual sessions, just as it does in traditional settings.

Conceptualization

Psychic life is constituted by the desires and fantasies parents have about their unborn child, society's expectations of the child, and the effect that these unconscious forces have on the body and mind of the infant. This psychosomatic background is the basis of transference, which occurs in the production space of psychoanalysis when at work with these constituent forces. During the analytic encounter, the libidinal body, the free association of the patient, and the abstinence of the analyst during the analytic dialogue are the essential elements in the formation of the analytic transference relationship and the circulation of the unconscious between them. All these elements are in place whether the analysis is conducted in a traditional setting or online.

Transference is the updated edition and experience of the enigma of the parental couple and the primal scene. Analysis creatively reopens the enigma in fantasy in conjunction with the analyst. If this analytical situation is created, whether in the analyst's office or in cyber communication, an analytic process will occur.

Two fundamental concepts

In thinking about the practice of teleanalysis, I find useful two concepts: the *distortions of semiotics* (Liberman, 1971, p. 577, 703 and 875) and *dispositif* (Foucault, 1977, p. 229).

Distortion

Liberman noted the quality of patients' communications and described three categories of distorted speech.

Syntactic distortions

Patients who show syntactic distortions speak in a manner that is detrimental to pace, intensity, modulation. Meaning is preserved and they do conserve articulated language with slips and omissions (usually seen in neurotic conditions).

Semantic distortions

When emotion invades the system of values and ideals of speech, the various verbal and paraverbal elements that make up the phonic mass of speech (such as clicks, sighs, uhms) distort the meaning and the structure of the language. These distortions overwhelm the articulated communication (usually seen in schizoid and depressive conditions).

Pragmatic distortions

Pragmatic distortions refer to speech affected by the speaker's changing the mode of expression and the content according to the impact of the speech on the listener during the whole conversation (usually seen in psychopaths).

Dispositif

Agamben (2006) uses *dispositif* in psychoanalysis to mean "anything that somehow has the ability to capture, determine, guide, intercept, mold, control and assure the gestures, behaviors, opinions and speeches of living beings" (Agamben, p. 14).

I study this network of elements from the perspective of 14 years of clinical observation of the transformations that develop over long periods of analytic process, particularly in teleanalysis.

The practice of teleanalysis

On 13 December, 2002, I began the first remote treatment at the behest of my patient. It consisted of three weekly sessions in my office with telephone sessions during two weeks every two months, and it lasted four years. Currently, I conduct 90% of the remote sessions by teleconference, either with or without video. Several treatments are progressing favourably and seem to me to involve recognizable analytic process. This finding made me wonder what my main criteria for defining analytic process are. Given that I am using an alternative setting, have I learned anything from my teleconference experience as to where to place the emphasis as to which elements are essential and whether a patient has truly undergone analysis or not? I believe that there has been some slippage in demonstrating analytic process in traditional settings. Too often it is held that the defining factor in psychoanalytic treatment is the setting. There has been less importance attributed to emphasizing what happens *inside* the setting, namely in the *dispositif.*

This has been partly due to the fact that the term "setting" refers to an aspect of the analyst–patient link, which is ideally fixed and stable in the pragmatic sense, and therefore supposedly more scientific and measurable according to logical positivism. On the contrary, I think that the better the work develops within this link, the more mobility of unconscious communication and metapsychological change can be observed. Therefore, for some time now, in Buenos Aires, the concept of *dispositif* is preferred. *Dispositif* implies the whole relationship, that which is said and not said in the analytic encounter, the impact of the sociocultural context, and the forces of multiple heterogeneous powers and areas of knowledge in the analytic dyad. Awareness of the inter-relation of power and knowledge, especially in a training analysis, is essential in studying the transference–countertransference dialectic in relation to an omniscient analyst. The power gradient is often exacerbated in the analytic relationship while using technology and must be carefully addressed. My idea is that patients with more ego weakness and altered states require narcissistic reassurances. The physical presence and constancy of the analyst favours that effect in the office. Online we can build a similar reliable network to support unstable ego states, with the exchanging of sms, whatsapps and e-mails to bridge any gaps in online communication so that when the analytic situation is reinstated there is support for responding to the novelty of a specific comment and the surprise of an interpretation.

When Anna O. defined her treatment as *the talking cure*, she was talking about speaking and listening without the element of touch (Freud & Breuer, 1893). She was referring to her experience of encounter with the other. Over the years, Freud and subsequently others discovered that the conflict emerges in the *dispositif* where the transference may serve as resistance or may itself be resisted. There-fore, it seems that the value of cure depends on the talking and not so much on the pragmatic setting itself. From my experience of analysing individual adults, chil-dren, adolescents, couples, and families, using sessions in my office, online, by telephone, including e-mail communication, I have a broad perspective on what I value in an analytic relationship, whatever the setting may be.

Expanding and improving on Anna O.'s definition of analysis as the talking cure, we can say: the analytic experience is understanding and being understood by a valued partner. This experience enables patients to become able to question themselves, speculate about their internal processes, and have full access to think-ing, feeling and motor skills for formulating, expressing and managing conflicts through the use of everyday speech, within the context and socio-cultural norms of that moment in time.

When beginning a teleanalytic treatment, I consider whether to include the trans-mission of a visual image. My decision will depend on the patient's comfort, and we can make any modification as the process develops. For example, a male patient considered my image absolutely necessary when we began analysis, but a year later, he stated that we would no longer need it. Clearly, his first preference was based on preformed transferences and paranoid anxiety, which after a year of analysis had shifted. The analytic work had eased his anxiety and his semantic distortions of the analytic relationship. With a visual image or without it, the patient uses technology to bridge the physical distance between us so that we can relate at conscious and unconscious levels of interaction, as if we were together in my office.

I have noticed that patients begin by perceiving the difference in the analysis space. They find that something happens there that did not happen before. Fur-thermore, they feel that they need it and benefit from it, and therefore they defend it and respect it. Analysis is invested with libido. The analytic space can become libidinous within any technology. This space, which is new for patients, promotes the development of transference, whether it be retrospective (a repetition of ear-lier ways of relating) or prospective (an anticipation of a new way of relating). The resulting psychoanalytic process based on an emotional-intellectual encoun-ter leads to achieving greater availability for thinking with another.

I try to listen "without memory and desire" (Bion, 1969, p. 679). I aim to be fully present, tuning in to a sixth sense, and listening with the third ear (Reik, 1948). Analysts turn their therapeutic instrument towards receiving unconscious communication, and towards hearing their own voice in reaction to what their patient says. Working in psychoanalysis in the office or online, without precon-ceptions and without prejudice, allows one to de-dogmatize the settings, whether traditional or technologically assisted. If we become unduly custodial of the traditional setting and the regulating of the "correct" practise of analysis, we are employing a superego attitude to reassure ourselves of our value. We can face our critics' worst fears – wild analysis, unmonitored countertransference, and analyst acting out. If we try too hard to make analytic process seem as if it is hard science with measurable units, we are deceiving ourselves. But we can open it to critique. And we can try hard to describe it. We can go beyond that too and record it according to a standard protocol.

My colleagues and I in Buenos Aires are subjecting our work in teleanalysis to this sort of methodical review at different stages in the treatment, using Ricardo Bernardi's Three Level Model (3LM), which describes stages in transformation using close study of history, narrative and process notes from analysis. Specific questions for the analyst to reflect upon lead to a refined observation and description of changes at three levels of examination of the material. I found that Bernardi's Levels 2 and 3 presented standardized guidelines that were similar to those I had been using intuitively and freely. I employ the Bernardi model in examining the clinical effectiveness of teleanalysis so as to allow us to reflect on the indications and contraindications for teleanalysis as a variant of the traditional setting capable of sustaining the *dispositif* that is the essence of psychoanalysis.

Clinical material

I will present vignettes including direct speech from selected moments in a three-session consultation and nine-year psychoanalysis of a 46-year-old man who began treatment after two failed therapies. The patient, whom I will call Lisandro, has an obsessive and narcissistic character structure with remnants of a childhood psychosis that had been treated in adolescence. Lisandro is married and had one son when I first met him nine years ago. (Now he has another son and will soon have a girl.) He lives in the country 200 km from Buenos Aires and comes to the city twice a week to his office at the company he owns. It is important to note that in the course of these nine years the time required to move around the city and the suburbs has more than doubled. This change has propelled patients to request some sessions by teleanalysis, even though they are local.

Consultation conducted in person

The first interview

At the first consultation interview, Lisandro sat down and said: "It has been six years now since I last had treatment." Then he began telling me about his two previous therapies. The first therapy including parent and family work covered his teenage years from the age of 13 to 22 and the second one was from 22 to 31. He explained that his two previous therapists, now friends, had not been able to assist him "in deep, in the internal".

As if interpreting, he said of the first analyst,

> He had to take care of me in my daily life. He taught me how to deal with
> financial transactions and helped me to establish my business. (And by the
> age of 23, I had my own company.) But we could not work on my inside. He
> ended up having personal problems himself and could no longer take care of
> me. So I continued with another therapist, a very good woman. The moment
> had now come to work on my inside.

With the second therapist, the treatment relationship became very affectionate.
Lisandro said,

> But again the therapist ended up having personal problems and eventually
> she could not see me. She had many problems with her daughter and sister,
> and many times needed me to contain her. I did it gladly, because she was a
> very good woman, and because I had learnt to survive in the relationship with
> my father, but what about my needs? It was a little complicated, but I saw that
> logically she could not deny priority to her daughter. Then finally she was
> afraid of losing her place as the therapist with me, and we decided that it was
> best to finish. Now we are good friends. She knows how to calm me down
> and remove the drama that I usually make of things.

Every now and then Lisandro mentioned his family of origin. He is the eldest of
four. His second sibling is two years younger; the next one is six years younger;
and the fourth is ten years younger, each of them now living in a different country.
Lisandro says he was like a father to his youngest brother. Lisandro described his
72-year-old father, a lawyer, as "extremely manipulative" and his mother at age 67
as "closely narcissistic, authoritarian and dictatorial, almost psychotic, using
threats to deal with any frustration". His parents alleged that Lisandro was insane
and threatened to sue his first therapist for refusing to put him in the hospital.

The second interview

In the second interview Lisandro elaborated on his reason for seeking treatment
again, saying, "I'm more reckless than I should be, especially with my 4-year-old
son." He taught him to throw stones from a bridge and to feed the horse and the
dog from his hand. He left him alone near a pool and watched from afar to see
what he would do. Lisandro thought of these as tests of his son's courage "so that
he learns what danger is and develops survival skills". At the same time he suspected that they were forms of exposing the child to danger and exposing himself
to alarm. Lisandro said, "I was afraid to overdo it and not arrive in time to save
him." He justified such behaviour saying that his father used to have him walk a
horse when he was too small to be responsible for the large animal. Looking back

on it, Lisandro feels that his father did step over the line into child abuse, which Lisandro himself does not do.

Lisandro's speech was confusing, obsessive, and peppered with terminology to impress me, but it was sometimes used incorrectly. The flow was uninterrupted. I felt compelled to ask questions to stop the cataract of words that could "drown" me. I asked myself, "Was he leaving me at the edge of the pool?" In reporting these two interviews I found that I was making his speech more coherent, and that alerted me to the level of confusion of his psychic life. For the same reason, the passages of the sessions to follow reflect his actual speech, sometimes partly reconstructed by me for ease of reading.

Preliminary metapsychological considerations

Lisandro was locked in a narcissistic world which he justified to himself, and yet he was willing to go through treatment. He deals with conflict between his ego and superego by projecting his cruel superego on his parents, who alleged he was insane. In the here and now of the transference he was identified with an omniscient object, explaining everything to me. I felt that he was putting together a "theatrical representation", a defensive acting out that, more than making up for his deficits in making contact, had complicated his interaction with me because it removed him emotionally. He replaced true emotion and concern with pseudo-preoccupation, such as the planning of tests to toughen his son, which then filled him with anxiety instead of concern. It was his experience of anguish that gave me the intuition that in analysis he could overcome his dissociation of thought and feeling, and the misunderstandings and confusions that he was caught in. I thought that he would be able to connect with his psychic pain and start working through it.

The third interview

Lisandro continued, at his fast pace and without pause, with stories of everyday situations in which he obsessively blamed his father for how he was treated during his latency. I noticed he was trying to buddy up to me as if he could not bear the power gradient in which he was asking me for help. I noted again the strange syntax and began to think of his speech constructions as "psychotic restitutions". After only 15 minutes I interrupted to tell him that I had enough information and that I was going to explain to him what kind of treatment I could offer. Speaking slowly and clearly as we speak to children, I told him the fundamental rules of free association and abstinence, and set out the frame, giving details such as schedules, agreeing not to modify the schedule arbitrarily once it was set, how to request changes if needed, cancellation policy for public holidays and vacations, and forms of payment. I was not sure how much he would understand and remember.

He immediately responded,

> Perfect, it's clear. Yes, it is, it is, yes. I am a little lost so these rules are better for me. To speak, I think that I try to have a bit of control, to speak of something that is or seems relevant, because it's really a silly thing, and it could be easy, because already there is a method in place, and then I'll go concentrating . . ." [This is translated from the Spanish, of course, but it is an unaltered report of his syntax.]

I added that if he were to lie down on the couch, instead of sitting in front of me looking at me, he could more easily focus on what he was thinking and talking about without distraction. Lisandro replied,

> Well, possibly in the future. Yes, the couch is a very important factor that I remember. I did very well lying down in therapy, the time I was working with my first therapist, at the beginning. I have a very good previous experience. I felt that I could talk a lot. I think that I will do that this time too.

I also chose to detail the dynamics of our relationship to modify the semantic distortions. I said,

> My function is to add something that you alone are not being able to realize, so you can continue thinking and developing your ideas. They are not policies, or rules, but a contribution to expand your options on how you might proceed here.

Lisandro replied,

> Good, well . . . Yes, it is clarifying for me because, let's say, I have been out of practice. It has done me well and I have the wish of . . . I know that there is another world beyond the area I try to control . . . or things are . . . There are always concerns, about entering that world. It is like dreaming . . . one has concerns and suddenly falls asleep.

Then he began to talk about the frame and his need for holidays. He said that for two or three months per year he was normally out of the country visiting family. "To me it is a major break because my adult obligations wear me out very much during the year." This sounded bizarre. I pointed out that a disruption of three months per year, in addition to my two months' of travel each year, would not provide enough continuity to support the treatment. He offered not to spend more than two months, and I suggested the possibility of working on the phone as long as it was productive in his case. He accepted my suggestion immediately and said that it was a matter of getting used to it and that several of his friends did that. I myself doubted my suggestion would be effective because of the nature of his character and problems, but those problems told me that there was no way he could be out of treatment for four months every year.

I will present passages from four sessions, years apart. I transcribed them to show the confused nature of the patient's speech and the shift in his syntax over the course of treatment.

The first analytic session (in person)

LISANDRO: How are you?

ANALYST: Hello

LISANDRO: [walking in and showing me what he wears] I came a little informal because I could not go by the house or I wouldn't make it. [he lies down, silence] First thing I think, that is, first thing that comes to my mind is that I continue with the theme of my father. Some new memories came to me that day I came here. Hence I think there is something quite nuclear in my daily existence. I have an adviser of mine in my company, but he is not my employee, he is an external advisor, but he often advises me also. That is the first thing that comes to my mind – a kind of interlocutor with my father to see if he could make him understand or make contact through third parties, and then came another idea that I had – that a little bit of my father, who is full of anger with me as I am with him in many respects, but it is a matter of irrational anger – that is, either it is a very strong hatred and for me it was better business to feel guilty because in that way I wouldn't lose him but in reality I do not feel guilty, don't think objectively that I am. My father is so crazy that . . . and I don't have him anymore, but I think that unconsciously something presses me, some fantasies of dialogue with him, ok? I just had one that goes like this: 'You were with me, you loved me, you used to take care of me, and suddenly you abandoned me, you were not there anymore, or it became difficult for you to be so stable with me and so attentive to my life' and well, after that I left and I looked away. That dialogue appeared in my mind.

ANALYST: I think that you are also trying to tell me that you wonder whether I'll be able to be a moderator between you and this image of father you have inside you so these ugly fantasies and feelings can change so that you are not guilty.

LISANDRO: I am guilty of everything, guilty that he doesn't give me more place in his life. In other words, I am the guilty one – that is, for me the relationship ran out as it was going on. I don't know, I guess because of his immaturity he sold out and ended it. Yesterday I had a fantasy in the pool which I think has to do with him. It is quite ugly, the one I had . . . but my son is very complaining and I am like him in being demanding, but he goes on about wanting to go to the pool, and I do not want to be alone with him in the pool because I sometimes have ugly fantasies or have attention problems – nothing will happen, but it is better if my wife is there. I'm teaching him to swim (he is a year and a half old) and then I grab him so he moves his legs. He begs me 'More, more, more daddy!' I don't know how to put limits, and in a moment I change the game. I think that's my mistake, trying to satisfy him to the point of wearing me out a bit. It was when he jumped in and he almost hit his leg on the edge that I had the fantasy. The fantasy was that if it happened and hurt him, he would loosen his demand on me a little. Do I explain myself? He would want to jump less often into the pool because of the pain. Then I had countless reflections around it, because I remembered that my father often hurt me so I would stop asking things of him. He used to do something that could hurt me so he could tamp down my demand. It was like a perverse game that does not give anything and messes up the playing field as well. Then when I told him that, I began to exit the relationship – that is, I looked for another father. When I could do it, it was, like, a very strong thing that happened with my father in the field of rivalry and rupture. I suppose that if my son calls me for something that I can't give him and he finds it somewhere else. On the other hand anyway I agree to it if others can give it him. I will accompany him, as I did with my younger brother who meant much to me – (and he sought his horizon differently than I did, or I would have followed him) and he did very well. I . . . I will not deny my, *his* place in me, or mine in him. Now we are more like brothers. Before, we were more father and son, and well, I somehow feel that I have an old wound with my father that is not resolved or at least not entirely. Then I do not know to what extent this might affect me with my son, if I have not resolved it.

ANALYST: You are scared that you are like your dad with your son, and you don't want to be like that. But with me perhaps you're afraid to be too demanding in case I treat you as your father did.

Friday 20 March, 2009. On the phone

LISANDRO: Well, here I am at home, after all I stayed. Otherwise it's too much traveling. Yesterday I was . . . there in your office, and then I was . . . I went to the country to meet this sister I don't want really to see and her daughter. But well, after that I came home and I was too tired to return today to Buenos Aires, wasn't I? And I'm not seeing the kids, so I stayed here. Since yesterday I've not been thinking about all this, have I? Perhaps I was very, very immature, or very weak, but I haven't faced it. I don't know, it seems like it is . . . or is not . . . not . . . or somehow is . . . not . . . Perhaps I get the feeling it is better not to confront it. On the other hand, it seems to me that it is time to grab the bull by the horns, because I have the clarity to at least talk about it because I think that it is better for me that I move forward with this. Now, for example, where it shows up most is with the kids, doesn't it, in being able to give the necessary time to that situation. Somehow there is always something which is essential to me what with my need, or my commitment to myself, or my internal order, any type of order. I do not know if there is an order, but some order, and I don't know, well, sometimes I feel good that there's going to be this harmony between, between, between what my son needs and what I need, and that life is that way, and my life today really is that way. I think the situation with my father and everything that happened put me a bit at risk and showed me my destiny, and – at least irrationally, unconsciously – showed me that I was sort of there in the trenches in search of interaction with someone who could help me.

ANALYST: It seems that if you do several things one after another coming and going from here to there, some of them unusual and others new, you become spread too thin and feel tired, especially if you have to come and explain them to me. Then finally if you remember and tell me about the burden of the discussions with your father, whether you won or not, brings you back to the familiar feeling of heated discussion.

LISANDRO: That is now, that I'm grown. If I lost, it would open a panorama of why, where, and what new things my father would move on to, because he was also revengeful. Those were my recurring fantasies. Once I spent three, four days like that with many . . . I devoted myself to this paranoia, filled with destabilizing ideas and writing them down and looking for the answer about what things my father might have in mind to relate to me in a perverse way and complicate my life.

Wednesday I July, 2015

LISANDRO: I gave you the option of talking yesterday by phone or today on Skype so I could talk with my latest model iPad, but yesterday I still didn't know how to put the Skype in this new iPad. I already solved almost everything else, it's cool . . . The subject yesterday . . . was the phone. I could not call by phone, because my brother-in-law was delayed. Then I thought that you could decide if we would go on Skype or go by phone, because I could use the phone, as there is a place there where I can sit and talk, but I prefer Skype. You prefer Skype too, don't you? [an example of symmetrizing the need] Anyhow thanks for the appointment time changes. I sent you a WhatsApp . . .

ANALYST: [I had noticed that he was making the need for the phone symmetrical – he wanted me to prefer it as much as he did – but I simply said Yes, I received it . . .]

LISANDRO: Really what happened is that a friend invited me to play golf and it was a nice day. Well and now I have a new racing car body. I bought the spare parts for it and they will give them to me on Thursday, so everything will be good from next week on. I have many resources, don't I? [Long silence] . . .

ANALYST: Having in mind that you have many resources will also help the treatment. You'll take more benefit of it, not needing so much of me.

LISANDRO: Certainly, and yes, because otherwise I'll depend on someone else . . . I don't know, the point is that it's a long process because – did I tell you? – I decided to buy all the spare parts for my old car so I'll rebuild it. [long

silence] Today I find you very lucid but I'm half and half. I can't find anything to talk about . . .

ANALYST: [Instead of taking up his comment about my lucidity, which implied
that I had not been lucid at other times, I focused on the activity of his mind.]
You get impatient waiting for your thoughts to come.

LISANDRO: [He nods. Silence] . . .

ANALYST: But of course, you need to take advantage of them and use them, and
do not exclude any.

LISANDRO: No, no, what comes to my mind I tell you. [brief pause] Now I'm more
relieved, but in the morning I felt that thing again, I don't know, that thing
about the time passing, and how I need to be taken care of. I felt a little helpless. But at 7 pm now talking with you I believe that it has to do more with
old experiences than with current reality, because I slept well enough. I could
sleep until 10:30 am. I think I'm getting fixed. Yet I'm always scared of not
having someone to talk to who would care for me a bit, as in this case you. I'm
always afraid of that, and now it's time, perhaps, to realize that it will not happen, that I will always find someone, and that, besides, people do not disappear. And besides I have more resources. Yes!!! I can hold myself together for
longer periods of time, perhaps much longer. I called a friend of mine today.
She has a friend in prison, and she visits him. This guy had addiction problems
and now he is in jail – it's been a year now. He is cured of all that stuff. He is
much more serene now. The jail was a blessing for him. And I felt identified
with him up to a point, like this: perhaps to me the isolation, assuming that
I would go to jail or something similar, would not be bad for me either. Not
bad to realize how much I fear lacking resources and accept that perhaps
basically I have them as a person, accept that I have strength, recognize that
I don't have to walk around with so much fear or begging for help. I have
no problem with the feeling of needing help, but I do with the feeling that
everything is at stake in every human relationship, as if they were all opportunities of finding people who will help me, or withdraw affection, or pass me
to someone else who could take care of me. So my mental muscles are very
attentive to any mistreatment by anybody towards me, or to any opportunity
of . . . of . . . of . . . of having a link with someone. And suddenly I realize
that I don't even need it. I don't know if I'm clear. Or with friends also, I suffer too much when a friend doesn't invite me to dinner and then it turns out
that he had invited me, and I didn't pick up the phone message and had been
mistaken. In other words I suffer when I feel I don't belong or I feel almost
like a pariah. As a child I must have somehow felt – I guess – almost helpless,
mustn't I? Then I do not know if the thing goes through also . . . I don't know,
I felt – as I said – if I was imprisoned for a year, perhaps at the end I would
realize that I had succeeded, that I have the resources I need inside myself.
Perhaps I'm looking out fearfully, always afraid that I'll find nobody.

ANALYST: I believe that you keep up the conviction of not having sufficient
resources so you can ask for more and more and more to calm down. But you

don't want to feel guilty for that and so prefer the explanation of having been forsaken and the solution of finding others to solve your problems. But the price that you pay is high because you go into panic that no one will appear at the very moment of need . . .

LISANDRO: That's true . . .

ANALYST: . . . Or pay the price of imagining going to jail to force yourself to find out how many resources you have and use them. But you continue giving priority to expectations that others will solve your problems because of the addiction to the conviction of helplessness.

LISANDRO: [Long silence] . . . Well, it may be that. Let's say I'm afraid of not having the resources myself. Yes . . . and that I'm looking outside [pause]. Yes, when you say "solve your problems" what actually happens is that I have a panic about being alone or helpless.

ANALYST: Because you immediately associate being alone to being helpless.

LISANDRO: That's true [silence]. Yes, it is like a fear that grabs me, and I need someone to take me off the panic attack. The reflective process does not exist here. There is suddenly a feeling of fear invading me.

Saturday 21 November, 2015

Lisandro starts saying that since he woke up he feels less constrained. Now he feels full like the wind, more permeable, as he does when on vacation. Additionally with good news, they are finishing the luggage carrier he designed for his car. Enthusiastic and nicely hopeful about small things, he feels a change, as if he had received an inheritance. He received the news that they are renting his field so that he will not spend a lot of money to keep it free of weeds. They also taught him that he could keep it free of weeds by using a special roller, a very cheap solution instead of using expensive chemicals. The grain prices improved, probably thanks to the new government. He has also paid his debts. His wife's pregnancy is going well, and so on.

LISANDRO: Right now, I find myself saying, "Now what am I going to invent to worry about?" I go to the seaside with the kids and enjoy myself! The truth is that kids are wonderful. There is an initial stage of raising them that takes a lot of push [pause]. I had this insight about all that I have been telling you.

ANALYST: It seems that you acknowledge that you found several solutions to your problems.

LISANDRO: Yea, exactly . . .

ANALYST: On the one hand, the boys are growing well, your wife is healthy, and her pregnancy is good, so you can stop worrying that you feel bad because of the past.

LISANDRO: Of course, it may be.

ANALYST: On the other hand, yesterday you could think back on your dad and your sister from your present point of view as if to put an end to old wounds, instead of returning to the past and feeling yourself abused by both of them. And you were able to resolve your current problems. You admitted that you do not know a problem that bothered you for a long time, and yet you didn't recognize it.

LISANDRO: Yes I didn't know, really I didn't.

ANALYST: So learning about and being able to solve everyday problems allowed you to let the past go by. You are even enjoying the present.

LISANDRO: Yes! Yes, I would have hooked in another problem. I would have involved some labour situation or something – right? But now I can say, "Let's stop. I'm going on holiday, let's enjoy it." The main thing was I could say "stop". That is also an improvement. I could not tell you why but I think I calmed down [long silence]. It might have to do with many things. I don't know if there's a moment of maturity that came to me also. [long silence] Also I spoke with my father again as I told you. I spoke for an hour and a half, two, and that's very tiring, isn't it? And since I have been in analysis, the difference with my sister and my dad is that I assume the second place with my father. I always used to have rage about that. Now I say, "Well, if I came out second to my father, ok. It's time. I had the first place and suddenly went to the second. That is the truth: It is time to accept it." And that is a great sorrow and a great pain, but it is an irreversible reality. [he smiles] But that doesn't mean that I cannot be happy.

ANALYST: Nowadays.

LISANDRO: Of course . . .

ANALYST: Because now you're not only second to your father, but first in your own family.

LISANDRO: Yea, both.

Saturday, 16 January, 2016

LISANDRO: Strange, last night I had a dream that I seem to recall. I must always dream but I never remember. I think that the dream was about one of the families that fostered my personal and emotional life. There was a lady, a very good lady, who was the grandmother of a friend of mine and used to invite me to their house, very friendly, very good, and I still miss her, but hey, basically it was a very large family! And it turns out to be that it still is. As I was walking down the street, we were looking for her apartment with one of her many grandchildren but we could not find the key and there was as a veil of guilt over me, that I had grabbed the key or done some dishonest act. I do not remember exactly. I believe that the old lady's daughter had said it, and then I had the sense that she was scrutinizing, evaluating, and suspecting me. And I said, "No, I don't have it", but as if I wanted to be accused of something. [long silence]

ANALYST: Do you remember anything else . . . also of this family?

LISANDRO: No, no, no. Yes, it makes me . . . No! The feeling was terrible because I was in the dock again.

ANALYST: Again?

LISANDRO: I do not know, I do not think that means . . . It sounds very familiar. First, we were talking yesterday about my father, about how my father accuses me – and used to accuse me when I was a kid – in such a cold way as if to say he thought I was a bad person. That was very hard for me. I don't know what can happen with my child, but I always maintain a foundation of trust, and I do not think that he can make something of hidden codes in my speech. When my father seemed like a private investigator accusing me, he seemed to be on another planet. What made me think about this and got me thinking was . . . do you remember Rachel's son-in-law, David, who stole money?

ANALYST: Yes, Yes. Well, but you told me that her daughter and David had just been using her money, not stealing it.

LISANDRO: No, no, no! He stole it because no one gave him permission to touch that money. In his mind he believed (auto-convinced himself, right?) that he could use that money. The daughter did not know about it. She wouldn't take anything that was not hers. He seized that money. It is robbery to some degree. [pause] Yes, Yes, Yes! It's a theft, a theft. There is something else: there were two episodes about money. Rachel kept money in the safe and in some other place. Suddenly the money disappeared from the other place, and that was when Rachel called me, that was four years ago, and she said, "The only person, who I can hardly think of distrusting, but who it may have been, is David, my son-in-law." Now you tell me, what sense is there in this? Rachel has left him a keychain with the key of the house and the key of the safe too. Is Rachel putting her neck on the block, or what? I don't know. That's what I told her.

So Rachel says, I'm pretty sure that that money was spent in my family. It is not that he went to Las Vegas alone. Let's say that he was not generating any income, lived on that money, and kept up with the family a kind of fiction that he generated money. [brief pause] I don't know; it's confusing because how can anyone imagine that Rachel let him have the key after she had already gone through that previous episode? And if you want to go deeper, we can delve so much more into the issue, and even find some humour in it. I told you that Rachel was a little dramatic in recent years, and well, her sister died too, and she sometimes conveys experiences that are not reality in my view. So I tell her: 'Look Rachel, you are the one living in this situation where somehow your daughter and your son-in-law seem to be the ones holding you in this crazy state of mind.' I have a very personal relationship with her. She is like a mother. I say, 'Obviously you have to have paid 30 thousand dollars at least!' [he begins to laugh] 'Quick, put more money in that safe so they can pay for the therapy you obviously need.' In other words we laughed a lot about this situation, and at the same time it is serious. I don't know if I explained the scenario properly. I mean Rachel is at boiling point.

ANALYST: It seems that yesterday's session fired up the dream, and introduced themes of accusation in a covert way, now in the form of Rachel accusing her son-in-law (your father not the only accuser now) and of the lady in the dream insinuating that you have stolen the key. With different characters from different periods comes the same theme of accusation about various misappropriations, and these are summarized in this dream. We should expand on whatever else has been condensed in this dream.

LISANDRO: It may be so. Yes. I fully agree that the theme has to do with accusation, because what I associate. [long silence] I also associate to this, that later I spoke with David, referring to it tangentially by talking about how he needs to inhabit the world of work and finance. He is a carpenter, and it's not so easy to get a good carpenter who does restoration. Then he began to specialize in that and managed to get many jobs, and he is keeping that up, or at least that's what he tells us, but I do think he is. And what he told me is that his father worked in the Montevideo police (he is Uruguayan) so he was constantly making deductions and investigating people as if he was a detective. [pause] Well, somehow his head since childhood was turned that way. And I think . . . here is my impression that I'm going to say: I think that his father accused him too. He accused him about something, anything, or at least kept him in a scrutinizing relationship; let's say a relationship that shouldn't be like that. Just like my father used to question me, questions to his son as if they were from a jailer to a prisoner, and I was no more than 7, 8, 9 years old. But the way he spoke to me . . . David broke a rule in his adulthood. But I imagine that it happened also to him when he was a kid. That is my impression. So the father in some way . . .

ANALYST: . . . Accused him when he was a child.

LISANDRO: He accused him in my opinion because it was how he made himself important, but was lost as the father. I notice he is desolate without a father, someone to guide him, and in that state of anxiety he takes that money because he needed to be checked because he has unresolved guilt in him. [brief pause] I don't know how to say . . .

ANALYST: Now these examples would be that David . . .

LISANDRO: . . . and myself. Notice that I started with a dream where I was accused.

ANALYST: So you become what you are as adults because of being treated as you were in your childhood. So David stole the money because his dad challenged him when he was a child, scrutinized and investigated him because of being a professional detective.

LISANDRO: No, no, I'm not saying that. He is desolated because when he was a kid his father tried to put himself before him. No, no, I'm not doing things that way at all. I am conveying to you . . . maybe what I am realizing now is . . . what I am conveying is that my father always put himself ahead of me. In other words he wasn't trying to educate me lovingly but doing it in a depraved way. I am giving you these examples to be able to convey to you how my father was, nothing more, nothing to do with any theory.

LEVEL I: PHENOMENOLOGICAL DESCRIPTION OF THE TRANSFORMATIONS WITH REFERENCE TO THE SESSION OF 21 NOVEMBER, 2015

Do aspects of material suggest the existence of changes positive, negative, or non-existence of changes? Which are predominant?

Without going into the content, the change in the type of his speech is striking. In the first years of analysis his speech had phrasing that appeared to be restitutions from a childhood psychosis. Now his speech is that of a predominantly obsessive neurotic. Referring to this session, the patient adds that he feels more uncompressed, fuller, permeable, and he can view the present undistorted by the past.

What are the changes that can be observed in the course of a session? And over time between different sessions?

He considers that these new sensations "are a step forward" because after solving problems he could say to himself "let's stop" when new problems came forward, and then he could calm down.

In what areas is it possible to observe changes?

a) capacity to love and sexuality

He hardly mentions his love for his wife or the quality of their sexual relationship.

b) family and social relations

He now enjoys playing with his children (a 10-year-old boy and a 3-year-old boy) and his wife is in her seventh month of pregnancy (of a girl). He discriminates between each child's tastes for games and entertainment. After having not spoken with his father for 15 years, he now visits him every month and takes his children. Although he persists in considering him a manipulator and a psychopath, he does it calmly, trying to understand ("he also has had a terrible childhood") and forgive him ("I want to end well with him, he is already over 80").

c) work and leisure

In the employment area, both commercial and agricultural, his mistrust regarding partners, employees and colleagues has decreased. As the analyst admits ignorance about the care of fields and asks him to explain it, the patient admits not knowing all he needs to know about necessary tools and accepts help without being suspicious that everybody would take advantage of his weaknesses.

d) interests and creativity

He recognized his skill in negotiations. Last year was devoted to designing a racing car and a roof rack for his 4 x 4. He also did a course on gardening, and now during his leisure time he takes care of things for himself and friends.

e) symptoms and subjective well-being

His physical symptoms when waking up with feelings of betrayal and per-secution have decreased. Now they last less than an hour, so he feels free to strike up a conversation with someone outside the house. He has many moments of well-being, since he has also paid his debts, organized and rented the fields, his kids have completed the school year with good grades, and conflicts with the neighbours have been clarified. As he says, "Now what will I say to myself to give me problems? I'm going to enjoy the holidays."

What is the patient's perspective about these changes?

Now he doesn't think that everything is because of the past. He acknowl-edges current problems as separate from past problems, and he can enjoy solving current problems.

Changes in the analytic process in relation to:

a) How the patient uses the analyst

In his two previous analyses, the patient had to dedicate his efforts to orga-nizing his life and ensuring his livelihood. He says he needs to verbalize infantile conflicts and recover memories that had been lost to awareness, but he tries to present his memories as "theoretical" explanations for blaming his parents for paternal abuse and for fraud, and to justify the defence of surviv-ing in solitude.

b) How the patient uses the analyst and his interventions

He says he feels himself heard because the analyst manages to make him think. He tries to get confirmation and endorsement that his current difficul-ties are due to having been abused by his parents from the ages of approxi-mately 5 to 30.

c) How the patient uses his own body and mental resources

He uses his mind and body to substantiate his arguments.

LEVEL 2: DIMENSIONS OF CHANGE

Subjective experience of disease and contextual factors

What is the subjective experience of the patient, his beliefs and expectations about his problems and treatment? To what extent does the patient accept his problems? Where does he see possibilities for change? Where do analyst and patient agree on expected transformations?

Lisandro now says that the reason for his malaise lies in his being the object of abuse in his infancy, latency and adolescence after the paradise of the first five years. His theory is that being "orphaned" he had to teach himself to survive by being compliant – not demanding, complaining–or hiding his achievements to "not awaken envy". In puberty, his parents tired of him and sent him to treatment, intending to make him obey them. Finally he entered into legal conflict with the therapist, who refused to admit him to hospital. Lisandro was clinging to him. Currently he attributes any conflict with third parties to their fears of being harshly judged or betrayed by him as it had been with their parents.

Are there any contextual factors affecting the therapeutic process (e.g., situations of crisis, traumatic experiences, somatic diseases, drugs, etc.)? How capable is the patient to cope with these situations?

Such contextual factors are not of importance, but each unexpected eventuality is experienced as traumatic, since he has suffered at the hands of capriciously arbitrary parents during childhood. Sometimes he recognizes that he exaggerates his paranoid fears (due to his narcissism), but he frequently projects into others, including his wife, and identifies them as the source of his difficult feelings.

How do these aspects change? How would the understanding of the patient of his problems and his possibilities of change be modified?

It was necessary for years to address his competitiveness and ambivalence while tending to his sensitivity to injury to his self-esteem.

Patterns of interpersonal relationship

How are the patient's close and intimate relationships?

With his peers (siblings, friends, and wife) he does not recognize any rivalry. If he is the needy one in a relationship, he reverses the situation by establishing some asymmetry in other fields where he is the needed one. So he never feels a frank appreciation from others for what he does for them. With his children he describes an almost idyllic relationship, but he finds it wearing. He often has in mind a dialogue with his father where he shows him how he should be a good father and proves that he is much better than him ("That's the pure truth"). It is not clear whether he is a good father to "avenge" his father or to express true love for his children. He gives the impression that he can feel love only for the children. In nine years, he has never made a comment of affection, love or attraction towards his wife or any other woman.

How does the patient experience others and himself in relation to others? How do other people experience the patient and themselves in relation to the patient (both in the transference–countertransference and other significant links)?

The patient sees others (except children) as hazards against whom he should be cautious and defensive, never trusting too much. Now he feels adequately equipped for that defence. He can never accept a critique from anyone. In the transference relationship he almost always presents an anecdote, an idea or a feeling as "something interesting to work on" but never as a question about himself. Instead he uses it as affirmation of an earlier question about his innocence and proof of being the victim of childhood abuse and handling by psychopathic parents.

The countertransference in turn is often overloaded and prevents the analyst from addressing the relationship without memory or desire. The patient always denies his innocence rather than be at fault in the eyes of his analyst. The analyst often feels as though he is being perceived as a detective, not an analyst. The analyst sometimes sees the patient as a helpless and homeless child completely occupied by his fantasy. The analyst's major effort is in discriminating between the past and present and between fact and fiction. Analysis often starts with the present and gradually reveals the repressed past. In this analysis, however, the present is taken into account only as proof that the narrative of the past was fact, not distorted by fantasy.

To what extent can the patient relate his current relational patterns to experiences in his childhood and the transference relationship.

The patient blames all his current relational patterns on actual infantile experiences rather than discriminating between unconscious infantile dynamics and current responsibility, claiming to have learned to "survive" the abuse and manipulations of the father. Regarding the transference relationship, the only fear to which he admits is the fear that the analyst will stop seeing him. To guard against this fear, he asked his analyst to recommend colleagues as possible successors, just as his first therapist had recommended the second one.

How have these aspects changed?

His expectations of betrayal and persecution began to change when he became able to accept his ignorance of a subject instead of hiding his ignorance or turning the situation into one where he did know the answers. Also his fears of failure, punishment and revenge dimmed when he could accept that he had caused offence or engaged in tortuous, duplicitous conduct. But these changes are yet to be consolidated.

Major intrapsychic conflicts

What are the main conflicts?

His main conflicts occur over dependence, control, self-reliance, self-esteem, guilt, Oedipal conflict, and identity.

What are the dominant unconscious fantasies that can be inferred from the conflicts and relational patterns?

In relationships where he is not treated as special he doubts whether he is wanted or feels mistreated and deprived of his "natural rights". For example, for many years he did not accept that many of his conflicts with others stemmed from his reaction to the birth of his sister when he was 2 and her becoming his father's favourite when he was 5. He tended to dismiss this fact in favour of "other much more serious mistreatments". When he has been given benefits or has successes, he fears that they can be removed from him and given to another, as happened when his father was favouring his little sister. Another denied fantasy was that he feels made inferior by the success of others.

Are the dominant defences appropriate and flexible or dysfunctional, distorting or restricting internal and external experiences?

They have been dysfunctional for a long time to hold onto the paranoid orientation. Approximately one year ago they began to be rectified.

How did change in these aspects occur?

These aspects have begun to be modified through tolerating the pain of the loss of his "paradisiacal childhood" illusions at the age of five. He has begun to recognize that others are actually others: they are different from him, and have aspects to them that are inaccessible to him and therefore unchangeable by him. This has implications for the solving of marital conflict.

Structural aspects of mental functioning

What is the level of mental functioning in the following areas?

Perception of himself and others: Identity

How capable is the patient of perceiving his own internal states and those of others?

He has achieved a few stable insights. He can perceive and accept the internal states of others if they are not restrictive to any need of his. He can generally accept them in children.

Is he able to empathize, tolerating and understanding different points of view?

He can be empathic and tolerant only as a strategic manoeuver in any negotiation that might have some gain for him. Every conflict or rejection causes an explosion in his identity and self-esteem, a narcissistic paranoid wound and not a depressive self-reflection.

Does he have a built-in sense of his own identity open to the possibility of unconscious aspects?

He has a precarious integration and does not tolerate the surprise appearance of unconscious fantasies. These need to be introduced gently so as not to surprise him, then he could accept them.

What are the characteristics of defenses (especially the pathological)?

He uses projective identification to defend against the unwanted unveiling of the unconscious.

Can he manage to connect with his past and give direction to his life with a sense of agency, feelings and objectives both short and long term?

After working with his analyst on differentiating past and present for years, he has begun to discover that he can be happy now even if he is convinced of his unhappiness during the latency period of childhood. It is a new sense of discovering what his life can be. On the other hand he has difficulty believing that he is allowed to be happy today, because (through projective identification) he thinks others may envy him.

Affective regulation

Is the patient able to regulate properly his impulses, his feelings, and his self-esteem?

He can regulate his impulses, feelings and self-esteem at times, when he feels particularly valued and not in need of repair.

Do his ideas and values allow him to process his emotions? Can he regulate his self-esteem against internal and external demands? Can he achieve a proper balance between his interests and those of others?

He achieves a somewhat precarious balance between his interests and those of others because he intends to consciously or unconsciously hide his intentions for his own benefit. He is quick to invoke the sense of justice whenever it benefits him.

External and internal communication and symbolization

How rich is dialogue with self and others, based on affective experiences, body, fantasies, dreams, sexuality, symbolic representations, and ability to play and be creative?

He is creative, playful and affectionate in relationships where the external object needs him. In other words he relates creatively to children, loyal employees, accommodating country labourers, and former analysts.

Links with internal and external objects

How deep, stable and distinct are the relationships with internal and external objects?

He can keep relationships if there is asymmetry and he is the needed one. He cannot build a link with a peer who is independent of him. He cannot tolerate rivalry with peers, nor accept differences.

How far can he begin and end relationships and tolerate separations?

He approaches relationships from a narcissistic position. He has problems finishing his projects because he does not work hard, waits for others to finish what he should have done, or is accused of not working hard. He doesn't tolerate relationships.

How does he handle the relations that imply the existence of a third party?

He does not tolerate them, if the third is a peer. He is unduly critical and accuses the other of injustice if he is not the preferred or favoured one. He will never admit that he is extremely jealous.

How did these aspects change?

These aspects have changed somewhat thanks to the analyst's constant care and careful handling of his narcissistic convictions and their effects on his self-esteem and paranoid anxiety. Further change will not be possible until his fantasies of parricide and homosexuality are more approachable.

Type of disorder

a) Is it possible to identify a type of personality or other physical or mental disorder?
b) How severe is the personality disturbance? In what way is the analytical work conditioned by the structural vulnerabilities of mental functioning?
c) How do these aspects function?

At first the diagnosis was narcissistic-paranoid personality with obsessive fea- tures. It seemed necessary to protect his self-esteem so it would be possible to address multiple semantic distortions. But the slightest approach to his negative transference led to pragmatic distortions. He felt subjected to a "climate of pros- ecution" and used to use psychotic restitutions, taking general norms and ideals out of context. Apparently neurotic psychic structure that had seemed analysable soon revealed an ego fragility guarded by a rigid and still severe superego. The patient tried to combat this superego by questioning and fighting its judgements and petitioning a higher authority. This structural panorama of his mental func- tioning meant that his analytic work progressed much more slowly than expected initially.

LEVEL 3: EXPLANATORY HYPOTHESIS OF HOW AND WHY CHANGE HAPPENED

On which aspects did the analyst focus his interventions primarily?

At first the analyst aimed his efforts at organizing the patient's speech. He tried to help him describe his everyday life without quickly finding "reasons" in the past. He worked on the patient's paranoid aspects and his defence against the pain of frustration or exclusion, and on the projective identi- fication in which he felt himself victim of treacherous strategies of others (especially his partners at work) or victim of their disregard (especially his wife). The patient used to take various issues out of context or make "reflec- tions" on his interior life with impersonal statements and generalizations which the analyst regarded as psychotic substitutions. Some of his confu- sions were legitimate: others were defences. The analyst helped him clarify that his resentment, hatred and calls for justice were based on his expectation of being highlighted as the "special" or the "preferred" one. Discriminating ego/non ego, past/present, and various other confused categories, the analyst helped the patient cover many themes and acknowledge his feelings, includ- ing his feeling of loneliness for not having "real friends".

Did they change his explicit or implicit assumptions and his interven- tions throughout the treatment?

Only those assumptions that had nothing to do with the primary figures and especially the father showed much change.

What could other theoretical hypotheses or interpretative strategies be? Which of them fit the material convincingly?

No other hypotheses strike me as useful.

What is the nature of the observed change, its depth and its probable stability?

New clarifications are much more stable than corrections of old certainties. It is obvious that his current speech is coherent and understandable and rarely alters. But he is unstable emotionally when he feels questioned or has done something objectionable or on the edge of being illegal.

Conclusion

We see a degree of complexity in the relationship with the patient, depth in the elaboration of his pragmatic, semantic and syntactic distortions, and he has started to bring up dreams. From these findings we hold that a psychoanalytic process is occurring. It is long, slow and torturous but changes of the mental structure can be shown. I have presented these teleanalysis sessions in depth, and examined them in terms of Bernardi's Three Level Model of psychic change to provide evidence for discussion as to whether the *dispositif* is successfully established within the teleanalysis setting, and whether analytic process is shown to be equivalent to that which can occur in a traditional analytic setting.

References

Agamben, G. (2006). What is an apparatus? In: *What is an Apparatus? And Other Essays* (pp. 1–24). Trans D. Kishik & S. Pedatella. Stanford: Stanford University Press, from the Italian *Che Cos'e un Dispositivo*. Rome: Nottetempo, 2005.

Bernardi, R. (2014). The three-level model (3-LM) for observing patient transformations. In: M. Altmann de Litvan (Ed.), *Time for Change: Tracking Transformations in Psychoanalysis* (pp. 3–34). London: Karnac.

Bion, W. (1967). Notas sobre la memoria y el deseo [Notes on Memory and Desire]. *The Psychoanalytic Forum*, 2(3): 679–681.

Foucault, M. (1977). *Dits et Écrits 1964–1988*, vol. iii 1976–1979. Paris: Editions Gallimard.

Freud, S., & Breuer, J. (1893). Case histories: Fraulein Anna O. *Standard Edition*, 2: 21–47.

Liberman, D. (1971). *Lingüística, interacción comunicativa y proceso psicoanalítico*. Buenos Aires: Galerna.

Manguel, A. (2015). Letter from Mesopotamian mountain dweller of the 12th Century AC, Alberto Manguel: Personal interview, *Revista*, 26 December, 2015.

Reik, T. (1948). *Listening with the Third Ear: The Inner Experience of a Psychoanalyst*. New York: Grove Press.

Chapter 6

Proximity and distance in teletherapy

Liliana Manguel

What do we mean by teleanalysis? When we speak of teleanalysis, also referred to as distance psychoanalysis and remote psychoanalysis, we begin to contemplate the experience of nearness or distance and feeling close or far apart. And we encounter many questions: Can teleanalysis be considered psychoanalytic? Is a committed encounter between a patient and an analyst at a distance analysis workable? What moves a patient, who could have a face-to-face analysis, to look for distance analysis? In teleanalysis, is the connection between patient and analyst no more than superficial, or is it intense and deep? Is it possible to achieve a sense of presence while patient and analyst are physically distant, even though they can see each other on the screen when a webcam is used? What does the encounter with the analyst mean for patients who choose distance analysis? Is it indicated and contra-indicated for certain patients? Can virtual reality allow the patient a closer emotional experience, despite – or because of – the absence of the body of patient and analyst in the same room? Can patients achieve a true closeness in analysis online?

In my opinion, the sense of closeness in the analytic pair does not necessarily depend on physical proximity. What is essential for the sense of closeness is a true encounter. Reading Freud's letters to Fliess, it is clear that, without meeting as embodied minds in the same room, Freud and Fliess maintained such a true encounter. Freud invested his trust in Fliess, and Fliess was privileged to receive and respond to his epistolary communications about dream life and family and professional circumstances. Nowadays typed emails and online verbal communication take the place of handwritten letters as devices for bridging the distance between people in different locations. A similarly close encounter is possible using technology.

If teleanalysis can support a true encounter, can it affect personal change? Over several years, I have been studying this with a group of colleagues, reviewing cases and applying the Three Level Model (3-LM), a protocol for assessing intra-psychic change on three levels (Bernardi, 2014). We proceed by observing the psychoanalytic process, medical history, treatment, several consecutive sessions, selected facts from the material, and records of the countertransference. As Bernardi says:

The description of transformations or changes occurring in patients throughout the analysis is of great theoretical and practical importance. This model aims to observe and describe changes in the patient using three successive levels of analysis. For this reason it is called the "model of three levels" to observe the transformations of the patient (3-LM). From the point of view of the heuristic, it is expected that this method will serve to enhance and refine clinical observation and description of the changes that occur during long periods of analysis or in the course of a full treatment. Also it will serve to measure the difficulties and limitations and assess the potential of new developments

(Bernardi, 2014, p. 1).

Psychoanalytic process, even in traditional settings, is difficult to convey and harder yet to measure. Through using 3-LM, Bernardi hopes to remedy this situation. Applying 3-LM to patients in analysis, my colleagues and I in Buenos Aires study analytic process in teleanalysis using a standard protocol. I will give vignettes from the treatment of Diana, applying the Bernardi 3-LM model to the material.

CLINICAL HISTORY, FIRST INTERVIEWS, AND OPENING PHASE OF TREATMENT

The referral

Diana's request for treatment came to me through a desperate email in which she exposed practically all her life to me an analyst she did not know. She did not even know if her email would arrive. She explained that, even though she was supposed to come for a few days to Argentina in ten months' time, she was not sure that she would, because she was afraid to return. She could not wait to see me then, but needed to start treatment right away to help her finally improve her "quality of life". So she was seeking an analyst she could consult on Skype or by telephone.

Diana, age 49, was born in Argentina but now lives in a country in the northern hemisphere. She said she needed an analyst of the same nationality, language, and culture, and got my data from a friend and colleague of mine. She had been in treatment with local analysts at her location, but she preferred me, an analyst in her country of origin – I guessed because she was unconsciously trying to resolve her ambivalence with her roots, country, and parents.

The history

Diana said,

> I've taken many turns along my life. I feel really lost, and I think that if I write to you, it can help me. I was born in Argentina, a country from which I escaped after I finished high school because my parents fought a lot, and I could not stand it, so I got a scholarship to study art abroad. I said goodbye

to Argentina, I finished a degree in Art History and Visual Arts, and I have not been back for 30 years.

Ten months after starting her psychoanalytic therapy with me, she was able to make the flying visit to her birth country for the first time in 30 years, and we met twice in my office. She told me that she does not have friends in Argentina or any social life anywhere at all. "Do you know that people are very bad? Everyone has turned away. People who were my friends do not talk to me any more – I do not know why."

Diana's father died of cancer years after her migration. She says she was very much affected by his death because she was his favourite child and confidant. Diana said,

> I loved my dad, but sometimes he played with me in a very strange way. When I sat in his lap, the way he used to stroke my legs felt weird. I did not feel it was the natural and spontaneous caress of a father. My mother was also very complicated: she noticed what my father did and said nothing.

She described her mother as a paranoid woman who suffered a postpartum depression after the patient's birth, and so a nanny raised Diana during her first year of life. Diana's two maternal uncles are schizophrenic, and she was always terrified of having some of their genes.

In the country to which she migrated, she met her first husband and had two children with him. At the time treatment began, she had been divorced from him for 16 years, and her sons were 23 and 17 years of age. While maintaining a strong bond with her two children, her love life had not fared so well.

> I got divorced from my first husband 16 years ago. I took the kids and moved from the country. I managed to arrange it that my ex-husband kept the house in exchange for my taking the kids far away. I established a contract in which I managed to exchange the house for the children and my ex-husband agreed not see them again. I lived there for six years, away from my family of origin and my husband. I fought with my parents because of their behaviour. I also have a younger sister I do not speak to since my mother died in 2007 because of issues of money. In late 2005 the man who would be my second husband came along. He is a prominent businessperson and his work caused us to move again to another country even further away. My eldest son is an anthropologist and lives with his girlfriend in the same country but in another city. My younger son is in high school and lives with me. I have a very good relationship with my sons.

When we began therapy, the children had not seen their father in years. After Diana's third year of psychotherapy she accepted that her children wanted to visit their father for the first time.

Her anguish had been heightened ever since her youngest son started having epileptic seizures a year before she consulted me. She said,

I had escaped from my ex-husband, who was a very sick and deranged person, but fate played a trick on me because despite of all my efforts, my ex-husband is still present all the time through this disease. Do you know that my youngest son inherited the disease from his father? Luckily, my eldest son is healthy and helps me face this.

According to Diana, before her son had seizures, she lived a quiet life writing her thesis and studying. She had no constraints of any kind. She complained, "This very surprising disease of my son has made me feel sad! I could not control it. I am always many steps ahead so that nothing bad happens to me, but I did not expect this!"

She tried various psychoanalytic treatments at the place where she lives, but she declared, "They were a failure. I feel that none has helped me at all." She also reported having persistent panic attacks, fear of going outside, tachycardia, and insomnia. For six months, she had taken medication prescribed by a psychiatrist who treated her without significant results, and only then did she decide to start her treatment.

Diana said she needed to "make remote therapy" early in the morning so that her husband would not be aware that she was having therapy – and she does not want him to know. This issue was to reappear periodically throughout the treatment, particularly linked to the transference field. Diana did not want to be asked any information about her husband. She deflected any questions by saying that she would tell me about him later. She only said that they are living in the same house, in separate rooms, go out to dinner together twice a week, and the rest of the time her husband works and travels.

I had the sense that Diana used the need to maintain secrets and lies in relation to her husband as a pretext for requiring distance analysis. I accepted her request, well aware that it was unusual to begin a psychoanalytic treatment without having met the patient. I was convinced that it was the only way the treatment could get started.

From my countertransference, I established the following questions:

1   Why does Diana prefer teleanalysis?
2   What role do the secrets, lies and covenants have in her life?
3   She is a patient who lives her life escaping and making sharp cuts. Could no one help her, or did she not allow them to help?
4   What does "meeting me" mean to her?
5   What does it mean that she needs to be sure that her husband is not around when she talks to me?
6   Is there a latent reason that Diana needs distance therapy?

Discussion

The analyst accepts the conditions in order to get the treatment started. Diana lives in isolation, with a paranoid view of the world and a history of cutting off relationships with family, friends, and previous therapists, and even erasing relationships, as she did with her ex-husband. The wall against him allows Diana to maintain a fantasy of control, which shatters with the discovery of her son's seizures. When we learn about the sexually intrusive father and the by-standing paranoid mother, Diana's need to control the setting begins to make some sense. We get a sense of her as a woman with deep cuts inside herself alongside poor internal boundaries against overwhelming affect. She expresses these internal cuts externally as soon as relationships become intimate, leaving parts of herself in various countries. The analyst may get cut off too, but unless she gets the treatment started, she has no hope of working on the problem.

The contract

With such thoughts and many other questions, I began to discuss the setting and the arrangements for teleanalysis. I asked Diana to talk from the quietest and most comfortable place possible. I made it clear that I would talk to her from my office, and that she should choose a similarly private, consistent space. The sessions would last 50 minutes. I said she could tell me everything that comes to her mind, although some things may seem shameful or fearful. I said that speaking freely, telling me everything including dreams, current experiences and past memories would help me help her. I told her she would need to ensure adequate internet bandwidth, and if for some reason this failed, she could use my office phone or my cell phone. If she had to change an appointment or leave me a message, she could contact me through my email. If for travel reasons either of us needed to change the time of the appointment, this had to be notified in advance, taking into account time differences. The payment would be done by Western Union in Argentina, made out to my name, or by bank transfer to my account. I asked her if she wanted to ask me any questions about my résumé or psychoanalytic experience, and she explained that before the consultation she had already learned all about me on Google and on my website. (I learned later that she had assured herself that I had no debts!). We agreed to begin teleanalysis using the telephone twice a week. Diana speaks from home when no one is in (and if they are in, she goes out to speak to me) because she is afraid that her son, her husband or her housekeeper would hear the conversation. I later find out that the alternative place she uses to make her call to me is a coffee bar. The dialogue in the vignettes is written in very short paragraphs to reflect her way of separating her thoughts in time, even though she may carry on a theme across a number of paragraphs.

Discussion

The analyst sets out clear instructions for creating a suitable setting, and the patient chooses a bar. It is hard to imagine a bar, even a coffee bar, as a quiet, private place, but she must have found a way to feel isolated there. Her choice of "bar" seems to refer to her longing for a barrier, given that her boundaries have not been respected. Perhaps she was seducing her analyst to meet her at the bar, as her father seduced her. She escapes from relationships and uses distance to preserve herself in life, and now to safeguard her access to treatment. But will she also wall off her analyst? It will be difficult to make interpretations, because Diana will first need to develop a containing mind.

Diana: A session from the third year of treatment, first session of the week

DIANA: Hello Liliana. Are you there? I was thinking all weekend about two words from our last session: imposition and perseverance. I know persevering is not enough to get me what I want if I keep making bad choices in my love life and in my emotional life, and it is also true that I keep imposing on my children to follow me in my madness. However, I want the best for them. I do not want to harm them.

I am still very paranoid about my youngest child having another seizure; time has passed, but I am terrified.

Although he is already 19, I wear a watch to remind him to take the medication. Now I have been giving him the pill that heals him. Yet for two years I fought with doctors because I did not want him to take any medication.

I also started taking something to sleep, as I have insomnia.

I have got rid of that terrible headache I had for 10 days. Even so, we can no longer endure living in this country – neither of us. This place is killing us. But today I woke up much better, I do not know why.

[Long silence] . . .

ANALYST: Maybe knowing that today we were having a session helped you get up feeling better.

DIANA: Probably.

I was thinking that my youngest son M will now begin university. He will live away from home. I wonder if he will be able to do so. I do not know. This is an unfriendly country. We do not have friends.

And I fear for him. What if he cannot do it?

ANALYST: I notice you feel distressed. You are probably wondering if you will be able to be alone, without him. Your voice sounds sad. I can tell you are sad thinking about his departure.

DIANA: I have great pain in one hand. I am on medical treatment because of the pain I have had in my hand for three weeks now. I avoid being on the computer, but I need it a lot. I am studying art and then writing about it.

I have many conferences to attend and I will have to travel a lot. I am afraid to leave him alone. Well, with my husband – he is a manipulator; he stops talking to us for days, for weeks. I do not care anymore . . . as long as he pays the bills, I am ok. I do not know how much longer I can endure this state. I know that I cannot live anymore like this.

I have to make a decision, but it is not easy. There were many years of poverty.

I have never been materialistic. I do not want to be like that.
We all deserve a better life.

ANALYST: But today, thinking about our meeting, you felt better. Perhaps part of your improvement is to encourage yourself to accept what you want to choose for your life, with all that this implies. You say that you choose to stay with a husband with whom you feel even more alone. Without any relationship, without sex, without fun things to do together – only money. Moreover, your child is leaving to go to a new school far from home.

DIANA: The pain in my hand is not hypochondria. It really hurts. But it is true that I am getting sick of nonsense all the time.
But . . . what you say is real. The illness of my son was caused by the illness of my ex-husband. Epilepsy is genetic.
It is painful all that you are saying. But it's so true . . .
I escaped from the father of my children and took them far away so they do not know anything about him, and yet his illness chases us.
And now the two boys told me they want to travel to meet him!
[Long silence] . . .
I do not know if this treatment is doing me any good or if it is bad for me. My world is changing.
I no longer understand anything . . .
My children are growing. They are more independent.
Now I'll have to go back to Argentina soon. Did I tell you?
I was asked to do an exhibition there.
I have not returned for many years and now things arise all the time.
I like to include literary notes on the images that I display.
But I was wondering: What am I running away from away all the time?
I don't know . . .

ANALYST: Mainly you are running from the impact of your son's having to take medicine for two years and his illness being associated with someone who is tough for you.

DIANA: These things have hurt me so much in my life!
See, what if I expose myself and I get hurt again.
I could not stand it.

ANALYST: What memories do you have from when you were younger?

DIANA: I never had limits in my childhood. I had to impose limits on myself. My parents wanted to raise me so freely that it was terrible! Neither my father nor my mother imposed any limits on me. Nowadays I think they could not take care of me because they were too busy fighting between themselves . . .
They were too busy seeing which of them was right! Dad had me as his ally; he spent all his time telling me how much he hated Mom. My mom was paranoid. She has a brother, schizophrenic. I was always too afraid of madness.

I grew up in a world of secrets and lies. Did I copy their behaviour?
They never finished anything: three majors each, but they dropped out in the middle of each one. Mom painted but never finished a picture. My dad wrote, but he never finished anything. I wanted to escape from that. That is what I am starting to believe now.

ANALYST: And did you really escape?

DIANA: [Long silence] . . .
I am persistent, creative, and that helps me, but it is not enough.
I feel very lonely [begins to cry].
Each work project that I start is truncated.
I thought it was the fault of others . . . that they did not value me. Now I wonder: What role do I play in it?
I know I have a good résumé, I am hard working, and I have good ideas. People like what I do . . . but then they do not call me again.
I think I get offended too fast: I answer back. I am impulsive. I get bored of it all. Although I am persistent in what I want, I do not know how to manage the social contact aspect of my work. I do not know how to maintain contact over time.
I find something in everyone and end up fighting with everyone, just like my parents.
Is my genetic inheritance chasing me too?
I want to go to Argentina and meet all the people I love.
I want to be better, get less sick and I feel that my life should be more than being a good mom.

So ended the first session of the week. I am always feeling that every session will be the last, and yet here we are in the third year of treatment, and I have not yet met the woman.

Discussion

Diana is perpetuating the lies and secrets from her family of origin and bringing them into her analysis right away. No limits were set by her warring parents, leaving Diana feeling unsafe and filled up with their fight. She expresses her longing to be dependent by babying her younger son and shows her grief at losing her eldest to college through psychosomatic pain. She not only cuts off relationships but she cuts off projects too, unable to finish. She identifies with the analytic attitude in looking at her role instead of blaming others. We note that Diana is a visual artist, who must be responsive to images, and yet she prefers to conduct her treatment using audio communication on the telephone and not online connection with web camera. Perhaps the deprivation of visual communication means that she can more easily reveal her hatred while she can hide herself behind a wall, and at the same time exert control over her analyst. Or was she taking care of her analyst by reducing the full impact of her possibly seductive presence? Local analysts felt too threatening and close in on her. Diana chooses distance analysis because of her narcissism and particular defensive constellation.

Diana: A session later that year

DIANA: I am very happy. I have become a member of the Association of Visual Arts. The president is in Argentina and I have already sent my articles.

If my son gets the confirmation to do the cinema and photography course for three months, we will come once more to Argentina in March, and this time I will stay for a month, and he will stay for three months.

Isn't that good? We will meet again at your office, and this time we will have many sessions before I leave!

After Argentina, I have to travel to Europe for a conference at the end of March. On December 20th, I will travel with my husband and my youngest son for a month. It will be very difficult for me to connect with you then. There I'm meeting my friends. I'm very happy about that.

I'm feeling that everything that I have been planning finally is working out.

I am in touch again with old friends. With my Argentinian friend too. That was always me. I had lost it but I'm getting back there. I'm recovering my social life. My dynamic part.

It has not happened for a long time.

[Long silence] . . .

ANALYST: When did that part of you evaporate?

DIANA: For years, I did not want anything that identified me with Argentina. This is very crazy.

Now I'm getting that beat back, and with some push from Facebook I also got my social part back. That makes me really happy.

I lived in X for a long time; it's a very hypocritical country. That made me withdraw. Now I realize that my complaints are not coming from paranoia: X is truly a hypocritical country.

I have already sent my writings to the various countries. If all goes well in late July I'm going to give lectures.

It was difficult to learn the different cultures, the different rhythms, and different languages. I thought a lot about you the other day . . .

[Long silence] . . .

Once you told me I had lost my spontaneity. It is true. I thought a lot about it. It still does not come naturally. But it is true that I had lost some of my features that I liked.

ANALYST: As if you had ironclad yourself and a part of you closed down.

DIANA: Through Facebook I met several former boyfriends. Now that I am traveling, at times when I'm alone, I want to meet with several of them – when my husband is not around [laughs].

ANALYST: When your husband is not around?

DIANA: My husband is very jealous. But I love having several male Facebook friends again.

I feel pretty again.

I want you to help me to know about myself when I lost everything. What happened to me? When was that? Did I lose my life due to my drastic cuts, my fleeing, my conflicts, and drama?

Every time I moved to a different country, I left everything behind. I wanted to make drastic cuts, to start over, and now I realize that I was wrong.

[Silence] . . .

ANALYST: You wanted to have a new birth in each place. A new life. And what you needed and did not have was continuity. That's what you did not allow yourself to achieve at that time. It's like along the way in the different countries where you lived, you left a large part of you . . .

DIANA: I needed to forget. That's what I loved.

[Long silence] . . .

My resentment killed me. My hatred killed me. Sometimes I felt calm in excess. I invented a personality that I do not have. I wanted to learn not to care about anything as my sister does.

I believe that for me, that's impossible.

I was shifting about, changing like a chameleon, until I got lost.

When I used to live in Argentina, I thought I had found a friend. One day I was very bad and sad and called her, and she said, "What do you need?" as if she did not know me. And so, I closed even tighter. I thought I was selective with people. Now I realize I was alone rather than selective.

It is funny, isn't it? There were more than 15 years between my first residence, the other country where I lived with my first husband, and the last place where I live now.

And the truth is, I have nothing left. Or almost nothing.

ANALYST: Well, you have the experience. If you can take advantage of it . . .

DIANA: But Liliana, what happened to me?

Why so much hate? I was not like that . . .

I know Mom lived with reproaches and resentment.

[Long silence] . . .

ANALYST: What are you thinking?

DIANA: No. Nothing.

Well, yes. Something. I do not know.

Probably I was repeating a story that was not mine. A story that I bought from other people. Their story. My parents?

My mother has several crazy people in her family.

Crazy, crazy.

Institutionalized.
And she quarrelled with her mother about an issue of fraud and money and
did not talk to her until her death.
Then, it was too late.
Neither of my parents was successful.
They ended up at odds with friends, neighbours, family.
My dad was a weak man and my mom was terrible.
I am afraid that my children also take that hatred and resentment from me as
I took it from my mother.
I would not forgive me . . .

ANALYST: Perhaps the same hatred grabs you at times with your husband or others
in general when you do not feel noticed.
Instead of showing pain, you show hatred and anger.
[Long silence] . . .

DIANA: I was thinking that when I first learned about my son's convulsions,
I started choking, losing memory, feeling lost. But I never cried. When he did
not recognize me after his seizure, the impact on me was terrible.
If I do not have memory, I do not have to remember things that hurt me and
make me sad.
I complained for many years that my parents and sister left me very lonely.
I very much hated them, until now.
Was it really hatred or, as you say, the pain of not having them?
[Silence] . . .
What's done is done. My sister does not help me, because she hated me, and
my parents are dead.
But if deleting and having no memory is no longer the solution, is feeling
pain the solution?

ANALYST: That solution seems to be something again imposed on you. If the pain
comes or not, we will see later. We'll see what comes . . .

DIANA: It is already time, isn't it? Time flew by today.

Discussion

Diana regrets her way of being, her feeling of having nothing left, and her loss of
spontaneity as the cost of her closing down to defend against pain. Now that she can
mourn this, she can begin to open up to social interaction. The continuity of the treatment is letting her express her rage. She still feels hated by her parents and her sister,
but now she can think about why she is so filled with hatred. The analyst tries repeatedly to show Diana that she uses her hatred to cover the pain of not being noticed,
of not feeling acknowledged by her parents. We note that Diana remains resistant to
feeling and working through her pain. Diana concludes that she has picked up her

parents' pain, and that they probably picked up the pain of their parents. We do not yet learn any details of this transgenerational transmission, but it seems hopeful that Diana is able to conceive of a world outside her own reality.

We note that analysis is helping Diana to reintegrate the fragments of herself that she left behind. Diana is curious about why she has made drastic cuts. Her analyst interprets that she moved on to have a new birth, and a new life in a new country, and tells her that the cost was that of leaving parts of herself behind, thus impoverishing her integrity and capacity to engage. Diana has become able to contemplate a return to the country of her birth (and of her trauma) and she even anticipates going to the analyst's office! She will meet her for the first time and have many sessions. But her habit of cutting off is expressed in shortening the visit by touring in Europe afterwards. It seems that the intimacy of the in-the-office sessions cannot be sustained, and we wonder what will happen when teleanalysis resumes after Diana's vacation.

APPLYING 3-LM TO THE SEQUENCE OF TWO SESSIONS

LEVEL I: PHENOMENOLOGICAL DESCRIPTION OF THE TRANSFORMATIONS

Which aspects of the material suggest change is occurring?

The patient has changed her mood.

She has become able to return to Argentina after 30 years.

She becomes able to meet me in person.

She has a more expanded socio-emotional life. Thanks to Facebook she has reconnected with friends and family. Now she can accept that people want to be with her without her feeling so exposed.

In this last stage of her treatment, she manages to trust her husband, revealing to him the secret that she is in treatment.

She begins to have work success and continuity without quarrelling with her colleagues.

She is less often physically sick.

What transformations are in the course of the sessions over time and in which areas (ability to love and enjoy sexuality, family, social relations, work and leisure, interests and activities, symptoms and well-being) from the perspective of the analyst and of the patient?

Symptoms and well-being

The patient has gone from being permanently distressed and resentful, projecting blame on others, to beginning to wonder if their behaviour towards her has something to do with her. She has become happy and hopeful.

Sexual relations

Diana does not discuss sex.

Social relations

She accepts her intolerance with others as the reason that she has been left alone.

Work

She now sees that her behaviour made her lose job opportunities. She now gets calls to give lectures.

Family relations

She can tolerate her children daring to tell her for the first time that they want to see their father.

From Diana's perspective she has much better physical health and family, work and social relations, but she does not yet trust that the analytic link has helped to secure these changes. She doesn't know still if her therapy will be doing right or wrong by her and prefers to attribute her positive social changes to Facebook.

Are there changes in the analytic process in relation to the use of the analyst and her interventions, and to their own bodily and mental resources?

Relation to the analyst

Diana has established a closer link with the analyst, wanting to meet her in person, and yet she cannot tolerate the feeling of needing her. She is more reflective. She asks about her hatred as one of the possible causes of her solitude.

Like her parents who could not bring any of their activities to a good conclusion, Diana cannot continue her progress in each country of residence but after a time starts over in yet another new country.

Selected clinical facts

The patient has fled any stable ties for fear of becoming dependent on relationships.

The constant fighting between her parents robbed her of a good climate of containment. Her sister cheated her out of money and friendship.

She has felt threatened frequently by fears of being tainted by her mother's family psychosis and her first husband's neurological disease.

She needed to keep her analytic treatment secret from her husband and engaged her analyst as an accomplice.

She has a symbiotic relationship with her youngest son, which is reflected in her experiencing his physical symptoms (panic attacks, feeling of being lost, and paraesthesia).

After intense sessions with thematic elaboration and emotional closeness, the analyst experienced a repetitive fantasy that each session would be the last. Thus in her countertransference, she experienced the patient's need to cut off.

LEVEL 2: DIMENSIONS OF CHANGE

SUBJECTIVE EXPERIENCE OF THE DISEASE AND CONTEXTUAL FACTORS

What are the patient's subjective experience, beliefs and expectations regarding their problems and treatment?

To what extent are the problems manifest in the treatment?

Where do you see possibilities for change?

Do analyst and patient have the same expectation of transformation?

Diana has a poor recognition of her problems with a large predominance of projective aspects.

She has ambivalent feelings about her husband, her son, and her analyst.

She wonders if the treatment will have positive or negative effects for her. Sometimes she accepts that feeling better is thanks to her treatment but simultaneously thinks that nobody has ever been able to help her as she hoped.

Having a husband who seems not to require emotional contact is the only way for her to be in a relationship.

Are there any contextual factors affecting the therapeutic process? (Example: situations of crisis, traumatic experiences, somatic diseases, drugs, etc.)

How capable is the patient of coping with these situations?

Diana insisted that her analytic treatment was kept secret, assuming her husband would not allow it.

Childhood traumatic history (abuse by the father, the withdrawal of a mother due to postpartum depression) is the probable cause of her great need to get away from her objects in life and in the transference.

She reacts to stress with illness and paranoia.

How changed are these aspects?

How is understanding of the patient, her problems and the possibilities for change modified at this point in the treatment?

The analyst's flexible frame for distance analysis offered good containment.

Change was not continuous but rolling, and occurred through transference work.

PATTERNS OF INTERPERSONAL RELATIONSHIP

How are the patient's intimate relationships?

Diana maintained control, regulating the proximity and distance in relationships to various degrees. For instance, she overprotected her children and kept a huge distance from their father, who she perceived as dangerous.

How does the patient experience others, and herself in relation to others?

How do others experience the patient and themselves in relation to the patient (both in the transference–countertransference and other significant links)?

Show the countertransference and the role of the analyst

Diana was avoidant of others, and could barely tolerate the analyst's presence.
   She manipulated others, using seduction as a way to placate.
   Dealing with Diana's abrupt cuts and disruptions, her friends became disoriented.
   Her analyst experienced great difficulty in calibrating the proximity distance with the patient.
   The role of the analyst was to tolerate the patient's disappearances on travel or following a close and deep intervention and to bear feeling impotent. The analyst had to respect Diana's defences in order to set the context for analytic process to occur.

Extent to which the patient can relate her current relational patterns to experiences in her childhood and the transferential relationship

Diana was gradually taking into account that the bad link in her interpersonal relationships was not so much due to a hostile external world but was in response to her defences, which were similar to her parents' paranoid defences.
   She is achieving a greater insight into her difficulties through analysis, linking her abrupt cut-offs with her fear of dependence on the analyst.
   She shunned new experiences such as returning to Argentina.

MAIN INTRAPSYCHIC CONFLICTS

What are the main conflicts? (Example: individuation vs. dependency, submission vs. control, need to care vs. self-reliance, self-esteem, guilt, Oedipal conflict, conflict of identity).

What are the dominant unconscious fantasies that can be inferred from the conflicts and relational patterns?

The main conflict is between self-sufficiency and dependence.

Her motivating unconscious fantasy is that her self-sufficiency will release her from the hold of all internal and external objects.

She has a fixed belief that her mother's family psychosis and her ex-husband's neurological disease will follow her, and that, since her father damaged her, everyone she meets will damage her too.

The fantasy that any long, stable relationship will be a danger to her impels her to cut off relationships, turning the abandonment she experienced in childhood from passive to active.

In each relationship she kills and she is killed with different abrupt cuts, then she resurfaces like the Phoenix.

The fantasy of having been abused by her father drove the fear of emotional closeness and continuity and so, turning passive to active, she abused, assaulted or left others.

Are the dominant defences appropriate and flexible, or dysfunctional, distorting, or restricting internal and external experiences?

The defences are projection, paranoia, and hypomania.

There is some change in the extent to which she resorts to projective and paranoid defences.

How have these aspects changed?

Diana fights less with others and can own her own contribution to her hardships. With awareness of the complications of projection, the projective identification defence is failing. Diana is on her way to achieving greater integration.

STRUCTURAL ASPECTS OF MENTAL FUNCTIONING

What is the level of mental functioning in the following areas?

Perception of herself and others' identity

How capable is the patient of adequately perceiving her own internal states and others'?

Can she empathize, tolerate and understand different points of view?

Does the patient have a built-in sense of her own identity and is she open to the possibility of unconscious dynamics?

What are the characteristics of (especially pathological) IDs?

Does the patient connect with her past and give direction to her life with a sense of agency and desire of short and long term goals?

Diana gradually began to differentiate her internal states from her perceptions of the external world but still does not tolerate the opinions of others if they are different from her own.

She does not have a built-in sense of her own identity.

Her identifications are with a paranoid and pessimistic mother and with a seductive and manipulative father.

Her amount of projective identifications has begun to decrease.

She is very slowly building a better link with the external world.

She is starting to be able to unite past and present.

AFFECT REGULATION

Is the patient able to properly regulate her impulses, affects, and self-esteem?

Do her ideas and values allow her to process her emotions?

Can she regulate her self-esteem against internal and external demands?

Can she achieve a proper balance between her own interests and those of others?

Avoidance of affect is a major defence.

To some extent, the patient has begun to regulate her emotions, impulses and self-esteem with her children (except when her younger son identifies her with his sick father and genetic disease in general).

Diana is a self-centred patient with difficulty in seeing the needs and perceptions of the other.

EXTERNAL AND INTERNAL COMMUNICATION AND SYMBOLIZATION

How deep is the dialogue with herself and with others, based on affective experiences, body, fantasies, dreams, sexuality, symbolic representations, and ability to play and be creative?

Her communication is intellectually rich. At times it is megalomanic and omnipotent in relation to herself and others and is lacking at the emotional level.

LINKS TO INTERNAL AND EXTERNAL OBJECTS

How deep, stable and distinct are the relationships with internal and external objects?

Can she maintain relationships and tolerate separations?

How does she deal with a relationship that includes a third party?

Diana's links with others fail to be deep, stable, and differentiated. If they seem to be moving in that direction, she interrupts them to prevent closeness.

She has poor relationships with others. She cannot bear closeness, but she cannot tolerate separation either.

How changed are these aspects?

Diana has begun to question if all the danger in relating is always located in others. This is happening most obviously in the area of work, where colleagues and institutions have resumed inviting her to seminars and conferences, and she has begun to sustain these work connections over time. In the social realm, she has made contacts through Facebook and various social networks.

TYPE OF DISORDER

Is it possible to identify a type of personality or other physical or mental disorder?

Diana is a brilliant but severely disturbed patient with significant ideo-affective decoupling.
   The diagnosis is Borderline Personality.

How severe is the personality disturbance?

Where is the analytical work by the structural vulnerabilities of mental functioning conditioned?

Diana is seriously unstable, and her persecution anxiety has always affected her ability to receive and use analytic interventions. So the analyst had to titrate her interventions to the patient's state of mind and receptivity.

How changed are these aspects?

By modulating the prevailing anxiety of the patient, the analyst helped the patient discriminate fantasy from reality thus decreasing her paranoia.

LEVEL 3: EXPLANATORY HYPOTHESIS OF CHANGE

What was the main focus of the analyst's interventions?

Did the analytic hypothesis and interventions change explicitly or implicitly throughout the treatment?

The main focus was on the need for secrets, distance from some (husband, analyst, Argentina) and symbiosis with others (son), avoidance of affect, conversion of emotion to physical distress, and the use of projective identification as a source of conflict at work and in social relationships.

The analyst allowed the patient distance, understanding it as a unique and necessary way of engaging the patient and gathering the conflict in the transference, where the resistance could be analysed. In transference terms the analyst worked on Diana's confusion between the analyst and her primary objects. This de-linking facilitated the patient's return to Argentina after 30 years.

Could there be other theoretical hypotheses or interpretative strategies?

Other previous analyses in traditional settings had failed for Diana. Teleanalysis helped the patient to begin treatment and then to engage in a process of analysis, as she managed the virtual and the real, the spaces between parts of herself, and her conflict over proximity and distance in relationship, including in the analytic relationship.

Conclusion

Diana tends to want to escape when she feels well in relation to the analyst. She finds the need for love humiliating. She confuses pleasure in the proximity of love with fear of seduction. The closeness and warmth of a deep link with another propels her into a fantasy of incestuous seduction. She sacrifices any link that involves such a threat. Diana was able to untangle her current objects from primary objects sufficiently in order to visit her homeland after 30 years, but the confusion persists. She is still afraid of reconnecting with relationships from her youth.

Follow up

Diana decided to move with her youngest son to Argentina for two years. She came to my office several times a week, until one day she suddenly telephoned me saying that she didn't want to continue her psychoanalysis and that I shouldn't email her or speak to her ever again. She was feeling wonderful. Now she had a lot of friends and good jobs. So she wanted to cut the relationship with me. She didn't give me any opportunity to work with her on this dynamic.

After all this, I continued thinking that she couldn't tolerate being near to me. She could have a better life but still she needed to have the illusion that she could control her life and make people disappear whenever she wanted. She could only be close to many people provided she made me disappear. This is the way she could deal with her life. As her analyst, I realize that her work life and her relationships are much improved, but her conflict is still in place. Perhaps it was made more acute by our meeting in the traditional setting – in the same room, in the same country. The conflict over proximity and distance is still in place awaiting further work.

Reference

Bernardi, R. 2014. The Three-Level Model (3-LM) for observing patient transformations. In: M. Altman Litvan (Ed.), *Time for Change: Tracking Transformations in Psychoanalysis* (pp. 3–34). London: Karnac.

Chapter 7

Technology and private practice

Christopher Vincent, Mary Barnett, Louisa Killpack, Amita Sehgal, and Penni Swinden

What is the impact of technology on clinicians' private practice of psychotherapy? To answer this question five independently practising psychotherapists in the U.K. established a study group to review their practice across the first six months of 2015. The range of technologies studied included websites, email, mobile phones, and Internet-based banking services for payment and receipt of fees, and Internet-based video software (or Voice over Internet Protocol/VoIP software) for providing therapy and/or establishing supervisory and training links. We were well aware that with the current rate of such technological innovation, our findings might well be out of date by the time the results were published, yet it seemed worthwhile to mark the effect of technology on clinical practice for a defined period. We funded the study ourselves, used research methods and an ethical framework that reflected the realities of all the participants working in private practice, and drew on the codes of practice of each participant's professional body to safeguard the material.

We designed a questionnaire which was then completed by each member of the group as well as by two experienced colleagues external to the study group. The feedback from the participants' questionnaires drew attention to the ways that technology has challenged conventional ideas of the therapeutic frame. We found that technologies have had both positive and negative impacts on professional practice and were managed in various, idiosyncratic ways. We noted the lack of professional training about these issues and we highlighted a few changes essential to redressing this situation. At the time of the study, there was little evidence of participants asking for or being offered continuing professional development training on these matters. This suggested that there was a learning gap to be filled.

The evolution and rapid development of telecommunications technology has transformed the way we communicate and transmit information in daily life. We commonly use mobile telephones for many activities, from conversing in person through voicemail or Short Message Service messages (SMS, commonly known as "text" messages) to watching television and surfing the Internet. Advances in Internet technology have not only made information more available to people but have made people more available to one another too. The Internet now offers us new ways of managing relationships as well as managing information. These developments have brought about unprecedented changes in the human condition (Fonagy, 2014). The widespread use of the mobile telephone, coupled with increasingly sophisticated methods of electronic communication, like email, text messages, social media messaging and image sharing, powerfully affects the way we conduct our daily lives.

We wanted to contribute to an exploration of how this technological revolution was impacting on the psychotherapy profession in particular. Could we harness its power, be alert to its pitfalls and dangers, and think in an open-minded, analytic way about its effect on practice?

We realized that many technological advances have become integrated within private clinical practice almost without conscious awareness. For example, the steadily increasing use of email instead of snail mail has had a major impact on the speed of communication between clients and therapists, with the consequence that there is often an erosion of the boundaries between therapists' work and private hours. In our study we noted that we had not given adequate consideration to how the ease and speed with which emails are sent might argue for clarifying the working hours within which our clients might expect replies. This was one example of the ways that technology has crept up on therapeutic practice in recent times (and is likely to go on doing so). For this reason we thought it timely to take a snapshot of how we were managing the impact of these innovations.

Alongside developments which have replaced former methods of communication – such as email replacing letters, mobile phones replacing land-lines and, to some extent, Internet-based banking services replacing the use of cheques – there are those technologies which have added new opportunities to the ways therapists might communicate with clients and colleagues. These technologies include websites, social media (e.g. Facebook and Twitter), and VoIP software, which allow face-to-face contact via the Internet. Therapists can decide whether and how they integrate these new ways of communicating into their professional lives. We found that study group participants made different choices about utilizing these new technologies for various reasons, some of which we will discuss later.

Method

Participants

We were seven senior and experienced psychoanalytic psychotherapists, five female and two male, who agreed to fill in the questionnaire. The mean average of post-qualification experience was 22 years. The age distribution was as follows: two male and three female clinicians were in the 61–70 year age group; one female clinician was in the 51–60 year band; one female clinician was in the 41–50 year band. All of the group were couple therapists in addition to working with individual clients.

We suspect that the seniority and experience of the respondents had a strong bearing on the results. Therapeutic practice is shaped and moulded by basic trainings which for most of our group took place in the pre-Internet age. In discussion we acknowledged that the older members of the group had a more cautious and questioning attitude to taking on new ways of working, especially when these challenged long-established practices. These older "digital immigrants" readily acknowledged their hesitancy and anxiety in tangling with complex new technologies, which they suspected would not be the experience of their younger colleagues, who having grown up with these technologies have the confidence of "digital natives" (Palfrey & Gasser, 2008; Prensky, 2001).

Design

The range of technologies selected for evaluation in our study reflected the practices of our group members. None of us employed social media in our professional lives, although Balick (2016) recognized that some psychotherapists do. One colleague briefly had a Facebook page for her private practice which she soon took down, feeling uncomfortable at the degree to which she felt exposed by it. All participants had varying degrees of involvement and levels of interest in the use of websites and VoIP software.

The questionnaire evaluated the experience of having a dedicated practitioner website and of being listed on organizational websites; the use of email in communicating with clients (ranging from point of first contact to scheduling consultations, maintaining contact between sessions to delivering invoices); the use of mobile telephones in conducting some of these functions; delivering psychotherapy using VoIP software and, finally, the employment of online banking services for invoice payments.

The questionnaire sought to assess how these technologies operated in clinical practice, and included the process of making referrals, providing supervision and conducting training events. The study did not set out to give an in-depth examination of any one technology but, instead, to take a broad overview of an array of technologies and to record their major effects on the clinical practices of a defined group of psychotherapists practising at a particular point in time.

Procedure and method of analysis

The findings from this study were generated in an iterative way. The seven completed questionnaires were distributed among the five members of the group, each of whom took responsibility for analysing subsections of the questionnaire data and writing up summaries of emerging themes (Braun & Clarke, 2006). Their written summaries were then discussed in seven group meetings spread across a period of ten months. From these discussions successive drafts of the study report emerged, each one worked on and revised by the group members.

As a consequence of the study group members being geographically spread out, the monthly research discussion meetings were conducted online using group videoconferencing software, VSee. Communication between meetings was conducted using mobile telephones and email.

There are now available for private and professional use a range of software programmes for individual and group videoconferencing (Weitz, 2014). We chose VSee as it is compliant with the Health Insurance Portability and Accountability Act (HIPAA), a piece of American legislation which sets minimum standards for protecting the confidentiality of electronic health information (http://www.vsee.com/blog) (General Data Protection Regulation GDDR standards have since been introduced as of May 2018).

Results

Websites

Five of us were included in at least one organizational website, while two members had set up their own. This pattern was partly shaped by financial considerations, as inclusion in organizational websites was generally more economical than setting up one's own. Websites can be expensive to build and require regular investment of time and money to maintain and update. Additionally, it also felt difficult to turn down the invitation to join a group website listing colleagues (who wants to be an outsider?), and it was thought that being part of a collective listing felt less exposing and, hence, safer than having one's own dedicated site.

Opinions about listing and describing clinical services offered on websites were mixed. Concerns were expressed about giving enough information so that clients can be appropriately informed before embarking upon therapy (for example, location, fees, time commitment, therapeutic orientation) but not creating unrealistic expectation by providing a surfeit of information. Moreover, an important aspect of working psychoanalytically involves the therapist limiting disclosure of his or her professional standing in order to allow the client's conscious and unconscious phantasies to emerge and be worked with. However, as it is becoming difficult to control the increasing amount of personal information posted on the Internet, therapists are proving less able to put a cloak of anonymity around their professional selves: we all leave digital "footprints". Commenting on this phenomenon, Gabbard is quoted as stating, "The classical view of psychoanalytical anonymity is dead" (Caparrotta & Lemma, 2014, p. 16). This exposure also applies to clients, when therapists, too, can easily obtain information via the Internet about their clients. This raises important questions about whether it is appropriate for therapists to access data that has not been personally volunteered by clients. Putting aside the therapeutic implications of whether therapists act in this way, there seems little doubt that prospective clients (especially younger ones) are increasingly browsing websites to access therapeutic services and are using the Internet to research the backgrounds of prospective therapists (Balick, 2014).

Overall there was a general view that websites could prove helpful for clients and colleagues at the point of referral. One of our group described a dedicated website as a "virtual business card" that referrers might use to direct clients to obtain more information on the therapist, thus shortening the amount of time involved in phone discussions. Additionally, it was thought that when couple therapy is being considered, access to website information could assist the client initiating the referral to engage their partner in a discussion, especially if there is some shared ambivalence about commitment to a first assessment session.

One disadvantage of having an online presence is that it presents the risk of uploaded material being misconstrued. Some of our study group were concerned that websites might convey over-idealized expectations of what therapy might provide. One colleague reported she had to work hard at the assessment interview with a client who having closely scrutinized her website photograph complained she was "less friendly" than her uploaded image had conveyed.

Email

Study group members reported that their use of email had increased enormously over the preceding five years and had replaced other forms of communication to a significant degree. This development was attributed to the ease and the speed with which messages can be sent and received, especially when on the move; email correspondence provides an audit trail of earlier discussions; emails sent and received on password-protected machines ensure privacy and confidentiality of the exchange; a significant advantage in communicating with couples is that emails can be sent to more than one recipient.

However, the ease and speed with which messages can be sent has produced a culture in which there is a high expectation of receiving a similarly speedy response. During our group discussions colleagues regularly commented on how this implicit expectation has affected their professional practice and resulted in the erosion of professional boundaries. Colleagues described how over time their behaviour has changed so that, in their private practices where they are unprotected by time boundaries imposed by "going to work", they tended to reply to work-related email messages from clients and colleagues at all sorts of times, including weekends and evenings.

Discussion about how email was used revealed a range of different practices. Two colleagues made explicit with their clients the hope that emails would be limited to scheduling appointments. Another two referred to having taken up their clients' excessive use of emails between sessions as part of the therapeutic dialogue. One colleague working with couples made it clear at the initial assessment that all email correspondence would be addressed to both partners. This practice encourages transparency of communication between therapist and couple, and also takes into account any oedipal tensions that might arise as a result of one or the other partner feeling excluded. It also maintains clarity about any practical arrangements that may be being discussed. As well as recording our practice, we also found that our discussions influenced our practice: two members decided that it would be helpful in the future to be more explicit than they currently are with clients about how and when emails would be answered.

A concern voiced in discussion involved email messages either going astray because the wrong addressee had inadvertently been selected from an email address list, or waiting for expected emails to arrive only for them to be discovered later in the "Junk" mailbox. Some concern was also expressed about what is included in emails: participants were aware that emails leave a record which can be accessed by third parties whether legally sanctioned or not.

Participants in the study revealed that they now rarely write letters in hard copy to clients. Some, having initially resisted resorting to email communication, gradually realized that email has become an indispensable means by which therapists and clients communicate. One respondent noted that five years ago nearly all her initial enquiries were by telephone, in contrast to the present day where email predominates. It was thought that this development may be linked to clients having found the therapist via websites where email addresses are provided.

Six therapists in our sample indicated they now routinely use email in establishing initial contact with clients and, post-assessment, in making arrangements for on-going therapy. Once regular therapy is underway, emails assist in rearranging session times when necessary. One colleague reported that reliance on emails could mean that postal addresses, and hence an awareness of where clients live, might not be recorded.

It was interesting to note the exceptions to this upward trend in the use of emails. Two therapists stated that they communicated with clients using the medium that their clients used when first contacting them. Another singled out a requirement to communicate with General Practitioners by letter because doctors' surgeries often do not publicize email addresses. Two in our sample stated that where they had to cancel a session and had a choice they would prefer to communicate this by telephone. This was particularly the case when appointments had to be cancelled at short notice, and it was felt preferable to communicate this personally, partly to ensure that the message was received and partly to convey the importance the therapist attached to having to cancel.

The use of email as part of the therapeutic dialogue

All of the study group members preferred engaging face-to-face with their clients, only using email as part of an on-going therapeutic dialogue when necessary. Two situations were identified where it was thought that the use of email was necessary and helpful. In one, the therapist continued to exchange daily emails between sessions as a way of containing his client's otherwise unmanageable feelings. During sessions this client felt debilitated by feelings of extreme shame that prevented him from talking about certain events in his life. Between sessions this client would describe these events in an email as a prelude to bringing this information into therapy. In the therapist's view, this use of email enabled the client to defuse the emotional charge of the material in a creative way, a view supported by Litowich and Gundlach (1987) and Gabbard, who observes that "email communication allows one to overcome shame and other inhibiting factors that prevent direct expression of embarrassing feelings in person" (Gabbard, 2014, p. 43). However, our study also reported on situations where the use of email could have the opposite effect. In one clinical example, the client, who walked out of her session in an enraged state, promptly sent the therapist a vitriolic email. On returning to the next session, she seemed to have very limited awareness of what she had felt or how angrily she had behaved after the previous session.

Both the creative and defensive uses of email, as illustrated by these two situations, alerted us to the difficulties of being dogmatic about its value and heightened our awareness of the importance of considering email and other technologies as holding significance within specific therapeutic contexts.

Mobile phones

All members of the study group used mobile telephones to communicate with clients and colleagues, and most of the group acknowledged that their usage had increased in the last five years, often replacing land lines. A minority found their use of mobile phones in clinical practice had not increased as much as their growing reliance on emails.

Three of our group found the mobile phone to be an inexpensive means of setting up a dedicated professional phone; all participants felt it provided an effective and confidential means of exchanging phone and text messages with clients. This confidence could, however, be threatened in a number of ways. For example, like emails, texts could be mistakenly sent to the wrong recipient, and there was a potential for phones to be misused. One of our group reported that, unbeknown to her, one of her clients recorded sessions on her mobile phone. In fact, the client's use of the recording was subsequently taken up in the therapy in a creative way, but the experience was a reminder that there is a potential for the privacy of conversations to be broken and for recordings to be used in both perverse and creative ways.

Mobile phone use among the group varied. Some of the variation in use was shaped by client preference and behaviours. For example, texting, with its convenience, brevity and immediacy, was noted to be especially favoured by younger clients, who have grown up with it, and who use it to communicate as a matter of course. Where texting was used by therapists, it was generally in reply to last minute practical changes to session times invariably initiated by their clients.

Within our group there seemed to be a broad difference between those who only used mobile phones for establishing or modifying the boundaries of the therapeutic frame – like making referrals, or making or changing appointment times – and those who, in addition, had used the phone to make therapeutic interventions. Such actions were usually made in high stress circumstances. One colleague reported using texts when a client stormed out of a couple session, and an exchange of texts helped the client return. Another described getting drawn into texting with a high risk young client who really needed psychiatric help alongside her therapy but felt unable to access it. As a result the therapy took on the function of crisis management. In the daily exchange of texts the client had felt temporarily contained by the therapist's replies. For this disturbed woman the increasing frequency of text exchanges thought necessary during a crisis created an unrealistic expectation that the pattern would be maintained when the crisis had passed. When this proved not to be the case the patient reacted by withdrawing from therapy. The therapist felt that the pressure on her to respond to the barrage of texts was related to her anxiety about containing a very troubled patient at a point of crisis and judged that the complications that arose as a result of the text exchanges significantly damaged the therapeutic frame and were ultimately unhelpful.

It was noted that the mobile phone's advantage in facilitating very rapid and sometimes immediate contact with others carries with it the potential to become an intrusive and persecuting object. Stadter observes that when patients enter his office they commonly turn off their smartphones and tablets, "This actually and symbolically creates a space for reflection . . . uninterrupted by the intrusions of the internet, social media and communications technology (calls, email and texting)" (Stadter, 2013, p. 3). In our study, this capacity of phone messaging to breach boundaries was experienced by therapists often feeling that calls, like emails, had to be answered very quickly, perhaps mimicking behaviour in their non-professional lives. The consequence was a growing awareness of how over time many of the group had allowed the boundary between work hours and personal time to break down. Few in the group had made it explicit with their clients that calls were to be answered in working hours only. We wondered whether this is likely to be a particular problem for therapists in private practice who do not benefit from working in an organization, where boundaries about where work begins and ends are more clearly drawn.

Voice over Internet Protocol (VoIP) software

Perhaps more than any other of the technologies reviewed in our study, the use of VoIP software in delivering therapy stirred up the strongest feelings and concerns. There are now a growing number of software programmes generically referred to as VoIP programmes that enable audio-visual communications between one or more participants. This practice has been challenged because it is said to be particularly vulnerable to outside surveillance (Churcher, 2012; Weitz, 2014).

The use of VoIP software in work with clients echoed a much broader phenomenon that we began to become aware of as our discussions progressed. Our study showed that while levels of use were quite high – four out of seven participants in our study reported using Skype or VSee in delivering therapy – it was acknowledged that this practice was highly innovative and posed challenges and uncertainties that were faced without training or discussion in post-qualifying professional seminars. In this context, the study group discussions provided a much needed thinking space for us all. As our work progressed we realized that other therapists were likely to be in a similar position. A limited survey of members of the British Psychoanalytic Society showed that about a third had experimented with telephone and/or VoIP analysis (Fornario-Spoto, 2011) and yet there is reported to be a reluctance to be open about this practice (Caparrotta & Lemma, 2014, op. cit.).

At the beginning of our study, six of the seven participants used video software for linking up with colleagues, while three had used the technology as a medium for delivering therapy. Encouraged by the experience of others and the discussions that centred on this way of working, another member of our group began offering therapy over the Internet as the research unfolded. Some colleagues were explicit in not wanting to use these technologies, having been put off by fears that the medium was not secure from outside surveillance and by reports that the technology itself can be unreliable. These colleagues stated that they would only consider working in this medium with existing clients who for any reason had to relocate.

In total six clinical cases were referred to in our discussions, four being work with individuals and two with couples. The most commonly cited single reason for using VoIP software was geographical distance preventing face-to-face contact continuing. One colleague also described working with a couple where a video link was used when one of the partners went through a debilitating episode of depression, and leaving the home was difficult. In relation to couple work one of our group also felt that for couples who are both working and have family responsibilities, a home-based computer link may be the only viable means of fitting in therapy with other commitments.

Those colleagues who had used video links as part of therapy reported significant technical challenges which included difficulties in setting up the connection. It soon becomes obvious that clients themselves have to take responsibility for establishing their end of the connection. This contrasts with the conventional therapeutic setting, in which the therapist takes responsibility for shaping the physical surroundings of the consulting room. By contrast in VoIP-mediated therapy, the client has a central role in deciding how their end of the connection is set up. These decisions will include positioning the video camera, choosing a room in their house, and considering whether the space can be guarded against intrusions by other household members or pets. The power balance in the therapeutic relationship is thereby altered, and whether this is a helpful or unhelpful consequence is likely to vary from case to case.

When working with couples a choice has to be made whether one computer link or two is used by the partners. Using one computer screen requires a couple to sit either quite close together or further apart but at a distance from the computer's video camera. How this decision is made has implications in the work of a dynamic and technical nature. Some couples may value being seated close together, while for conflicted couples this may be an anathema. Sitting further from the camera can result in poor sound quality, but this may be compensated by the benefit of gaining a fuller view of both partners.

Once the set-up has been established, further technical challenges were reported in the questionnaires and study group discussions. These challenges fell into two broad categories: firstly, the losses associated with this type of work (which one respondent described as a loss of the "total situation" (Joseph, 1985)) as compared to working face-to-face and, secondly, the anxieties that therapists and clients have to live with in using this new technology.

So, for example, there was a concern that this way of work limits the therapist's confidence in feeling that he or she is sufficiently well attuned to the client's emotional state (Scharff, 2012) and, in parallel, can trust their countertransference. Loss of image definition and distortions to voice quality play into this problem. Moreover, the abrupt beginnings and endings of sessions mean that important information is lost about how clients enter the consulting room, talk of their journey to therapy and then exit the room at the end of the session. Lin (2015) explores the impact of the VoIP setting on the analytic frame in detail, discussing whether such a connection can provide a "good enough" setting for therapy. He describes how VoIP (or "teleanalysis", as he terms it) reduces the journey to therapy to just one click of the computer mouse, making it seem more like a magic game than making a real, serious connection. Once a computer session is started there are questions about how we as therapists relate to the computer screen and to this "virtual space" (Balick, 2014, p. 32) imagined to exist between us and our clients. There is a self-consciousness associated with using a video camera, reinforced by simultaneously being able to see a picture of oneself on the screen as one talks. The experience of feeling less emotionally attuned to the person at the other end of the line coupled with the self-consciousness that comes from observing oneself can heighten the feeling that the conversation tends towards a narcissistic or solipsistic exchange. Balick (2014, op. cit.) makes the point that in feeling less emotionally connected to the person at the other end of the line, there is a greater opportunity for participants in computer-linked conversations to experiment with projecting different identities. One study group member thought that the couple he worked with using VoIP used their screen to present an over-idealized image of themselves to themselves and to their therapist: that of being a linked couple (they used one video camera and sat closely intertwined on a sofa at home), which was at odds with the reality of their non-relating. Another colleague reported that a web camera exchange involved seeing her client in her night clothes and sitting up in bed. These presentations of self and couple were possible because of the clients' control of the web camera location and use. In both cases, the therapists pondered hard on whether these presentations helped or hindered the therapeutic task.

Anxieties stirred up by using VoIP software were often caused by the failure to make or maintain a connection, a point underlined by Isaacs Russell (2015). Colleagues reported on this problem being particularly burdensome when working with clients who could be thought of as showing patterns of insecure attachment.

Both Lin (2015) and Wallwork (2015) echo these concerns, advising caution in using VoIP technologies with clients demonstrating more serious problems in forming and maintaining relationships.

VoIP and professional links

Participants in our study used VoIP software fairly extensively in their communications with colleagues. All seven reported using this medium for either supervising others or being supervised themselves. It was also apparent that a range of post-qualifying professional development programmes were delivered using this medium. Four colleagues were using it to offer training and three had stated that they had participated in training webinars. We were also conscious that the work reported on in this paper was made possible by meeting regularly in a video-conference format.

One significant advantage of using the medium of VoIP was its cost effectiveness. Travel costs and travel time to meetings no longer need to be accounted for. Set against this powerful advantage was the difficulty in feeling the emotional pulse of the meeting, whether a one-to-one meeting or a larger group. There was also a recognition that participants need to be vigilant in safeguarding the confidentiality of clinical material, but it was felt that this could be protected with adequate disguise and, where necessary, by encryption (for example, when encryption is used to protect the exchange of process notes between supervisee and supervisor).

The use of online banking

All members of our study group offered the options to both clients and supervisees of using Bankers' Automated Clearing Services (BACS) for payment of fees. The percentage of clients paying in this way varied; some therapists reported the percentage to be as high as 100% whereas for others it was as low as 10%. One colleague noted a decrease in the popularity of cheque payments alongside an increase in payments via BACS and cash.

The advantages of bank transfer payments were convenience, speed and transparency of transactions, which clients, overall, liked. The disadvantages were that, by removing the payment from the consulting room, opportunities can be lost or sidestepped to consider the meaning of paying for services; the process may become sanitized with a fear of therapy being devalued. Close attention to account payments is also required, to check when invoices have been paid, and this can cause problems when there is no identifying reference on the invoice or when partners in a couple therapy take turns in paying.

Conclusion

Our study reported on developments in clinical practice brought about by technological change. Most of the developments discussed in this report have become accepted into practice in two ways. First, there were those developments that had crept up and become part of day-to-day practice almost without conscious awareness. The use of email and mobile phones seemed to fall within this category. But, second, there were those technological innovations where psychotherapists have exercised choice about whether and how to integrate them within their professional working lives. Social media, websites, VoIP software and payments by bank transfer fell within this group.

When thinking about these technologies it became apparent to us that they all comprise elements of the therapeutic frames within which therapy takes place and that the changes they have brought about raise questions in a number of important areas.

Firstly, they have had an impact on therapeutic boundaries. All the technologies we discussed have made communication easier, faster and less costly than the methods they have replaced. We have tried to spell out how we as practitioners experienced the advantages and disadvantages of faster communication. We were all surprised by the incremental manner in which some of us had allowed this acceleration to blur the boundaries between work and private hours in unhelpful ways, raising the possibility that, at assessment meetings, expectations about response times to emails and texts need to be clarified.

Secondly, changes to the therapeutic frame influence what happens within that frame. We have considered some of the advantages and disadvantages of using email, mobile phones and VoIP software as part of on-going therapy. In exploring these possibilities we were struck by the inhibitions to openly discussing these interventions, perhaps because they challenge long-held conventions about how as therapists we ought to practise. These inhibitions need to be overcome so that we can explore the dynamic issues that working with these technologies present.

Thirdly, we are aware that important ethical and legal questions are raised by the use of these technologies (Wallwork, 2015). Should practitioners be formally trained in the use of new techniques like VoIP software? Do professional indemnity insurance policies cover psychotherapeutic work using video software, particularly if this work crosses international boundaries? Should therapists be registered with the Office of the Information Commissioner as Data Controllers under the U.K. Data Protection Act as has been strongly argued (Weitz, 2014)? These are just a few of the questions raised by our study. As far as we could tell, the professional bodies of which respondents were members at the time of the study (January to June 2015) had not issued any practice guidelines or advice in this area.

We set up this project when we became aware that our practice was changing under the sway of technical innovations, and we believed that these changes needed to be benchmarked and discussed. We recognized the paradox that while technology was altering the nature of the therapeutic frames within which we practised, there was little written about how different technologies interact with one another to shape the overall psychological containment we are able to offer our clients. We thought such a deficit warranted taking an overview of our practices. We were aware that such an approach could be criticized on a number of grounds. By taking a broad overview of technological innovations, the analysis could be considered superficial in that each of the technologies mentioned could have been examined at greater depth. We also concede that the analysis is essentially descriptive and does not explore the dynamic significance of these technologies within detailed clinical situations. In taking this extensive and descriptive perspective, we hope that we have laid some groundwork for more in-depth research.

Methodologically the study can be challenged for utilizing VoIP software as part of the research method when also claiming to evaluate its effectiveness. Nevertheless, the research group felt that communicating with one another via VSee brought to life many of the dilemmas which we were attempting to describe and understand. We describe how we, as a particular group of therapists who undertake couple and individual psychotherapy in private practice, are thinking about the implications for us of recent technological changes. The hope is that by describing our experiences, we will help others to reflect on the impact of technology on their own clinical practice. We hope to facilitate a much needed professional dialogue, and to call attention to a gap in the provision of continuing education about the use of technology for psychotherapists.

References

Balick, A. (2014). How to think about psychotherapy in a digital context. In: P. Weitz (Ed.), *Psychotherapy 2.0: Where Psychotherapy and Technology Meet* (pp. 23–40). London: Karnac.

Balick, A. (2016). twitter.com/Dr AaronB. Last accessed 10 July.

Braun, V., & Clarke, V. (2006). Using thematic analysis in psychology. *Qualitative Research in Psychology*, 3(2): 77–101.

Caparrotta, L., & Lemma, A. (2014). Introduction. In: A. Lemma & L. Caparrotta (Eds.), *Psychoanalysis in the Technoculture Era* (pp. 1–21). London and New York: Routledge.

Churcher, J. (2012). Skype and privacy. *International Journal of Psychoanalysis*, 4: 1035–1037.

Fonagy, P. (2014). Foreword. In: A. Lemma & L. Caparrotta (Eds.), *Psychoanalysis in the Technoculture Era* (pp. xv–xxi). London and New York: Routledge.

Fornario-Spoto, G. (2011). Analysis and supervision by telephone and Skype: A valid alternative, a stop-gap measure or best avoided? *Bulletin of the British Psychoanalytical Society*, 47(7): 26–32.

Gabbard, G. (2014). Cyberpassion: E-rotic transference and the internet. In: A. Lemma & L. Caparrotta (Eds.), *Psychoanalysis in the Technoculture Era* (pp. 33–46). London and New York: Routledge.

Isaacs Russell, G. (2015). *Screen Relations: The Limits of Computer-Mediated Psychoanalysis and Psychotherapy.* London: Karnac.

Joseph, B. (1985). Transference: The total situation. *International Journal of Psychoanalysis*, 66: 447–454.

Lin, T. (2015). Teleanalysis: problems, limitations, and opportunities. In: J. S. Scharff (Ed.), *Psychoanalysis Online 2* (pp. 105–120). London: Karnac.

Litowich, B. E., & Gundlach, R. A. (1987). When adolescents write: Semiotic and social dimensions of adolescents' writing. *Adolescent Psychiatry*, 14: 82–111.

Palfrey, J., & Gasser, U. (2008). *Born Digital: Understanding the First Generation of Digital Natives*. New York: Basic Books.

Prensky, M. (2001). Digital natives, digital immigrants. *On the Horizon*, 9(5): 1–6.

Scharff, J. S. (2012). Clinical issues in analysis over the telephone and internet. *International Journal of Psychoanalysis*, 93: 81–85.

Stadter, M. (2013). The influence of social media and communications technology on self and relationships. In: J. Scharff (Ed.), *Psychoanalysis Online* (pp. 3–13). London: Karnac.

Wallwork, E. (2015). Thinking ethically about beginning online work. In: J. S. Scharff (Ed.), *Psychoanalysis Online 2* (pp. 83–92). London: Karnac.

Weitz, P. (2014). The role of confidentiality and security for working on-line. http:// www. pwtraining.com/resources/v02.

Commentary

David E. Scharff

Christopher Vincent and his colleagues offer an impressive overview of the pervasive influence of the explosive development of technology in the modern world, as viewed through the lens of private psychotherapy practice. The authors acknowledge that they do not examine the dynamics of this multifaceted phenomenon in any detail, but this is also the strength of their article. They offer a bird's-eye view that complements the detail they give about the interaction of technology with the psychodynamics of the therapeutic process in the several modalities that are considered. Their discussion sets the stage for detailed examination of our own experiences of distance therapy and delineates the context in which our private clinical and social experiences take place.

For this reason, I regard this article as an essential companion to those detailed examinations of technology-mediated individual psychotherapy sessions and courses of treatment, processes of individual psychoanalysis and couple therapy, and distance teaching of psychodynamic concepts. In each of those cases we are free to examine the dynamics as we would do when studying material from traditional clinical settings. But in the background of contemporary experience in the digital age lies this ubiquitous technology that affects the life of us all, not only in our practice of psychotherapy and psychoanalysis but in family life, business and social interaction.

As I start to write this brief discussion, I have most poignantly in mind what happened to me over the past weekend. A mandatory update to my iTunes account on my iPhone essentially killed the phone. The message from Apple then told me that all of my data would be erased in the process of restoring the phone. Never mind that I was unable to restore the phone by logging onto the website because their processes for restoring the phone all involved communicating to the phone in order to verify that I was who I said I was. In the process of this mini-trauma – which caused me an almost sleepless night – I had the sudden full realization that my iPhone had become an object in my inner world. It had entered with a certain excitement and now had become a very unwelcome persecuting object. The genius at the Apple store did fix it, which was a relief, but it only goes to show how dependent we are on technology and technical assistance. With this experience in mind, I want to echo the authors' plea for acknowledging the impact of this development of the last 20 years. We cannot escape the importance of technological advances and the effect on us of our entry into a technological world, the likes of which humankind has never known before.

The authors have covered a great deal of territory in an even-handed, thoughtful way, using a qualitative research approach in which their results, thoughtful speculations and conclusions have been validated through extensive discussion amongst themselves and are now shared for all of us to think with them. Let me now add a couple of thoughts that came from my reading of this interesting and important chapter.

First, I can see that we urgently need an expanded literature about the use of distance technology in all of its forms, including email and VoIP communication, Internet banking, the use of mobile phones for communication and texting, social media – and the new forms of technology usage that will no doubt emerge between the time this book is sent to press and the time that it appears in print. This chapter, and this whole book, is really about the impact of the rapid pace of change in the technological world that seems at times to be out of our control and to have taken on a life of its own. Witness, for instance, the way in which there is an emergent journalism about the five great Internet forces (Google, Facebook, Microsoft, Apple and Amazon) monopolizing a huge swathe of our global technological connectedness with an economic and social power beyond that of national governments. These forces bring great benefits but have substantial drawbacks. Their power over us surely is something that has an effect on our experience of technology and on our choice to use it for technology-mediated therapy. For instance, we are rightly afraid that our communications can be hacked or spied on, which leads us to depend on encryption technology for security – but as we now know, it cannot guarantee complete privacy.

So I repeat that we now need a contemporary literature about technology in psychotherapy and psychoanalysis with a breadth and depth comparable to the literature of the early days of psychoanalysis on principles of technique focused on the use of the couch, the proper outfitting of the therapy office, dealing with resistance – for instance, treating a balky child outside in the car or waiting room, free association, and transference and countertransference. How is the technical equipment to be set up? Where is the webcamera placed in relation to the couch? How is resistance manifest in difficulty in arranging for adequate bandwidth? How is transference manifest in clicking the wrong icon and losing connection?

We also need a literature on the way that these various technologies interact. They can no longer be seen as a single technology employed on discrete occasions. For instance, we use email for the scheduling of appointments, or sustaining a patient who is too anxious to maintain herself in the interval between appointments. We use VoIP with a webcamera to mediate the therapy session. The use of text or email supports and interacts with our use of VoIP for conducting sessions for a patient who is in a different geographic location, travelling, too ill to leave the house, or who would miss sessions because of an ill child. What about the interaction between these uses of email and VoIP? How do we deal with young patients who include us in their all-day-and all-night communication? Do we set our mobile phones in the mode of sounding alerts when texts arrive during a session with another patient? Or do we turn off those alerts and risk missing an urgent communication? How do we think dynamically about our use and misuse of all these media? For instance, I realize that I no longer have the same urgency to provide substitute coverage when I travel. It is easy for me to be available by mobile phone, which works from virtually any place in the world. Now I can respond to the unlikely occasion of an urgent need for a session immediately. This is adequate because of the nature of my psychoanalytic practice, but it would not be adequate for therapists whose patients need crisis-oriented psychiatric coverage.

Finally, I come to my main point following Vincent and his colleagues' underscoring of the way in which the new technologies have changed the frame in which we work. Interestingly, they pose the question of how this will change the content of our work. Will our experience of treatment using distance technologies expand our capacity to analyse issues that we previously understood when we met with patients only in the office, physically in the room together? This of course is a matter of keen interest. It has been already explored in articles in this and previous volumes in the series, and deserves a great deal more study.

The point I want to make is that frame and content are always inextricably connected. The content of our sessions is a feature of the frame that we offer. The frame represents the most fundamental security of the therapeutic project. José Bleger (2013) holds that the frame represents what he calls the psychotic element in analysis, but, while I agree that it is the foundation, I think of the frame as representing the infantile elements on which all development rests. Because these technological developments have fundamentally changed crucial elements of the frame in which we work, even when we are not using a distance technology they change the content with which we work. For instance, it is common in my practice for a patient to take out her cell phone and play a piece of music or a recorded conversation, show me an email that came to her or an image she finds important for me to see or hear. This never would have happened 25 years ago. We have yet to fully understand the significance of importing experience from outside the consultation room directly into our offices and into our minds, whether from a handheld device or from the screen image of the personal environment a patient has set up for their distance therapy. This area of exploration remains before us as we face the exciting and daunting future of the use of technology in psychotherapy and psychoanalysis.

Reference

Bleger, J. (2013). *Symbiosis and Ambiguity: A Psychoanalytic Study.* J. Churcher & L. Bleger (Eds.). Trans. S. Rogers. London, Routledge [Original in Spanish in 1967].

Research on teaching, supervision and psychotherapy using video conference technology

Robert M. Gordon, Xiubing Wang, and Jane Tune

How do experts compare teaching, supervision and treatment from a psychodynamic perceptive over the Internet with in-person work? To answer this question, we designed a research study, its methodology based on online survey, qualitative review, and statistical comparison of the expert opinions of 176 teachers, supervisors and therapists in the China American Psychoanalytic Alliance (CAPA) who use video conferencing (VCON) with Chinese students. The results from our online survey indicate: 1. The longer teachers teach, the more effective they rate teaching over VCON; 2. Teaching, supervision and treatment were all rated in the range of "slightly less effective" than in-person work, with supervision rated significantly more effective than teaching and treatment over VCON; 3. When doing psychodynamic treatment over VCON the issues of symptom reduction, exploring mental life, working on transference, relational problems, resistance, privacy issues and countertransference are all equally rated in the range of "slightly less effective" than in-person treatment; 4. The highest significantly rated indications for treatment over VCON are: "To offer high-quality treatment to underserved or remote patients" and "When patient is house-bound or travel would be impractical"; and 5. The highest significantly rated contraindication for treatment over VCON is: "Patient needs close observation due to crisis or decompensation." Overall, this survey suggests that VCON teaching, supervision and treatment from a psychodynamic perceptive is a worthwhile option when considering its unique contribution to extending services where needed.

Psychological education, supervision and treatments over the Internet video-conferencing technology (such as Skype, ooVoo, etc.) provide services to students and patients who may live in areas that are remote or have a lack of qualified specialists, who may have impaired mobility, lack transportation. However, there is currently an uncertainty about how online services differ from the same process in the in-person relationship.

While video conferencing (VCON) psychological services have been an emerging twenty-first century phenomena since Skype began in 2003, universities began using the Internet for remote learning soon after the beginning of the Internet, with a great deal of success. Cowart (2010) reported that from 1991 to 2004, online university enrolments grew from virtually 0 to over 2.35 million students.

The teaching of psychotherapy over the Internet also has empirical support. Combining internet-based theory teaching with in-person supervision and personal experience, Tantam, Blackmore, and Van Deurzen (2006) found that both student performance and student satisfaction were higher in the eLearning psychotherapy programme when compared with a traditional in-person programme.

Supervision of treatment over the Internet has also been found effective. Jacobsen and Grünbaum (2011) studied situations in which distance supervision may be necessary and concluded that supervision via video conferencing (VCON) offers a good alternative to in-person encounters, and in certain ways it even seems to boost the growth of the supervisees. Savin et al. (2013) describe the collaboration between the Departments of Psychiatry at the University of Colorado School of Medicine and the University of Health Sciences in Cambodia. They conclude that VCON enhances psychiatric training across cultures and international boundaries in offering an effective and inexpensive approach to address disparities in global mental health.

Psychological treatment over the Internet is far more complex than distance learning and supervision. Treatment involves a more intense, subjective, therapeutic relationship and a greater need for privacy than didactic education or supervision. There is clearly a place for VCON therapy services for patients who do not have easy access to treatment. Godleski, Darkins, and Peters (2012) assessed clinical outcomes of 98,609 mental health patients before and after enrolment in remote clinical video conferencing of the U.S. Department of Veterans Affairs between 2006 and 2010. They found that psychiatric admissions of VCON therapy patients decreased by an average of approximately 24%, and length of stay decreased by an average of 27%.

Backhaus et al. (2012) conducted a systematic literature review of the use of video conferencing psychotherapy (VCP) and found 65 studies for their analysis. Their results indicate that VCP has been used in a variety of therapeutic formats and with diverse populations, is generally associated with good user satisfaction, and is found to have similar clinical outcomes to traditional face-to-face psychotherapy.

However, the more the treatment depends on a therapeutic relationship, as in the case of the psychoanalytic relationship, the more there may be problems with VCON treatment. There are few studies on the nature of the online therapeutic relationship. Sucala et al. (2012) reviewed the literature on "e-therapy", which is defined as providing mental health services via email, video conferencing, virtual reality technology, chat technology, or any combination of these. The authors searched PubMed, PsycINFO and CINAHL through to August 2011. From the 840 reviewed studies, only 11 (1.3%) investigated the therapeutic relationship.

The Internet would seem to create an interpersonal distance that might weaken the therapeutic alliance. However, Holmes, and Foster (2012) found that online counselling clients perceived a significantly stronger working alliance on the total Working Alliance Inventory–Short Form than did those who received in-person only counselling. Still, it is not clear from this study if the definition of a "working alliance" in counselling is generalizable to how psychoanalysts use the term.

Cognitive Behaviour Therapy with less emphasis on the working alliance and more emphasis on technique with cognitive learning as the goal would seem to be a natural treatment for the Internet. Empirical studies support this. Johansson, Frederick, and Andersson (2013) report studies showing no differences between Internet-delivered cognitive behavioural therapy and in-person cognitive behavioural therapy for mild to moderate depression, anxiety disorders, and somatic problems. But Donker et al. (2013) found that for the brief online treatment of depression both CBT and interpersonal psychotherapy (IPT) are both effective treatments, though they do not report studies showing that IPT online is as good as in-person IPT.

Bayles (2012) wrote that since therapeutic action is grounded in implicit, procedural, nonverbal communication, the entire body is implicated in the analytic dialogue. She believes that psychotherapy by VCON may limit the access to the information communicated by the body and the various sense modalities.

Although psychoanalysis and psychodynamic treatment requires more of a therapeutic "presence" than other psychotherapies, the Internet can still convey enough therapeutic effect to people who would not have such treatment otherwise. Several papers demonstrated the advantages to providing psychoanalytic treatment to remote areas lacking expert providers. Edirippulige, Levandovskaya and Prishutova (2013) looked at the use of Skype for delivering psychotherapy services in the Ukraine. Most of the practitioners thought their clients considered the services received on Skype to be good or excellent. The majority of clients and providers showed high satisfaction with the use of Skype for psychotherapy services.

Fishkin et al. (2011) reported on the China American Psychoanalytic Alliance (CAPA), which provides treatment, education and supervision to Chinese mental health professionals over the Internet. The lack of enough Chinese analysts and mentors has created an intense demand for psychodynamic psychotherapy training and the treatment that CAPA is addressing by using Internet communication technologies. They discussed not only the success of the programme but also the cultural issues, as well as aspects of the transference and countertransference that are shaped by the virtual nature of the technology.

The issue of privacy with providing treatment online is another area of debate. Churcher (2012) was concerned that we have knowledge about our immediate physical and social environment to make reliable judgements about whether a conversation is private, but this is less true of our virtual environment in cyberspace. However, Scharff (2013a) replied that we need to work on weighing the benefits against the risks with teleanalysis. She argues that there will be fewer concerns with more discussion at our association meetings, and more systematic research is needed as to whether teleanalysis can provide a secure setting and can meet the standard of being clinically equally effective.

Scharff also reports a recent study by the American Psychoanalytic Association that found that 28% of respondents reported using the phone, 9% used Skype for psychotherapy, and 4% used Skype for psychoanalysis. Scharff states that online supervision and online analyses are part of the repertoire of current practice, and when used with care, the Internet has the potential to allow teaching and treatment to occur when it would otherwise be impossible.

Paolo (2013) wrote that psychoanalysis over the Internet reflects on what we mean by communication between patient and analyst. He feels that online therapy is simply a different form of therapy.

Dettbarn (2013) discussed Skype as a third "secret sharer" in the analytic process. She wondered what feelings, fantasies and thoughts analysts and clients entertain when they hear each other's disembodied voices from a loudspeaker and observe the video transmission on a screen. Dettbarn posed these important issues: the absence of spatial and physical proximity and the development of trust, denial of the reality of separation and mourning, the Internet as a protection against the real dangers in a physical presence (violence, aggression, sexual seduction), and if transference, resistance and regression will seem more magical.

The less sense of propinquity in treatment may be why despite the effectiveness of online treatment there might be a higher drop-out rate as compared to in-person treatment as reported by King et al. (2014).

Caparrotta (2013) claims that digital technologies need to be embraced responsibly and with an open mind by the psychoanalytic profession. This seems to be occurring as indicated by two recent books on the topic, *Psychoanalysis Online: Mental Health, Teletherapy and Training* edited by Scharff (2013b), and *Psychoanalysis in the Technoculture Era* edited by Lemma and Caparrotta (2013). Scharff's (2013b) book emerged from an international workgroup of colleagues from the International Psychoanalytical Association (IPA) and the International Institute for Psychoanalytic Training (IIPT) studying the practice of psychoanalysis and psychotherapy conducted on the telephone and over the Internet.

While there are a few empirical studies on the perceived effectiveness of teaching, supervision and treatment over the Internet, presently there are no studies comparing them with each other. Teaching, supervision and psychodynamic treatment over the Internet each involve different roles, tasks, and degrees of intimacy. It would be useful to compare them in regards to the issue of object relations over VCON and the effectiveness of the services. It might take training and experience to become proficient in delivering these services over VCON. There is also a need for research that takes a more in-depth comparison of psychodynamic therapy online vs. psychodynamic treatment in person, with the issues of symptom reduction, exploring mental life, working with transference, working though relational problems, working with resistances, privacy concerns, countertransference issues, and indications and contraindications for doing VCON treatment.

We hypothesize the following: 1. The more experienced at teaching, supervising or treatment, the higher the service will be rated. 2. Overall, VCON technology should compare favourably to in-person work in teaching, supervising and treatment, and the nature of the relationship should affect the perceived effectiveness of the VCON work. That is, supervision, with the more personal relationship (as compared to trying to hold the attention of many students when teaching over VCON) and without the attachment and transference issues of the therapeutic relationship, should make it more effective than teaching and treating. 3. VCON technology presents special problems for psychodynamic treatment, but the overall issues of symptom reduction, exploring mental life, working with transference, working though relational problems, working with resistances, privacy concerns, and countertransference should compare favourably to in-person work. 4. The main indications for VCON psychotherapy should be about making it available to people who do not have access to quality care, or when meeting in person is not practical. 5. The main contraindication should be when the patient is in a crisis and needs closer observation.

Since these hypotheses involve the interaction of several complex variables, we felt that using expert opinion was an appropriate method for testing our hypotheses. Expert opinion can synthesize complex variables that are difficult to study with controlled experimentation. Laboratory methodology of complex systems that isolate variables out of context would also lack ecological validity. Cook (1991) argued that the use of expert opinion in scientific inquiry and policymaking is often the best methodology for understanding complex systems and technologies. Mosleh, Bier, and Apostolakis (1987) found in their review that expert opinion works best in practical decision-making settings. While case study is based on the expert opinion of one person, we used a high number of experts in the area of concern for greater reliability.

Method

Participants and design

Our expert participants were recruited from the email list of 300 past and present China American Psychoanalytic Alliance (CAPA) teachers, supervisors, and therapists. There were four consecutive email requests for participation. The email notices stated that participation is voluntary and anonymous. They were given a link to the online survey on SurveyMonkey, where their responses to the questions were automatically stored and exported to SPSS for analysis. The survey was kept very short, generally less than 5 minutes in the hope to increase participation. We stated in the survey:

> Answer only the questions as they apply to your work with CAPA. There may be issues with differences in education, language and culture between your CAPA students/supervisees/patients and your in-person American students/supervisees/patients. For the sake of this research, please assume 'all other things being equal' though this is not easy to do.

From the 300 email addresses, 176 took the online survey, roughly a 59% response rate (we could not be sure that all the email addresses were current). The respondents were 65% female, 37 % were psychologists, 33% were social workers, and 22% were psychiatrists. The teachers (n = 130) had an average of 18.35 years of experience (SD = 9.72), supervisors (n = 152) had an average of 18.63 years of experience (SD = 10.21), and the therapists (n = 163) had an average of 23.84 years of practising psychoanalytic treatment (SD = 7.44). Seventy-nine per cent (n = 175) stated that they have been using video conferencing (VCON) for 3 or more years for doing teaching, or providing supervision or treatment (M = 4.21, SD = 2.14). The executive members of CAPA initially screened all the participants for their expertise before they were allowed to offer their services to CAPA. Additionally, the results indicating the many years of teaching, providing supervision or treatment support our methodological assumption that this is a survey of expert opinion.

Results

We hypothesized positive correlations between years of experience teaching, supervising or providing treatment, with the perceived effectiveness. Our hypothesis is partially supported. The Pearson product-moment correlation coefficient is significant between years of teaching with their ratings of perceived effectiveness of their teaching (r = .286, p < .05, n = 79). The correlations of years supervising and treating are in the positive direction, but are not significant with their ratings of perceived effectiveness.

In particular we hypothesized that VCON technology would be more effective in supporting supervision than teaching or treatment, because supervision is an intimate situation with a focus on one person and so is more personal than teaching a class and less fraught with attachment and transference issues than individual therapy. All the ratings went from 1 = much less effective, 2 = less effective, 3 = slightly less effective, 4 = no difference (from in-person treatment), 5 = slightly more effective, 6 = more effective, and 7 = much more effective. Respondents were asked how much their teaching or supervising or treating over VCON differs from their in-person work in perceived effectiveness. (We used ANOVA with unequal Ns to analyse these survey questions, and focused paired t-tests for testing specific Post Hoc comparisons.)

Our hypothesis is supported. There was a significant main effect, F (2, 8.45) = 8.53, p < .0001). All three (teaching, supervising, and treating) are in the "slightly less effective" than in-person range. Focused post-hoc analysis with paired t-tests analysis shows that supervision is significantly rated as more effective than both teaching and treating (p < .0001). Teaching and treating were not rated significantly different from each other: supervision (n = 114, M = 3.16, SD = .97), teaching (n = 84, M = 2.62, SD = .88) and treatment (n = 101, M = 2.72, SD = 1.11). Supervision and teaching are most similar (r = .78), then supervision and treating (r = .68) and least similar are teaching and treating (r = .51).

The overall issues of symptom reduction, exploring mental life, working with transference, working though relational problems, working with resistances, privacy concerns, and countertransference should compare favourably to in-person work.

a   How does video conferencing compare to in-person treatment in reducing symptoms? ($n = 109$, $M = 2.86$, $SD = 1.05$)
b   How does video conferencing compare to in-person psychotherapy in exploring the mental life of the patient? ($n = 112$, $M = 2.89$, $SD = 1.04$)
c   How does video conferencing compare to in-person treatment in working on transference? ($n = 110$, $M = 2.88$, $SD = 1.16$)
d   How does video conferencing compare to in-person treatment in working through relational problems? ($n = 112$, $M = 2.89$, $SD = 1.06$)
e   How does video conferencing compare to in-person treatment in working with resistance? ($n = 112$, $M = 2.70$, $SD = 1.19$)
f   How does video conferencing compare to in-person treatment in creating a sense of privacy? ($n = 111$, $M = 3.03$, $SD = 1.34$)
g   How does video conferencing compare to in-person treatment in countertransference issues? ($n = 111$, $M = 3.08$, $SD = 1.19$)

Our hypothesis is supported. The ANOVA results do not indicate any significant differences between these psychotherapy factors in the VCON condition. They were all rated in the range of "slightly less effective" than in-person treatment.

The main indications for VCON psychotherapy should be about making it available to people who do not have access to quality care, or when meeting in person is not practical. We asked, "What do you think are indications for doing video conferencing treatment? (1 = not much, 2 = somewhat, 3 = definite indication, 4 = strong indication)."

a   To offer high-quality treatment to underserved or remote patients ($n = 105$, $M = 3.51$, $SD = .69$)
b   Comfort and convenience of environment ($n = 100$, $M = 1.90$, $SD = 1.03$)
c   Expectation that it will be more effective than in-person treatment ($n = 102$, $M = 1.16$, $SD = .52$)
d   Feel safer with a hostile patient ($n = 100$, $M = 1.51$, $SD = .82$)
e   When patient is house-bound or travel would be impractical ($n = 102$, $M = 3.38$, $SD = .83$)
f   Continuity of care when the therapist or patient is traveling ($n = 103$, $M = 2.91$, $SD = .94$).

Our hypothesis is supported. The ANOVA results indicate significant main effects, $F(5, 103.54) = 153.03$, $p < .0001$.

Focused Post Hoc tests show that both indications: "To offer high-quality treatment to underserved or remote patients" and "When patient is house-bound or travel would be impractical" are not significantly different from each other, but they are each significantly higher in their ratings than the other indications ($p < .0001$).

The main contraindication should be when the patient is in a crisis and needs closer observation. We asked, "What do you think are contraindications for doing video conferencing treatment? (1 = not much, 2 = somewhat, 3 = definite contra-indication, 4 = strong contraindication)."

a   Patient needs close observation due to crisis or decompensation ($n = 102$, $M = 3.32, SD = .90$)
b   Patient needs the supportive feeling of "a mommy in the room" ($n = 101$, $M = 2.56, SD = 1.14$)
c   Patient is very resistant and may use Internet problems as an excuse ($n = 102$, $M = 2.68, SD = 1.09$)
d   Patient is too concerned about privacy ($n = 100, M = 2.74, SD = 1.10$)
e   Legal issues about practice in other regions ($n = 101, M = 3.01, SD = 1.08$)
f   Malpractice concerns ($n = 100, M = 2.74, SD = 1.17$)
g   Problems with the reliability of service ($n = 102, M = 2.90, SD = 1.03$)
h   Language problems are too serious ($n = 101, M = 2.92, SD = 1.12$)
i   Bringing the therapist "home" can be seen as seductive ($n = 101, M = 2.12$, $SD = 1.17$)

Our hypothesis is supported. The ANOVA results indicate a significant main effect $F (8, 11.16) = 9.39, p < .0001$. Focused post-hoc paired t-tests showed that the highest rated contraindication for treatment over VCON is that the "Patient needs close observation due to crisis or decompensation". This is significantly higher than the other 8 contraindications ($p < .0001$ compared to b, c, d, f and i; $p = .001$ compared to h; $p = .001$ compared to g and h; $p = .012$ compared to e.)

Qualitative comments

Comment boxes were included in our online survey. We received 91 comments from the respondents with a wide range of concerns. The most consistent theme is that the effectiveness of teaching, supervising and treating over VCON varies widely and is highly dependent on the client characteristics ($n = 19$). The following are comments we feel are particularly helpful:

> In some ways the virtual world allows for more recognition of separation anxiety . . . But in other ways it disconnects the in-person experience of being with someone, heat, body posture, sense of a whole context. So it is not more or less efficacious, rather it impacts the treatment differently.
> On the whole I have been surprised at the effectiveness of treatment using video conferencing, including the fact the patient has chosen to use a couch. It is possible it worked with my patient so spectacularly because

of her particular dynamics. I don't know how it would work with a lower functioning patient.

The two patients I have treated over Skype seem to feel freer to express their negative transference feelings toward me over Skype. Maybe because we are half a world apart.

I actually believe it makes no difference, as I have experienced this material with the same amount of intensity as when working in embodied sessions. However, I do think some people need embodied therapy for many reasons.

It depends on the patient. I have had some patients who find it initially easier over Skype to talk about some things in the transference – especially erotic transference. But overall I think Skype is less effective than in person – for instance, over Skype there is no possibility of actual physical touch, which alters the pull of the erotic.

Depends on the patient and the defensive organization.

Face-to-face (over Skype) feels more intimate than does sitting across the room or lying on the couch.

With working with transference, I was surprised that I could still experience both the transference and countertransference with the same amount of feeling/intensity as if poor video (etc.) quality would somehow make it impossible.

I would personally suggest that teletherapy is most helpful when there has been a period of face-to-face therapy that allows for the establishment of a solid alliance, that then can "carry" the long-distance treatment. With patients in China, of course, this is not possible; and so it just might take a longer length of time to develop a solid alliance.

Most of the problems with teletherapy can be dealt with by interpretation and working through.

All resistances and transferences that are treatable can be addressed and should be address, regardless of video conferencing or in-person. We handle crises at a distance all the time. Language a problem? Seems a contraindication period, in-person won't solve that problem.

Discussion

We asked 176 experts to compare the delivery of teaching, supervising and treating from a psychodynamic perceptive over video conferencing technology (VCON) with Chinese students with their experience with their in-person population. This poses a difficult task with the confounding variables of language, culture, and perhaps different stages of education in psychoanalytic training.

We used the methodology of a large number of expert opinions that is likely to be able to account for "all other things being equal" when asked how VCON work compares to in-person work. Expert opinion has a long history of validity in both jurisprudence and in science and is a methodology suited to discovering an understanding of complex interacting variables that cannot be easily studied under strict laboratory conditions.

Since this study is not a randomized controlled trial (RCT) of service efficacy, it cannot address the cause and effect issues. However, a RCT methodology would involve a need for a manualized, time-limited treatment and the parcelling out of a great many interacting variables (i.e. in-person vs. VCON, culture, client characteristics, amount of sessions, nature of work, etc.) and difficulty with comparable dependent measures across the different conditions, which would require a very high number of clients, high cost, and may result in questionable generalizable validity given the complexity of the variables.

Our experts feel that, overall, VCON minimally reduces effectiveness. Individual client characteristics may be a significant factor in effectiveness. Ethically maintained frames can be flexible and its variations can be grist for the mill, if there is empathy, respect and knowledge of cultural differences. There is no perfect frame, and our psychotherapeutic techniques are robust and reliable.

Another methodological concern is that our scales compared teaching, supervision and treatment of Chinese students, with the cultural differences, language problems and Internet problems, with an in-person American client point of reference. This is likely to negatively bias our results, by pushing the responses to the lower end of the scale. We also helped to control for a positive bias by using a scale with the midpoint as "no difference (from in-person treatment)". We would rather have a conservative finding than bias in favour of the obvious. Most of our experts are currently involved with VCON teaching, supervision and treatment and would have rated them as effective. We wanted to look beyond the question of simple perceived effectiveness and into how the VCON medium differentially affects different types of psychoanalytic relationships (teaching, supervising, and treating). Also, it is unlikely that these findings are due to bias, since the teachers, supervisors and therapists were not simply reviewing their work over VCON but comparing it to their in-person work. The results showed that all three (teaching, supervising, and treating) are in the "slightly less effective" as compared to "no difference" than in-person range. We also found that supervision was perceived more positively than teaching and treating. Supervision enjoys a more intimate mentoring relationship, without the problems of diffusion of focus in a class and the difficulty of discerning nuances in nonverbal communication and creating the bodily sense of proximity for dealing with attachment issues and transference as in therapy using VCON. The theoretical issues that these results raise go to the very nature of psychoanalytic treatment and the issue of attachment in the analytic space. The object relations of the supervisory situation can foster professional identification through the process of idealization (Gordon, 1995), making VCON supervision an excellent resource that could be more utilized by training programmes. There is a need for psychoanalytic supervision for psychotherapists who do not want to become psychoanalysts but do want to enhance their skills and insight. VCON psychoanalytic supervision can become a popular form of education.

We found that the issues of symptom reduction, exploring mental life, working on transference, relational problems, resistance, privacy issues and countertransference are all equally rated in the range of "slightly less effective" than in-person treatment. The highest significantly rated indications for treatment over VCON are: "To offer high quality treatment to underserved or remote patients" and "When patient is house-bound or travel would be impractical". The highest significantly rated contraindication for treatment over VCON is "Patient needs close observation due to crisis or decompensation".

Of course statistical findings let us know about the typical finding and are insensitive to the ideograph situation. Our findings are valuable in making general statements about how VCON teaching, supervision and treatment compares to in-person teaching, supervision and treatment according to the opinion of our large sample of experts. However, the most consistent comment was that the effectiveness varies widely depending on the client characteristics.

A logical next step would be to test our hypotheses with the other side of this study – that is, with the students, supervisees and patients that have received the VCON services. It would also be valuable to discover which personality variables correlate with greater satisfaction with VCON services. Overall, this survey suggests that VCON teaching, supervision and treatment from a psychodynamic perceptive is a worthwhile option when considering its unique contribution to extending services where needed. There are few opportunities for many professionals who desire psychoanalytic education, supervision and treatment in many areas of the world. The Internet can fulfil that need.

References

Backhaus, A., Agha, Z., Maglione, M. L., Repp, A., Ross, B., Zuest, D., & Thorp, S. R. (2012). Videoconferencing psychotherapy: A systematic review. *Psychological Services*, 9(2): 111–131.

Bayles, M. (2012). Is physical proximity essential to the psychoanalytic process? An exploration through the lens of Skype? *Psychoanalytic Dialogues*, 22(5): 569–585. DOI: 10.1080/10481885.2012.717043.

Caparrotta, L. (2013). Digital technology is here to stay and the psychoanalytic community should grapple with it. *Psychoanalytic Psychotherapy*, 27(4): 296–305. DOI: 10.1080/02668734.2013.846272.

Churcher, J. (2012). On: Skype and privacy: Comment. *The International Journal of Psychoanalysis*, 93(4): 1035–1037. DOI: 10.1111/j.1745–8315.2012.00610.x.

Cooke, R. M. (1991). *Experts in Uncertainty: Opinion and Subjective Probability in Science* (Environmental Ethics and Science Policy). Oxford: Oxford University Press.

Cowart, J. R. (2010). Best practices in online instruction: Why practices work for some students and not for others. *Dissertation Abstracts International Section A: Humanities and Social Sciences*, 70(12-A): 4591.

Dettbarn, I. (2013). ". . . When the distinction between imagination and reality is effaced . . ." (Freud): Skype, the secret sharer, and psychoanalysis. *Psyche: Zeitschrift für Psychoanalyse und ihre Anwendungen*, 67(7): 649–664.

Donker, T., Bennett, K., Bennett, A., Mackinnon, A., Van Straten, A., Cuijpers, P., Christensen, H., & Griffiths, K. M. (2013). Internet-delivered interpersonal psychotherapy versus internet-delivered cognitive behavioral therapy for adults with depressive symptoms: Randomized controlled noninferiority trial. *Journal of Medical Internet Research*, 15(5): 146–161. DOI: 10.2196/jmir.2307.

Edirippulige, S., Levandovskaya, M., & Prishutova, A. (2013). A qualitative study of the use of Skype for psychotherapy consultations in the Ukraine. *Journal of Telemedicine and Telecare*, 19(7): 376–378.

Fishkin, R., Fishkin, L., Leli, U., Katz, B., & Snyder, E. (2011). Psychodynamic treatment, training, and supervision using Internet-based technologies. *Journal of the American Academy of Psychoanalysis & Dynamic Psychiatry*, 39(1): 155–168. DOI: 10.1521/jaap.2011.39.1.155.

Godleski, L., Darkins, A., & Peters, J. (2012). Outcomes of 98,609 U.S. Department of Veterans Affairs patients enrolled in telemental health services, 2006–2010. *Psychiatric Services*, 63(4): 383–385. DOI: 10.1176/appi.ps.201100206.

Gordon, R. M. (1995). The symbolic nature of the supervisory relationship: Identification and professional growth. *Issues in Psychoanalytic Psychology*, 17(2): 154–162.

Holmes, C., & Foster, V. (2012). A preliminary comparison study of online and face-to-face counseling: Client perceptions of three factors. *Journal of Technology in Human Services*, 30(1): 14–31. DOI: 10.1080/15228835.2012.662848.

Jacobsen, C. H., & Grünbaum, L. (2011). Supervision of psychotherapy via Skype™. *Matrix: Nordisk Tidsskrift for Psykoterapi*, 28(4): 337–349.

Johansson, R., Frederick, R. J., & Andersson, G. (2013). Using the internet to provide psychodynamic psychotherapy. *Psychodynamic Psychiatry*, 41(4): 513–540. DOI: 10.1521/pdps.2013.41.4.513.

King, V. L., Brooner, R. K., Peirce, J. M., Kolodner, K., & Kidorf, M. S. (2014). A randomized trial of web-based videoconferencing for substance abuse counseling. *Journal of Substance Abuse Treatment*, 46(1): 36–42. DOI: 10.1016/j.jsat.2013.08.009.

Lemma, A., & Caparrotta, L. (Eds.). (2013). *Psychoanalysis in the Technoculture Era*. London: Routledge.

Mosleh, A., Bier, V. M., & Apostolakis, G. (1987). Methods for the elicitation and use of expert opinion in risk assessment: Phase 1, A critical evaluation and directions for future research. Pickard, Lowe and Garrick, Inc., Newport Beach, CA (USA).

Paolo, M. (2013). Psychoanalysis on the internet: A discussion of its theoretical implications for both online and offline therapeutic technique. *Psychoanalytic Psychology*, 30(2): 281–299.

Savin, D. M., Legha, R. K., Cordaro, A. R., Ka, S., Chak, T., Chardavoyne, J., Yager, J., & Novins, D. (2013). Spanning distance and culture in psychiatric education: A teleconferencing collaboration between Cambodia and the United States. *Academic Psychiatry*, 37(5): 355–359. DOI: 10.1176/appi.ap.12120214.

Scharff, J. S. (2013a). "On: Skype and privacy: Comment": Reply. [Comment/Reply] The *International Journal of Psychoanalysis*, 93(4): 1037–1039. DOI: 10.1111/j.1745–8315.2012.00609.x.

Scharff, J. S. (Ed.). (2013b). *Psychoanalysis Online: Mental Health, Teletherapy and Training*. London: Karnac.

Sucala, M., Schnur, J. B., Constantino, M. J., Miller, S. J., Brackman, E. H., & Montgomery, G. H. (2012). The therapeutic relationship in e-therapy for mental health: A systematic review. *Journal of Medical Internet Research*, 14(4): 175–187. DOI: 10.2196/jmir.2084.

Tantam, D., Blackmore, C., & Van Deurzen, E. (2006). eLearning and traditional "face-to-face" teaching: A comparative evaluation of methods in a psychotherapy training programme. *International Journal of Psychotherapy*, 10(2): 7–14.

Commentary

Janine Wanlass

Optimal distance

What is the optimal distance with distance technology that allows us to provide training and treatment to underserved populations in an effective manner? Gordon, Wang, and Tune (2015) gathered opinions from experts about the relative effectiveness of technology-assisted teaching, supervision, and treatment of Chinese students affiliated with Chinese American Psychoanalytic Alliance (CAPA). Their research questions added empirical data to an emerging body of literature on telemental health, with particular relevance to models of distance training.

These researchers begin with an educative review of recent research examining technology use for teaching, supervision, and treatment. They note that universities began to use the Internet for teaching almost immediately after its discovery, adding research findings by Tantam, Blackmore, and Van Deurzen (2006) that document the successful use of Internet teaching of psychotherapy skills. Gordon et al. (2015) follow with a list of studies asserting effective Internet-based clinical supervision and treatment (Godleski, Darkins, & Peters, 2012; Savin et al., 2013; Sucala et al., 2012). Although the treatment outcomes for more concrete, manualized approaches like cognitive-behavioural therapy are strong, they wonder aloud if these outcomes can be sustained in less-structured, more relationally based psychodynamic treatments.

They also pose questions about the comparative effectiveness of distance approaches to teaching, supervision, and treatment, speculating that consumers would find technology-assisted supervision more effective than technology-assisted treatment or teaching. They hypothesize that clinical supervision provides a close enough relationship to manage the technological distance, while offering a distant enough relationship to escape the intensity and complexity of transference demands associated with mental health treatment. Drawing from the perspective of these researchers, we might conjecture that clinical supervision provides the optimal relational distance for distance learning. The supervisory dyad is containing across the miles, providing more holding than the virtual classroom attended by many students, yet less compromised by the limited or technologically distorted nonverbal data that is sometimes problematic for therapists of long-distance clients.

In fact, Gordon et al. (2015) found much of what they anticipated, with all forms of intervention (teaching, supervision, treatment) evaluated as slightly less effective than in-person methods and with supervision rated more favourably than either teaching or treatment. In considering treatment, they reported that "symptom reduction, exploring mental life, working with transference, working through relational problems, working with resistances, privacy concerns, and countertransference" all compared favourably with in-person work (Gordon et al., 2015, p. 7). Additionally, their findings suggest that the main contraindication for distance treatment is the need for close observation, such as a client who is suicidal or in crisis. The primary reasons for utilizing technology include making treatment available to an underserved population who cannot access quality care or when the client is unable to travel to the office. To those of us working in telemental health, these findings are not surprising and confirm both prior research and anecdotal experience.

Perhaps what is most interesting about this research is what is absent from the findings and present in assumptions made within the research design itself. Let us consider the make-up of the research sample. The researchers have an excellent response rate of 59%. These respondents were people who provided telemental health services in China as part of an ongoing programme and may lean towards seeing effectiveness, given their level of investment. In other words, those who would volunteer to teach, supervise, and treat via technology may have a predisposing belief in its effectiveness and a comfort with its use. Findings from another research study (Wanlass) in this volume suggest that those who use technology rate its effectiveness more positively than those who do not. Is this because those who use technology see its potential or because those who use technology are pulled to view it favourably? Who wants to consider that their teaching or treatment efforts have serious limitations? We need more information about perceptions from clinicians accompanied by outcome data from students, supervisees, and clients to help us interpret these findings.

This raises another question. Participants were asked to compare their distance trainees and patients in China to their American counterparts. Admittedly, finding a group of in-person Western colleagues treating in-person Chinese patients seems impossible. Certainly, Gordon et al. (2015) recognized that the comparison group was far from ideal, encouraging respondents to consider the groups as though all other factors but distance were equal. "For the sake of this research, please assume 'all other things being equal' though this is not easy to do" (Gordon, et al., 2015, p. 6). How can one dismiss cultural, geographic, and access differences? For instance, does the Chinese norm of respect for teachers influence views of effectiveness? Are American teachers somehow protected from negative feedback? Does lack of access to mental health treatment among Chinese infuse a more favourable evaluation of therapeutic effectiveness than would be true in an American sample using technology? Is "all other things being equal" (Gordon et al., 2015, p. 6) either possible or desirable?

The researchers ended their survey with an open-ended "comments" section. They noted that respondents raised a wide range of concerns and opinions; however, they highlight a prominent theme that teaching, supervision, and treatment effectiveness are highly dependent on client characteristics. This is a very important observation. Perhaps we should be looking closely at what client, therapist, and dyad characteristics predict for effective use of VCON for treatment. For instance, clients who have strong early attachment histories may be able to keep the therapeutic relationship in mind over the distance and more openly discuss transference issues magnified by the technology. They may more easily maintain a sort of object constancy and navigate technological drops. Or perhaps clients who are younger and more technology-savvy may find the distortions of image, voice, and movement less disturbing. Given the early stages of research in this area, we simply do not know.

In the comments provided to the reader for examination, the tone is clearly positive. Was this because most of the comments were favourable towards telemental health? Were negative remarks unconsciously excluded? Does this speak to a favourable bias towards technology use in the sample itself, as discussed earlier? Could the researchers represent, content code, or categorize more of the narrative response set?

Overall, Gordon and his colleagues should be commended for their efforts to better understand the impact of technology use in teaching, supervision, and treatment with Chinese students, supervisees, and clients. They improve our understanding of technology use, and they raise some interesting questions about the relative impact of technology on each of these interventions. The confirmed effective use of technology for supervision seems particularly helpful and supports more expansion of technology-assisted consultation. The need for optimal distance, which they suggest exists in supervision, has implications for teaching and treatment. For example, would smaller classes or technology features like "zooming-in" on students as they speak or more individualized instruction create results similar to that for supervision? If teachers attended more to the relationship, would outcomes improve? In treatment efforts, should we research client characteristics that predict a more favourable response? Do we need to assess – just as we do with variables like diagnosis, stability, or motivation – which clients would benefit most from this type of treatment? Is there a difference in rated effectiveness for clients in face-to-face treatment versus clients on the couch? Certainly, Gordon et al. (2015) invite us to think more complexly about technology use and to further investigate its effectiveness.

References

Godleski, L., Darkins, A., & Peters, J. (2012). Outcomes of 98,609 U.S. Department of Veterans Affairs patients enrolled in telemental health services, 2006–2010. *Psychiatric Services*, 63(4): 383–385.

Gordon, R. M., Wang, X., & Tune, J. (2015). Comparing psychodynamic teaching, supervision, and psychotherapy over video-conferencing technology with Chinese students. *Psychodynamic Psychotherapy*, 43(4): 585–599.

Savin, D. M., Legha, R. K., Cordaro, A. R., Ka, S., Chak, T., Chardavoyne, J., Yager, J., & Novins, D. (2013). Spanning distance and culture in psychiatric education: A teleconferencing collaboration between Cambodia and the United States. *Academic Psychiatry*, 37(5): 355–359.

Sucala, M., Schnur, J. B., Constantino, M. J., Miller, S. J., Brackman, E. H., & Montgomery, G. H. (2012). The therapeutic relationship in e-therapy for mental health: A systematic review. *Journal of Medical Internet Research*, 14(4): 175–187.

Tantam, D., Blackmore, C., & Van Deurzen, E. (2006). eLearning and traditional "face-to-face" teaching: A comparative evaluation of methods in a psychotherapy training programme. *International Journal of Psychotherapy*, 10(2): 7–14.

Chapter 9

The effect of distance training on the development of psychodynamic psychotherapists

Robert M. Gordon and Jing Lan

How effective is psychoanalytic/psychodynamic distance training over the Internet? To assess this, we surveyed graduates of the two-year and four-year programmes of the China America Psychoanalytic Alliance (CAPA). The main results of the 90 graduates' surveys showed that 77% of their work involves a psychoanalytic formulation of their cases as compared to other theoretical orientations. The degree to which graduates used a psychoanalytic formulation of their cases was best predicted by the number of years in training and the more days a week in their own treatment. Graduates highly rated the effectiveness of their own psychoanalytic therapy over video conferencing (VCON). Graduates' ratings of treatment with their patients over VCON positively correlated with years of psychoanalytic education, number of days a week in own treatment, years doing psychoanalytic treatment, and degree to which graduates worked with a psychoanalytic orientation. Graduates thought that therapist variables (skilfulness, warmth, empathy, and wisdom) were much more important in the effectiveness of their treatment than whether the treatment was in-person or with VCON, or the presence of cultural differences with their therapist. The graduates' ratings of how they are practising psychoanalytic treatment were highly correlated with how their own therapists practised psychoanalytic psychotherapy, as measured by the psychodynamic/interpersonal process items on the Comparative Psychotherapy Process Scale.

Institutes for the training of psychoanalytic therapists are mostly limited to major metropolitan centres. This presents a problem for the training of psychodynamic psychotherapists and psychoanalysts. Distance learning over the Internet could potentially bring psychoanalytic education to many who would not otherwise have access.

Psychoanalytic training programmes have three components: a personal analysis, a didactic curriculum, and intensive supervised psychoanalytic clinical work. The didactic education and supervision may be easier to provide online, as compared to conducting psychoanalysis over the Internet. Internet-based psychotherapy is a growing area, since it can help many individuals who do not have easy access to psychotherapy services due to distance, lack of transportation, physical disability, time constraints, etc. Barak, Hen, Boniel-Nissim, and Shapira (2008) performed a meta-analysis of the effectiveness of Internet-based psychotherapeutic interventions. They found 92 studies that involved a total of 9,764 clients who were treated through various Internet-based psychological interventions. The overall mean weighted effect size was found to be 0.53 (medium effect), which is similar to the average effect size of traditional face-to-face therapy. A comparison between face-to-face and Internet intervention as reported in 14 of the studies revealed no differences in effectiveness. De Bitencourt Machado et al. (2016) reviewed 59 studies of online psychotherapy compared with face-to-face therapies and found similar effects.

However, psychoanalytic treatment over the Internet by video conferencing (VCON) presents somewhat different problems than most other psychological treatments. There are the issues of how online treatment affects transference, countertransference, fantasies, resistances, etc. J. S. Scharff (2012) explored analysts' perceptions and experiences of using the telephone and the Internet. She focused on clinical concerns that arise, including the frame, fantasies, resistance, transference, and countertransference. Scharff concluded that conducting analysis via the telephone or VCON is a viable, clinically effective alternative to traditional analysis where necessary. J. S. Scharff (2013, 2015) explored the advantages and possible problems with not only online psychotherapy and psychoanalysis, but also training. She argued that the continuity, availability of the frequency of analytic sessions for in-depth analytic work, and outreach to analysands in areas far from specialized psychoanalytic centres is an important consideration despite the problems. Still, Migone (2013) argued that online therapy is simply a different therapy, in the same way as two therapies, both offline (or both online), may be different from each other.

Fishkin et al. (2011) reported on the China American Psychoanalytic Alliance (CAPA), which provides treatment, education, and supervision to Chinese mental health professionals over the Internet. The lack of Chinese analysts and mentors has created a demand for psychoanalytic psychotherapy training and treatment. Fishkin and colleagues concluded that the Internet-based programme has been a success, and any issues of transference and countertransference can be discussed as part of the therapeutic process.

D. E. Scharff (2015) reported that another distance-learning group, the International Psychotherapy Institute, has extensive experience in the use of video conference and telephone technology in the teaching of psychoanalysis and psychoanalytic psychotherapy with individuals and groups across the United States and other countries. D. E. Scharff concluded that the use of this technology for tele-education has facilitated the spread of psychoanalytic ideas, recruitment of psychoanalytic and psychotherapeutic trainees, and ongoing training for members living at great distances from training institutes.

However, there have been no studies of psychoanalytic training comparing the effectiveness of teaching, supervising, and treating students online by VCON with in-person teaching, supervision, and treatment. For this reason, Gordon, Wang, and

Tune (2015) surveyed the expert opinions of 176 teachers, supervisors, and therapists in the CAPA who use VCON with Chinese students. The main findings were:

(1) teaching, supervision, and treatment were all rated in the range of "slightly less effective" than in-person, with supervision rated significantly more effective than teaching and treatment over VCON;
(2) symptom reduction, exploring mental life, working on transference, relational problems, resistance, privacy issues, and countertransference were all equally rated in the range of "slightly less effective" than in-person treatment;
(3) the most important indications for treatment over VCON were the need for high-quality treatment for underserved, remote, or house-bound patients, and when travel would make treatment impractical;
(4) the most important contraindication for treatment over VCON is when the patient needs close observation. However, Gordon et al. (2015) did not explore the opinions of the recipients of the distance psychoanalytic programme; namely, the graduates of CAPA. This would be the logical next step and was the rationale for the current research.

Attempts to study the effectiveness of distance psychoanalytic training are limited by methodological and ethical problems. For example, invading the ongoing treatment of patients in psychoanalytic treatment can change the dynamics of the therapeutic relationship. In addition, many patients may wish to give their therapists good grades or bad grades based on the nature of the transference. We can mitigate these problems by using CAPA graduates, who received their psychoanalytic treatment during their training and are now providing psychotherapy themselves. This is a unique population that allows us to compare the psychoanalytic treatment graduates received to the treatment they are providing their own patients, and to assess how psychoanalytically oriented they have become in their own work since completion of their training and personal treatment.

METHOD

Participants and procedure

Graduates of the two-year and four-year CAPA programmes were invited in three separate mailings about a week apart to respond to a brief online survey (in Mandarin) that inquired about their experience in receiving psychoanalytic psychotherapy training and personal treatment over VCON. The survey stated,

> This survey research on psychoanalytic psychotherapy is for CAPA graduates who have had their own psychoanalytic treatment while in CAPA. Your participation is voluntary and anonymous. There will be four kinds of prizes for participating (a first prize of 500 RMB; 3 second prizes of 200 RMB; 5 third prizes of 100 RMB, and 14 fourth prizes of 50 RMB). Winners for

the prizes will be drawn randomly from the pool of the email addresses of respondents at the end of the data collection. Participation in the draw for prizes is voluntary. If you wish to participate in the draw, follow the instructions at the end of the survey.

We used an email list of 220 CAPA graduates with about 200 being valid email addresses.[1] Ninety-seven graduates responded (a 48.5% response rate); seven graduates were eliminated because they were not engaged in practising therapy. This resulted in a sample of 90 participants for most of the questions. The participants were recruited for the online survey in 2016. The study was approved by the IRB of the Washington Center of Psychoanalysis.

Of the 90 CAPA graduates who participated in the survey, 74% were female; the mean age was 40 (SD = 7.2) years. The other descriptives for the sample are as follows: number of years in the CAPA programme (M = 3.5, SD = 1.4); total number of years of psychoanalytic education (M = 6.4, SD = 3.6); number of years in personal psychoanalytic treatment (M = 4.8, SD = 5.4); number of days a week in treatment (M = 2.5, SD = 1.0); number of years doing psychoanalytic psychotherapy with patients (M = 5.5, SD = 2.9); percent of own therapy received over VCON (M = 77.6 %, SD = 32); percent of own work with patients done over VCON (M = 25%, SD = 21). The difference in percentages is because most graduates received their personal therapy from overseas therapists, whereas graduates practising in their own communities have less need for conducting therapy over the Internet.

Measures

The ad hoc online survey questions were: age; gender; total number of years of CAPA education; total number of years for all your psychoanalytic education; total number of years of your own psychoanalytic treatment; average number of days a week in your own treatment; total number of years doing psychoanalytic psychotherapy with patients; what percentage of your work with patients involves a psychoanalytic formulation of the case as compared to other theoretical orientations?; what percentage of your own psychoanalytic treatment was over video conferencing?; if you received your treatment over video conferencing, overall, how would you rate the effectiveness of your psychoanalytic therapy? (0 = lowest rating; 6 = highest rating); what percentage of your own work with patients is done over video conferencing?; if you do treatment over video conferencing, overall, how would you rate the effectiveness of psychoanalytic therapy over video conferencing? (0 = lowest rating; 6 = highest rating); rate how much you think each variable was important to the effectiveness of your own personal psychotherapy (0 = lowest rating; 6 = highest rating): warmth of therapist, wisdom of therapist, empathy of therapist, skilfulness of therapist, cultural similarity of therapist, and the use of video conferencing.

We used the 10 psychodynamic/interpersonal process items from the Comparative Psychotherapy Process Scale (CPPS) (Hilsenroth et al., 2005) in the survey. The CPPS also includes items about CBT interventions, which we did not use, since these items were not relevant to our hypotheses. This is a valid use of the individual items for research purposes, since an overall score is often not used for the CPPS. The CPPS has excellent reliability and validity (Hilsenroth et al., 2005) and is a standard assessment instrument in psychotherapy research. We asked the 10 psychodynamic/interpersonal process questions three times. The first set asked how much each intervention was used by their own therapist. The second set asked how much the graduates typically use these interventions with their own insightful patients. The third set of questions asked how helpful each intervention was for the graduate. The data from the responses from the third set of questions will be analysed in a future study. We set the survey to change the order of these three sets of 10 items from the CPPS. The questions are responded to on 7 point Likert scales ranging from "0 = not at all characteristic" to "6 = extremely characteristic". The survey stated: "Using the scale below, please rate how characteristic each statement is of your own therapist in CAPA."

1   Your therapist encouraged the exploration of feelings regarded by you as uncomfortable (e.g., anger, envy, excitement, sadness, or happiness).
2   Your therapist linked your current feelings or perceptions to experiences of the past.
3   Your therapist focused attention on similarities among your relationships repeated over time, settings, or people.
4   Your therapist focused discussion on the relationship between the therapist and you.
5   Your therapist encouraged you to experience and express feelings in the session.
6   Your therapist addressed your avoidance of important topics and shifts in mood.
7   Your therapist suggested alternative ways to understand experiences or events not previously recognized by you.
8   Your therapist identified recurrent patterns in your actions, feelings, and experiences.
9   Your therapist allowed you to initiate the discussion of significant issues, events, and experiences.
10 Your therapist encouraged discussion of your wishes, fantasies, dreams, or early childhood memories (positive or negative).

The second set of the 10 CPPS items asked, "Please rate how much you typically use these interventions with insightful patients?" (0 = not at all, 6 = very often). (NB These questions started with, "You" instead of "Your therapist".)

Statistical analyses

We used descriptive statistics for the demographic data and for ratings of satisfaction, and percentages to measure how much of the graduates' work involves a psychoanalytic formulation of their cases as compared to other theoretical orientations. Pearson product moment correlations were used to test the degree of relationship between the hypothesized variables. A stepwise regression was used to determine the strongest predictor of the use of a psychoanalytic orientation.

We used an exploratory factor analysis (EFA) and Varimax rotation for two factor structures. The theoretical justification for this method was to test our assumption that the therapist variables (warmth, wisdom, empathy, and skilfulness) formed a factor distinct from the parameters (if the treatment was in-person or with VCON, or the cultural differences with therapist). A Varimax rotation assumes a low correlation between the two proposed factors. Kim and Mueller (1978) suggest theoretical reasons for helping to determine number of factors and type of rotation in EFA. Varimax rotation and exploration using two factors made theoretical sense, since we were exploring categorical distinctions between therapist variables and the parameters. If the EFA produced two factors – therapist variables and parameters – then we thought we could use paired t-tests to specifically test the comparisons related to our hypotheses; namely, that the therapist variables are more important to patient satisfaction with treatment than the issues of cultural similarity and use of VCON. All inferential tests are 2-tailed.

Hypotheses

1   We hypothesized that CAPA graduates who are now practising will use a psychoanalytic case formulation in the majority of their cases and that the number of years of CAPA education would correlate positively with the number of years of the graduates' own psychoanalytic treatment, and the number of years working psychoanalytically with patients.

2   We hypothesized that VCON treatment will be considered valuable (greater than 3.5 on the 0–6 scale) both as a patient receiving VCON treatment and as a therapist practising VCON treatment; and that the effectiveness of VCON treatment would correlate significantly with how much the graduates use a psychoanalytic formulation in their work and how much they work with their own patients over VCON.

3   We hypothesized that the graduates would consider the therapist variables (warmth, empathy, wisdom, and skilfulness) as more important to the effectiveness of their own personal psychotherapy than the parameters of whether the treatment was in-person or with VCON, or cultural differences with the therapist.

4   We hypothesized that the CAPA graduates are practising psychoanalytic treatment in a manner that is highly correlated with the psychoanalytic treatment they received during their training, as measured by the 10 psychodynamic/interpersonal process items from the CPPS.

Results

Hypothesis 1 was supported. CAPA graduates indicated that about 77% of their work involves a psychoanalytic formulation of their cases as compared to other theoretical orientations ($n = 81$, $M = 76.5\%$, $SD = 25$). The number of years of CAPA education correlated significantly with the number of years of own psychoanalytic treatment ($r = .29$, $p = .005$, $n = 90$) and with the number of years working psychoanalytically with patients ($r = .27$, $p = .01$, $n = 90$).

The following variables were used in the stepwise regression analysis: total number of years in CAPA, total number of years of all psychoanalytic education, number of years of personal psychoanalytic therapy, average number of days a week in own treatment, and number of years practising psychoanalytic therapy. A significant regression was found ($F (5, 75) = 3.96$, $p < .003$), with an R^2 of .21. The results suggest that the strongest predictor of the degree to which graduates reported using a psychoanalytic formulation was the total number of years in CAPA ($B = 38.5$, $t = 4.0$, $p < .0001$. The next significant variable that offered a unique contribution to the prediction was the average number of days a week in the graduates' own treatment ($B = 9.99$, $t = 3.78$, $p < .0001$).

Hypothesis 2 was supported. VCON treatment was considered valuable both as a student/patient and as a practising therapist. The mean score on the rating of effectiveness of participants' own therapy over VCON was 4.73 ($SD = .97$, $n = 84$). The effectiveness of treatment over VCON correlated significantly with the percentage of therapeutic work using a psychoanalytic formulation ($r = .36$, $p < .001$, $n = 77$), and significantly with the percentage of therapy with patients done over VCON ($r = .22$, $p < .047$, $n = 84$). The mean score of the participants' ratings of the effectiveness of psychoanalytic therapy with their own patients over VCON was 4.44 ($SD = 1.05$, $n = 85$). Participants' ratings of the effectiveness of the psychoanalytic therapy they do using VCON correlated significantly with the number of years of psychoanalytic education ($r = .24$, $p = .03$, $n = 85$); number of days a week of own treatment ($r = .27$, $p = .01$, $n = 85$); years doing psychoanalytic treatment ($r = .22$, $p = .04$, $n = 85$); degree of working with a psychoanalytic formulation ($r = .46$, $p < .0001$, $n = 77$); and using VCON with their own patients ($r = .40$, $p < .0001$, $n = 85$).

Hypothesis 3 was supported. The therapist variables (warmth, wisdom, empathy, and skilfulness) were rated as much more important in the effectiveness of their own treatment than the parameters of whether the treatment was in-person or with VCON, or cultural differences with the therapist ($n = 90$).

Warmth of therapist	$M = 6.0$, $SD = 1.2$
Wisdom of therapist	$M = 5.9$, $SD = 1.1$
Empathy of therapist	$M = 6.4$, $SD = .85$
Skilfulness of therapist	$M = 5.4$, $SD = .96$
Cultural similarity of therapist	$M = 4.1$, $SD = 1.4$
The use of video conferencing	$M = 3.9$, $SD = 1.5$

The factor loadings for the effective treatment variables are displayed in Table 1. Whereas the therapist variables (warmth, wisdom, empathy, and skilfulness) loaded highly on factor 1, the parameters (cultural similarity to therapist and use of VCON) loaded highly on factor 2. There was no significant difference between cultural similarity to therapist and the use of VCON ($t = 1.4$, $df = 89$, $p = .16$).

Based on this distinction, we used paired t-tests to specifically test the comparisons related to our hypotheses; namely, that the therapist variables are more important to patient satisfaction with treatment than the issues of cultural similarity and use of VCON. The results, which are displayed in Table 2, support the hypothesis that the qualities of the therapist are far more important to patient satisfaction than cultural similarity issues or if the treatment was over VCON. All comparisons were statistically significant ($p < .0001$).

Table 9.1 Factor loadings of the effective treatment variables

Variables	Component	
	I	2
Warmth	.71	−.04
Wisdom	.58	.24
Empathy	.86	.06
Skilfulness	.57	−.08
Cultural similarity	.15	.79
Use of VCON	−.10	.80

Table 9.2 Paired t-tests of effective treatment variables

		Mean	Std. Deviation	Std. Error Mean	t	df	Sig. (2-tailed)
Pair 1	cultural similarity of therapist –warmth of therapist	−1.89	1.79	.19	−10.01	89	.000
Pair 2	cultural similarity of therapist – wisdom of therapist	−1.79	1.60	.17	−10.58	89	.000
Pair 3	cultural similarity of therapist – empathy of therapist	−2.23	1.50	.16	−14.13	89	.000
Pair 4	cultural similarity of therapist – skilfulness of therapist	−1.28	1.64	.17	−7.38	89	.000

		Mean	Std. Deviation	Std. Error Mean	t	df	Sig. (2-tailed)
Pair 5	the use of video conferencing – warmth of therapist	−2.14	1.98	.21	−10.30	89	.000
Pair 6	the use of video conferencing – wisdom of therapist	−2.04	1.82	.19	−10.63	89	.000
Pair 7	the use of video conferencing – empathy of therapist	−2.49	1.73	.18	−13.64	89	.000
Pair 8	the use of video conferencing – skilfulness of therapist	−1.53	1.81	.19	−8.05	89	.000

Hypothesis 4 was supported. The graduates' ratings of the personal therapy they received during their training, as measured by the CPPS psychodynamic/interpersonal items, correlated strongly with how they are practising psychoanalytic treatment with their own patients as measured by the CPPS items ($n = 90$): encouraging the exploration of uncomfortable feelings ($r = .50, p < .0001$), linking current feelings or perceptions to experiences of the past ($r = .43, p < .0001$), focusing attention on similarities with relationships repeated over time, settings, or people ($r = .51, p < .0001$), focusing discussion on the relationship with the therapist ($r = .42, p < .001$), encouraging the experience and expression of feelings in the session ($r = .34, p < .001$), dealing with the avoidance of important topics and shifts in mood ($r = .55, p < .0001$), suggesting alternative ways to understand experiences or events not previously recognized ($r = .69, p < .0001$), identifying recurrent patterns in actions, feelings, and experiences ($r = .56, p < .0001$), feeling free to initiate the discussion of significant issues, events, and experiences ($r = .61, p < .0001$), encouraging discussion of wishes, fantasies, dreams, or early childhood memories (positive or negative) ($r = .77, p < .0001$). The average correlation is $r = .54$ ($SD = 12.7$). Overall, these results suggest that the graduates are practising psychoanalytic treatment in ways that are very similar to how they experienced their own psychoanalytic therapists.

Discussion

This study assessed the opinions of CAPA graduates about the effectiveness of their distance psychoanalytic training. The population was unique in that the respondents had not only been students and patients but were now practising therapists. We were therefore able to explore what the graduates thought about the personal therapy they had received and the therapy they currently provide, and how much their training and personal therapy contributes to their work. Although the participants in the study had graduated from a single distance-training organization, the variables used in the study are universal to psychoanalytic/psychodynamic training. The findings, therefore, can most likely be generalized to any group that receives training via the Internet. That is, a long distance personal intensive analysis of several days a week, and several years of training via the Internet, appear to be highly effective in producing psychotherapists with a psychoanalytic orientation.

The response rate of 48.5% of the graduates who were invited to participate in the study can be considered an excellent internal (within a group) response rate. Mertler's (2003) review of internal response rates of web-based surveys with professionals ranged from 11–33%. Mertler found that the main reason given by non-responders was that they did not want to take the time to respond to the survey. We suspect that was the main reason for the non-responders in our study. Ninety responders answered 92% of the questions, but some of our results were based on *Ns* of 85–77, which is probably explained by the relevancy of the questions for some of the responders.

Our survey of the graduates of the two-year and four-year CAPA programmes indicated a high degree of support for distance training over the Internet. The results showed that 77% of their work involves a psychoanalytic formulation of their cases as compared to other theoretical orientations. The number of years of CAPA distance education correlated significantly with the number of years of personal psychoanalytic treatment, and also with the number of years working psychoanalytically with patients.

The extent to which graduates use a psychoanalytic formulation of their cases was best predicted by a greater number of years in distance education and the more days a week in personal therapy. This supports the idea that practitioners are more likely to become psychoanalytic in their clinical practice when they receive a longer period of training, as well as intensive psychoanalytic therapy themselves. The several-days-a-week analytic therapy likely gave the students more opportunity to explore their unconscious minds and gain a greater appreciation for a psychoanalytic orientation. Graduates highly rated the effectiveness of their own psychoanalytic therapy over VCON. Graduates' ratings of treatment with their patients over VCON correlated positively with the amount of psychoanalytic education, experience doing psychoanalytic treatment, number of days a week in own treatment, and degree to which they worked with a psychoanalytic orientation. This suggests that working with VCON treatment might require a high level of training and an understanding of the special issues that arise.

Many psychoanalysts are concerned that psychoanalytic treatment cannot translate well over the Internet and that cultural differences might significantly diminish the effectiveness of the treatment. However, the Chinese graduates thought that the therapist variables (warmth, wisdom, empathy, and skilfulness) were more important in the effectiveness of their treatment than whether the treatment was in-person or with VCON, or the cultural differences with their therapist.

The graduates' ratings of how they are currently practising psychoanalytic psychotherapy were highly correlated with how their own therapists practised psychoanalytic treatment, as measured by the CPPS items. The larger magnitude correlations were in the areas of exploring unconscious mental life, while the smaller magnitude correlations were in the areas that required emotional expression in the sessions. This may be a cultural issue in that many Chinese people may feel less comfortable expressing emotion than those in the Western countries (Dere et al., 2013; Zhu et al., 2007). This would be an interesting topic for further research.

Limitations of the study are that the data were collected with self-report questionnaires, and the findings reflect the subjective opinions of the graduates. In addition, most of the analyses are correlational, so that no inferences can be drawn concerning cause and effect. Nonetheless, the findings demonstrate that distance psychoanalytic/psychodynamic training is perceived by graduates as highly effective and can produce therapists who use psychoanalytic formulations and techniques in their work with patients.

Note

1 Thanks to John Fanning for emailing the requests and estimating the number of valid email addresses from the list.

References

Barak, A., Hen, L., Boniel-Nissim, M., & Shapira, N. A. (2008). A comprehensive review and a meta-analysis of the effectiveness of internet-based psychotherapeutic interventions. *Journal of Technology in Human Services*, 26(2–4): 109–160.

De Bitencourt Machado, D., Braga Laskoski, P., Trelles Severo, C., Bassols, A. M., Sfoggia, A., Kowacs, C., Valle Krieger, D., Benetti Torres, M. Bento Gastaud, M. Wellausen, R. S., Pigatto Teche, S., & Eizirik, C. L. (2016). A psychodynamic perspective on a systematic review of online psychotherapy for adults. *British Journal of Psychotherapy*, 32(1): 79–108.

Dere, J., Tang, Q., Zhu, X., Cai, L., Yao, S., & Ryder, A. G. (2013). The cultural shaping of alexithymia: Values and externally oriented thinking in a Chinese clinical sample. *Comprehensive Psychiatry*, 54(4): 362–368.

Fishkin, R., Fishkin, L., Leli, U., Katz, B., & Snyder, E. (2011). Psychodynamic treatment, training, and supervision using Internet-based technologies. *Journal of the American Academy of Psychoanalysis & Dynamic Psychiatry*, 39(1): 155–168. DOI: 10.1521/jaap.2011.39.1.155.

Gordon, R.M., Wang, X., & Tune, J. (2015). Comparing psychodynamic teaching, supervision and psychotherapy over video-conferencing technology with Chinese students. *Psychodynamic Psychiatry*, 43(4): 585–599.

Hilsenroth, M. J., Blagys, M. D., Ackerman, S. J., Bonge, D. R., & Blais, M. D. (2005). Measuring psychodynamic-interpersonal and cognitive-behavioral techniques: Development of a comparative psychotherapy process scale. *Psychotherapy: Theory, Research, Practice, Training*, 42: 340–356.

Kim, J. O., & Mueller, C. W. (1978). *Introduction to Factor Analysis: What it is and How to Do It*. Beverly Hills, CA: Sage.

Mertler, C. A. (2003). Patterns of response and nonresponse from teachers to traditional and web surveys. *Practical Assessment, Research & Evaluation*, 8(22): 1–17.

Migone, P. (2013). Psychoanalysis on the Internet: A discussion of its theoretical implications for both online and offline therapeutic technique. *Psychoanalytic Psychology*, 30(2): 281.

Scharff, D. E. (2015). Psychoanalytic teaching by video link and telephone. *Journal of the American Psychoanalytic Association*, 63(3): 443.

Scharff, J. S. (2012). Clinical issues in analyses over the telephone and the internet. *The International Journal of Psychoanalysis*, 93(1): 81–95.

Scharff, J. S. (Ed.). (2013). *Psychoanalysis Online: Mental Health, Teletherapy and Training*. London: Karnac.

Scharff, J. S. (Ed.). (2015). *Psychoanalysis Online 2: Impact of Technology on Development, Training, and Therapy*. London: Karnac.

Zhu, X., Yi, J., Yao, S., Ryder, A. G., Taylor, G. J., & Bagby, R. M. (2007). Cross-cultural validation of a Chinese translation of the 20-item Toronto Alexithymia Scale. *Comprehensive Psychiatry*, 48(5): 489–496.

Commentary

Janine Wanlass

Investment is the key

Gordon and Lan (2017) engage our curiosity about outcomes of technology-based distance psychoanalytic psychotherapy training by surveying graduates of two- and four-year training programmes offered through the Chinese American Psychoanalytic Alliance (CAPA). Specifically, the authors wanted to assess whether or not graduates were practising from a psychoanalytic perspective and to determine the relative importance of various demographic factors in predicting endorsement of psychoanalytic practice. Additionally, they speculated that the graduates' own experiences as patients in psychoanalytic treatment via the internet would influence graduates' opinions of tele-therapy effectiveness and influence ways of engaging as therapists in tele-therapy with their own patients. Lastly, they assumed that graduates would find therapist variables such as empathy, warmth, skilfulness, and wisdom more important in their own therapy experiences than cultural factors or the fact that the therapy was delivered via distance technology vs. in-person, in-office treatment.

Certainly, Gordon and Lan (2017) deserve praise for this research project, which moves beyond anecdotal claims of success by those providing training and treatment. In a creative design effort, the authors survey graduates about their training and treatment experiences and current clinical practices – a means of seeing just how distance training transfers to subsequent clinical work. They achieve a solid response rate of about 49%, leading to a participant sample of 90 graduates. Their hypotheses are all supported, offering some validation for the effectiveness of the CAPA training programmes in specific and for other distance learning video-conferencing programmes by extension.

But what does this study really tell us, and what issues or questions does it raise? First, the findings strongly suggest that investment is the key to learning. Those graduates who stayed longer in CAPA and worked more intensively in their own psychoanalytic treatment seemed to form stronger identifications with psychoanalytic treatment approaches as clinicians and expressed stronger beliefs about its treatment efficacy, whether delivered in person or via videoconferencing. This has implications for training design, as more in-depth training approaches likely allow for greater integration of theoretical constructs and practices, particularly with a less-structured treatment approach such as a psychodynamic one, which relies heavily on the use of the therapist's self. There is no manualized treatment directive about how to navigate the unconscious or make use of one's counter-transference. Only a strong investment in didactic approaches to theory, making use of the supervisory dyad, and exploring one's own issues in personal treatment can prepare the novice therapist for use of the self as a clinician.

Second, the authors found that CAPA graduates reported 77% of their work reflected psychodynamic case formulations. Additionally, they concluded that new clinicians described practising as psychoanalytic psychotherapists in a way that mirrors their own personal treatment experiences. This is not surprising, as graduates would identify with the treatment approaches they have been taught and with their own therapist's styles and assumptions about therapeutic action. However, this finding may not be as robust as it appears, as there is no outside verification that these graduates are employing a psychoanalytic approach in their practices. While the authors use items from the Comparative Psychotherapy Process Scale (CPPS) (Hilsenroth et al., 2005) as evidence, this is all self-report data. It suggests that these graduates practise similarly to their own established psychoanalytic therapists, but no session material was examined to establish that what graduates say they do in their clinical practice is in fact what they do, and no evaluations were included by supervisors or field experts, who could verify claims of psychoanalytic case conceptualizations. Additionally, extracting a subset of items from a scale rather than using the scale in its entirety does raise questions about reliability and validity for the subscale items.

Third, consistent with other research findings (Gordon, Wang, & Tune, 2015: Scharff, 2015; Wanlass, this volume), the authors found that those who use videoconferencing for treatment and training on a regular basis tend to view it as an effective alternative to in-person treatment and training. What does this finding mean? Are those who immerse themselves in technology-assisted treatment more effective practitioners using this medium? Are they more likely to be trained in the specifics of this treatment modality? Or does the fact that no in-person viable treatment alternative exists for this group of Chinese students cast a favourable lens on this form of service delivery? Does the high degree of investment required to participate in CAPA predispose participants to a favourable view of distance treatment? Certainly, as a practitioner of tele-therapy, I would argue strongly for its effectiveness, but as a researcher, I have to consider all possible explanations for a favourable finding, particularly when participants have little or no in-person experiences as a patient in a traditional in-office psychoanalytic treatment. There may be benefits to tele-therapy that exceed in-office treatment in some instances, or the two service delivery systems may be comparable. We just do not have enough of an empirical research base to draw firm conclusions. This research provides an empirical beginning, and speculations about the meanings of these findings could be explored in future research studies.

Lastly, the authors found that therapist characteristics were more important to their patients than cultural match or type of service delivery (in-office or technology-based). Again, this finding makes intuitive sense and is consistent with well-researched ideas about the importance of the therapeutic relationship, particularly in a psychoanalytic approach, where transference–countertransference issues are its essence. However, I wonder whether or not cultural issues were fully explored. Obviously, the authors could not construct a comparison group of Chinese psychoanalytic clinicians to provide treatment for CAPA students. This is a study for the future, when CAPA graduates become the treating group, which I know is already happening. Perhaps, when these Chinese practitioners become more experienced and treat more patients using a psychoanalytic approach, we can draw firmer and more complex conclusions about the importance of culture. As Western clinicians, we can learn about Chinese culture and consider these influences in our patients' unconscious processes, but our views are inevitably as outsiders looking in, influenced by our own cultures embedded in our self-development. Perhaps we need to consider creative ways to measure the impact of culture on the therapy dyad, not just in China but in our own backyards.

I want to thank Gordon and Lan (2017) for this thoughtful and interesting piece of research, which extends our knowledge base about the use of technology in training and treatment. I agree with the authors' contention that while this is a study of CAPA graduates, it has implications for other psychoanalytic training efforts that utilize technology-based delivery systems. We need more empirical studies to confirm or to refute our anecdotal observations about clinical training and to help us consider how to design strong, effective distance-learning programmes. Distance training and treatment are here to stay, so perhaps we should stop debating whether or not technology-based supervision, teaching, and treatment are viable alternatives and focus our research on illuminating effective technology-based practices, identifying important contraindications or necessary adaptations in the use of technology for providing mental health services, and understanding more about its effects on analytic process.

References

Gordon, R. M, & Lan, J. (2017). Assessing distance training: How well does it produce psychoanalytic psychotherapists? *Psychodynamic Psychiatry*, 45(3): 329–342.

Gordon, R. M., Wang, X., & Tune, J. (2015). Comparing psychodynamic teaching, supervision, and psychotherapy over video-conferencing technology with Chinese students. *Psychodynamic Psychiatry*, 43(4): 585–599.

Hilsenroth, M. J., Blagys, M. D., Ackerman, S. J., Bonge, D. R., & Blais, M. D. (2005). Measuring psychodynamic-interpersonal and cognitive-behavioral techniques: Development of a comparative psychotherapy process scale. *Psychotherapy: Theory, Research, Practice, Training*, 42: 340–356.

Scharff, D. E. (2015). Psychoanalytic teaching by video link and telephone. *Journal of the American Psychoanalytic Association*, 63(3): 443.

Chapter 10

Psychoanalytic teaching by video link and telephone

David E. Scharff

In this era of global connectedness, there is great interest in using distance video platforms such as Skype (which is unfortunately still in use even though it is now known to be insecure), VSee Clinic or Zoom (both secure), as well as the telephone, for conducting psychoanalysis and psychotherapy across geographic distance. Little, however, has been written about the use of technology for psychoanalytic education. The International Psychotherapy Institute has extensive experience in the use of videoconference and telephone technology in the teaching of psychoanalysis and psychoanalytic psychotherapy, including didactic teaching of infant observation, and individual and group supervision, with individuals and groups across the United States and overseas. Use of this technology for tele-education has facilitated the spread of psychoanalytic ideas, recruitment of psychoanalytic and psychotherapeutic trainees, and ongoing training for members living at great distances from one another and from the institute. This work is in many ways similar to ordinary psychoanalytic teaching and supervision, and yet presents significant differences in technique, opportunity, and group dynamics. Further implementation and study of this methodology can greatly aid in the dissemination of psychoanalysis and psychotherapy in the digital age. The digital age of global connectedness has been with us for more than twenty years. Recently, psychoanalysts have focused debate on the legitimacy of modern tools of communication as vehicles for the conduct of clinical psychoanalysis and psychotherapy (Lemma & Caparrotta, 2013; J. Scharff, 2012, 2013a, 2013b, 2015). At the same time, the literature has mostly ignored the unprecedented potential of telecommunication for education and the spread of psychoanalytic ideas and techniques, with the exception of a few articles, including two that discuss the use of Internet-based technologies for education and supervision in China (Fishkin et al., 2011; Alexander-Guerra, 2015). It is my contention here that we can no longer afford to overlook the use of these new vehicles for psychoanalytic education.

The opportunity to take advantage of evolving technologies is not new. The original spread of psychoanalysis from its beginnings in Vienna also took advantage of technology. In that case, it was the ready accessibility of international travel, especially within Europe, made possible by the nineteenth-century development of passenger railroads, and to and from North and South America by ocean travel. Trainees and disciples could make their way to Vienna on a scale not possible in previous centuries. During Freud's lifetime, the telephone became a common means of communication, but with the limited technology of its early days, it was not used to facilitate the further spread of psychoanalysis. Other developing technologies have aided in that dissemination: translations of Freud's works (especially the *Standard Edition)*, relatively low-cost printing that has facilitated the spread of analytic ideas, video interviews of analysts and recorded sessions of treatment for teaching, and even the popularization of psychoanalysis in the 1950s through depictions on film. The recent explosion of technology used for the dissemination of information and knowledge, and for the connection of people living at great distances from one another, has exponentially increased the possibilities for communication and the spread of ideas, offering new and revolutionary possibilities in many fields, including ours. To secure the future of psychoanalysis in the marketplace of ideas and therapies, it is up to us to take full advantage of this. We will need to study the possibilities and potential drawbacks, and understand the impact of evolving technologies on the educational process, as we would any changes in educational approach, while keeping a careful eye on the core of our work.

I will draw here on more than 20 years of experience accumulated in the use of electronic media for the education of psychoanalysts and psychotherapists at the International Psychotherapy Institute (IPI), based in Washington, D.C. I am not referring primarily to the use of the Internet or email to spread published materials, although this too is occurring to unprecedented effect. PEP web has made virtually the entirety of the psychoanalytic literature available to users without their having to leave their offices or homes. Other sites offer blogs, videos for purchase, interviews (e.g., psychotherapy.net), and lectures. The websites of major psychoanalytic and psychotherapy publishers sell eBooks, while other sites distribute free eBooks and lectures, and operate open-access online journals. At a site offered by our institute (www.freepsychotherapybooks.org) there have been more than a million downloads of free books for psychoanalysts, psychotherapists, and psychiatrists in more than 200 countries in the three years since it was launched.

But my focus here is on the use of video communication, and the old-fashioned telephone, in psychoanalytic education. Until recently, psychoanalytic training for the most part had been confined to large cities with a concentration of analysts. This was true even of training in psychoanalytic psychotherapy, which has often had to rely on analysts to teach the much larger group of therapists who desire to think analytically about their work. Professionals living in remote areas who wanted to learn psychoanalysis have had to travel to larger centres (Fonda, 2011), often at the expense of personal and professional hardship. Psychoanalytic candidates from unserved areas often permanently relocated to the larger cities where they trained, or would return to their home area to practise psychoanalysis in relative isolation.

In what follows, I will document the several ways my colleagues and I have used communications media for direct training and supervision. We have accumulated enough experience to describe the effective use of these media, ways of working with virtual classroom dynamics, and how to work with the legal issues and technical glitches likely to accompany its use. We now regularly employ these methods for training in psychoanalysis and psychotherapy. In addition, by teaching psychoanalytic attitudes and skills to psychotherapists in remote areas, we have been able to cultivate interest in psychoanalysis; indeed, several of our long-distance psychotherapy trainees have since become analytic candidates.

First steps towards adopting video technology

Almost 20 years ago, the idea emerged at IPI that it would be possible for students and faculty in various sites to connect in real time with eminent teachers in other states and countries by using the then novel videoconference equipment coming onto the market at relatively low cost (as little as a few thousand dollars). To serve students living all over the U.S. and in Central America, our training programmes had been based on having students travel to Washington, D.C., and some IPI faculty felt that the mounting costs of travel for students and faculty justified our experimenting with less costly ways of programme delivery. There was no pressure on faculty members who were not interested to join in this project, and for the most part those who were reluctant were agreeable to others trying things out. Because the initial venture was solely about teaching, legal issues pertaining to use of the phone or webcam to conduct therapy did not arise. (See the discussion of legal issues below.)

The next level of discussion that occurred with the institute's board of directors concerned issues such as legal considerations, the unproven effectiveness of such a venture, and the financial risks. Because we knew of no other institute widely using such technology for its educational programmes, one board member commented that there were considerable advantages to letting others test the waters first. Nevertheless, the board authorized the venture and its expenditures, asking that we give them regular progress reports.

We began with the purchase of Polycom videoconference equipment in the late 1990s. The equipment had the capacity to link up as many as four sites, with our master site in Washington connecting the other three. (The other sites did not need to have the same brand of equipment, as international standards have ensured compatibility between different brands.) Polycom was a secure service when the connections are run through a central piece of equipment known as a "bridge". Since then, Polycom claims to be "HIPAA-compliant", a designation for security that did not exist at the time of our initial purchase. With this equipment, we initiated a series of monthly seminars by linking the IPI centre in Washington with satellite centres at Westminster College in Salt Lake City, our IPI location in Port Washington, Long Island, and the Tavistock Clinic in London. Through our partnership with the Tavistock, we could draw on eminent analysts and analytic therapists from London for two-hour monthly live-time seminars in the other three cities, and could include students in London as well. Groups of students and faculty assembled in the four cities, each able to talk spontaneously with the other groups and with the invited presenter in lively discussion. Over time, we got to know each other, and when on occasion members of this virtual large-group seminar did meet in person, it was as if they knew one another, although they had never been physically together in the same room. The topics offered were a smorgasbord of analytic ideas and clinical presentations typical of analytic scientific meetings and continuing education courses. We also brought guest faculty to our site in Long Island, an hour's drive from Manhattan with its trove of eminent analysts, and brought local analysts to our national centre in Washington. When a guest was invited to teach in Salt Lake City, we originated the seminar from there.

On an occasion of teaching from London by Anne Alvarez, author of two well-regarded books on analytic therapy with autistic children (1992, 2012), some of the humorous and winning things her children said in therapy brought laughs simultaneously across sites. There was no question that Alvarez's personality and the quality of her clinical sessions could be transmitted through the airwaves, offering a shared and intimate experience of learning. Despite the geographic distance, the group felt connected to her and to one another. This kind of experience would be ordinary in a seminar held in one place in London or New York, but in Salt Lake, which at the time had no analysts, it was quite unusual.

Based on the success of this initial programme, we began two other distance education programmes. We wanted to initiate an infant observation programme for training our psychotherapy trainees and, beginning in 2004, for candidates in psychoanalysis. Lacking the local resource of a faculty member thoroughly steeped in the discipline of infant observation as practised at the Institute of Psychoanalysis in London and at the Tavistock, we arranged with the latter to provide an experienced faculty member to teach the course. The teacher who volunteered, Jeanne Magagna, was willing to face the initial technical difficulties in order to work twice monthly with our students, some of whom had to travel a considerable distance to our Washington or Salt Lake sites for the classes.

Because these programmes were established early in our experience, and also early in the development of the "intranet" (a broadband service used then that was separate from and parallel to the Internet offering a dedicated, more stable connection), there were many dropped calls and inferior connections. (We handled such difficulties by having a technician on standby so that participants could concentrate on the substance of their work together despite interruptions.) Faculty and participants suffered anxiously through these moments when the connection could not be continued on the telephone. However, what surprised all of us, faculty and students alike, was *how much* could be conveyed, communicated, and learned despite the maddening interruptions and technical glitches.

Right from the beginning, we learned that the dynamics of connection and interruption among the three sites of Washington, DC, Salt Lake, and London entered the group process and coloured the understanding of the infant–mother pairs being observed and discussed by the group. We all felt the anxiety attendant on the relative insecurity of the early electronic connection, and we learned to cope with it by speaking about it together. While this has become less of a problem with improvement of equipment and the development of the Internet, technical glitches and dropped calls still remain a factor in distance learning programmes.

What do participants see on the screen?

When our original participants were at a site, sitting with a few others looking at a large video projection screen or television set, they saw three or four squares side by side. Now, with more sites connected in our current use of platforms widely available at reasonable cost, such as Zoom, Webex or VSee, participants manage their reception of the programme, choosing to view only the speaker or the speaker and participants as a few selected sites or up to 25 sites, or speaker plus document or PowerPoint slide.

Examples of distance teaching

The following examples illustrate how we worked with these early experiences to learn about the psychodynamics of joining multiple sites across five thousand miles and three different time zones, as students learned the skills of psychoanalytic infant observation (D. Scharff, 2005a). The first vignette is intended to show a number of things. First, it was one of our early uses of videoconference technology, and shows how we learned to work with it. Second, it shows that a videoconference teaching and learning process is essentially the same as that of an in-person group. Third, I want to demonstrate how the leader and the group can amplify their learning by incorporating experience with the frame, as altered by technology, into the dynamics of its own learning. For readers not accustomed to thinking psychodynamically about group process, my comments about group may seem speculative or arbitrary, so I beg their indulgence. At IPI we have developed a set of theoretical guidelines for use in teaching in groups psychoanalytically, something that will be unfamiliar to many readers (Horwitz, 2014; Scharff & Scharff, 2000, 2014, 2017). The point of using group dynamic interpretations here is that it is our usual way of teaching; we have learned that the group itself can learn to think about its own experience towards the furtherance of learning. In the context of distance learning, thinking about the frame augmented by technology becomes simply one more dimension for study. Through these examples, I hope to illustrate both the ordinariness of the teaching and the attention to the expanded frame that enters into the student experience.

Example I

The first example comes from the initial meeting of the infant observation seminar, in which Jeanne Magagna introduced the methods of infant observation.

She described how students make weekly hour-long naturalistic observations of an infant at home, providing a mode of preparation for working with counter-transference in the conduct of psychoanalysis and psychotherapy. Infant obser-vation seminars had long been used for this purpose at the London Institute for Psychoanalysis and the Tavistock Clinic for training candidates and students (Bick, 1964).

In this first meeting of the seminar, Magagna reviewed the methodology (Miller et al., 1989) and then surveyed the anxieties of students as they contem-plated recruiting families. To detoxify their anticipatory anxiety, she used the educational technique of role playing to rehearse the first interview observers would have with parents. Although role playing was common practice in her small teaching seminars, this was her first experience using it to overcome the spatial separation of the videoconference medium. She made time for participants at both sites to voice their worries and ambivalence about asking families to let observers view their babies. Then, to get them used to communicating across the miles, Magagna suggested from London that the student who role played the would-be observer be in Washington, and those playing the parents be in Salt Lake. She asked other seminar members from both sites to report on their impres-sion of what they expected they would feel in the place of each of the role players. This educational method let the group members put themselves in the shoes of all participants of an observation, both the observer and the parents. (In this example, the baby to be observed had not yet been born.) More important in convening a seminar by video link, it placed students at sites geographically remote from each other in an intimate exchange as they conjectured about the psychology of the unfamiliar infant observation situation. The role playing was helpful in educat-ing students in their new venture, but it was even more effective in providing a bond for the learning project between students not in the same room. They found they were able to talk across the distance, use each other's empathy, correct each other's perceptions, and experience relief in finding shared anxieties. It also heightened the experience of asking an unknown person for permission to be in their intimate space, perhaps more so than had everyone been in the same room working together as local colleagues. One student commented that in this sense each person was a kind of "new baby" for everyone else involved.

In the next meeting, a student in Washington, the first to have located a baby to observe, reported on her first observation of the newborn with her mother as she would have done in an ordinary infant observation seminar with all students in the same room. The focus on this first infant let other group members secure their bond and learn about beginnings together. In each subsequent week, before that first student in Washington reported, Magagna asked a student in Salt Lake to review the observations from the previous meeting of the seminar and to give her own understanding of the issues. This arrangement allowed active partici-pation at both sites. I speculated to the group that this arrangement was analo-gous to pulling together a blended family, and through discussion of this point they generally agreed that they were in a blended learning family, separated by distance and by living in two rather different professional cultures, but joined through shared interest in an educational venture. From this point on, Magagna worked with the students in Salt Lake to support their recruitment of families for observation, and when the first of their members soon found a baby to observe, they felt a new sense of balance between the two sites. Soon several infants were being observed at both sites, and the two subgroups came to feel like equal participants. At this point, the story of the seminar became more or less the story of an ordinary seminar employing the infant observational method of psychoanalytic education. However, as in any group considered analytically, the dynamics of the group itself continued to be of interest in the study of the infants and their families. There were periods of friendly competition between the groups, with the interaction with Magagna representing a new triadic interaction, much like the expansion from a couple to a family with the birth of a baby. These matters were in the background, but Magagna or I occasionally called attention to them when we felt it might illuminate the learning. In each case the group would consider our process comments, discussing whether there was overlap in their experience that influenced how they understood the mother-infant pair under study. In this way we could see that the composition of the group made possible by the technology could be used to illustrate family and mother-child issues.

Example 2

My second example of the experience of conducting teaching and learning through the video link medium is meant to illustrate the action of group dynamics when more than one distant site is involved in the teaching. It concerns the study of that first baby, who I'll call Michele. She was born into a family in which her mother's attention was distracted by the rivalry of Michele's 2-year-old brother. The seminar participants at both sites experienced the drama of Michele's fight for room, striving to come to life in a family that was ambivalent about giving her space. It was difficult for the group to tolerate reports of the inattention of a mother who was preoccupied with a demanding older toddler, who at times seemed to our group members to be the villain of the piece. Nevertheless, the liveliness of the entire family, and of the student who conducted the observation, infused the group with energy and carried their hopes not only for the infant's development but also for their own progress and learning. This led to some idealization of the process. Over the months, the group was relieved to see that baby Michele secured her place with her mother by competing quietly but competently with her brother, who then seemed less like an imposing ogre and more like an anxious 2 year old.

During the seminar, I commented on how the dynamics of the two groups of seminar members echoed the struggles of the family they were observing. I speculated that the Salt Lake group might feel like a second child who did not have her own space because they did not yet have a baby of their own to observe, and so had to fight for space to relate to their teacher. There were also more students in Washington, and I was there with my own experience of infant observation, while our faculty member in Salt Lake, though skilled and enthusiastic, had never done an infant observation herself. Group members carefully considered my comments.

A member in Salt Lake said that though Magagna skilfully gave Salt Lake its turn and paid attention to students there, she felt they had been like the younger, lesser sibs. A bit later, as they began to present their own infants, they said they now felt they were coming into their own. I commented on the parallel with how baby Michele had claimed a space with her mother and the relief and pleasure the mother took in making a more secure bond with the infant, just as now Magagna and the Salt Lake students created a more robust working bond for which I could now see that the entire group had been saving space. Members in both groups confirmed my observation, and there was a kind of humorous pleasure in recognizing the parallel between the group process and that of the infant and her family. In this overlap of themes, learning about the infant and learning about the group's experience of itself were mutually strengthened. While discussions about the overlap of group dynamics and the dynamics of the mother and infant being studied do not come up often, they can be usefully addressed when they do.

Discussion

The dynamics of this seminar, divided by miles and joined by technology, resembled the dynamics of any learning group made up of subgroups. Use of videoconference technology and the existence of two geographic subgroups here amplified certain aspects of the group's unconscious anxieties which could then be used metaphorically to illustrate the situation being examined. They could be understood and worked with using the same internal monitoring processes that an experienced psychoanalytic teacher would use in teaching any seminar group. The members of the group were all steeped in IPI's use of group dynamics for education, and I had previously introduced the idea of having the group look at and process its own experience of the infant observation seminar as an affective learning group. That is our usual way of conducting learning groups at IPI (D. Scharff, 2005b; Scharff & Scharff, 2000, 2017). In this case we found that as long as we held in mind that the group was composed of subgroups at the separate sites, we could do the same work we would do with a psychodynamic learning group physically sitting in a room together.

The group members had to tolerate uncomfortable feelings as they observed siblings fighting for attention. This process parallels the need for analysts to contain the discomfort so often felt in the therapeutic encounter where reflection needs to replace a call to action. Indeed, learning about this capacity is one lesson that infant observation holds for future analysts, although of course there are many other opportunities in analytic education to build this capacity. But in this particular seminar, we also felt the impact of dynamics introduced by the technology itself, which could "drop us" by disconnecting us without warning. The experience of these "drops" had to be processed, as did the way the technological joining of groups represented a kind of new learning-family structure, in which we were all new, experimental babies, unclear *how* or even *if* our project would work. While this analogy may be a stretch for some readers, it seemed to the group's members to be a useful metaphor for thinking about themselves as subjects of this learning experiment. Using this analogy, the group was able to discuss how the anxiety infusing the whole experience mixed with the anxieties intrinsic to all infant observation and to the observation of the particular families we studied. I leave it to the reader to decide if the interpretations we made are convincing, but that is not my aim in introducing them. Instead, I wish to illustrate that the analogy gives a metaphorical language for discussing the tensions between subgroups operating at a distance. Because this was a familiar way of thinking for our group when learning in person, it could also be applied to the situation of distance learning made possible through video technology.

Further developments in videoconference and telephone supervision

Given the success of the video seminars and the infant observation programme, we next instituted distance group supervision. In Salt Lake City at the time, there were no resident analysts; an experienced psychoanalytic psychotherapist who had been one of our founding faculty members had been alone in teaching students at the site. With her active support, another faculty member and I used our videoconference system to offer psychodynamic supervision of individual cases to two groups of clinicians in Salt Lake. This supervision continued for several years and brought a level of experience to Salt Lake not otherwise available, helping to teach the process of analytic thinking about cases, and increasing group members' interest in analytic therapy. These meetings had the added benefit of solidifying a group of colleagues in Salt Lake who had had no vehicle for sharing their psychodynamic work and so had operated in relative isolation. After several years, some of these participants wanted analytic training that they could not get locally. So the early distance learning programmes led to the development of the International Institute for Psychoanalytic Training, an advanced four-year distance learning programme, and the current online courses stand alone and also recruit for the analytic programme.

An example from distance group supervision

The following example, like the one presented later of an analytic case conference, is meant to demonstrate that the work of analytic teaching and supervision is fully possible when assisted by technology. An analyst reading these examples might well feel that there is nothing unusual about them in that they are essentially the same kind of work usually done in face-to-face teaching. That is indeed my point in presenting them.

Some years ago, a group of six Salt Lake City clinicians requested that I supervise them via videoconference for two-hour sessions twice a month. Each of the six presented an ongoing case every third session, with an hour for presentation and discussion. One clinician, Colleen Sandor, has published her experience of this group supervision (Sandor, 2014) and has given permission for my use of her experience here. She presented a severely traumatized young woman whose mother had openly expressed wanting her dead, and who had been subjected to boundary violations from a previous therapist, who the patient had then attacked in fear and retaliation.

On this day, Sandor reported a turbulent session. The patient had begun by paying her, as she usually did, but on this occasion paid only half the usual amount. When Sandor asked about this, the patient got extremely angry. The anger mounted through the session, and Sandor's interpretive comments only seemed to drive the anger. She reported to the group (who were in Salt Lake City with her) and to me (in Washington, DC) that she felt she had lost her capacity to think. The patient talked about wishes to harm her, recalling another session in which the patient was shouting and Sandor had feared she might strike her. On the earlier occasion, one of the group members had been working in a neighbouring office and had considered coming to intervene.

From my point of view as supervisor, the situation was this: a talented but relatively untrained therapist, with the guidance of the supervision, was attempting an in-depth treatment of an exceedingly difficult and traumatized patient. I had found Sandor sturdy and thoughtful as she learned to tolerate the patient's hurt, longing and fear, the transference version of what the patient had experienced with her murderous mother. This session came after months of careful preparation in which Sandor had built up her tolerance of the patient's anger so it could be given space in the transference field.

Several times during the reporting of this session we paused to take comments from members of the group. In her published article reporting the supervision, Sandor commented on the differentiated and helpful role played by each member of the group. One member, acting as the emotional barometer, commented thoughtfully about the patient's anger. This helped Sandor think about the patient's hostility and her own anger in response, which gave her the feeling of being stuck in the middle of a power struggle. Another member identified with the difficulty of just staying in the room in the middle of the storm and commented on how Sandor's presence had allowed the patient to regress in safety. Another commented on the transference situation, while a fourth helped Sandor see how both she and the patient had "lost their mind" in the storm, increasing the amount of fear in the room. After facilitating and drawing out discussion about these elements, I pointed out the enactment in the opening discussion about the fee, saying that it was an attack on the treatment and on the therapist as a maternal transference object. In this attack, the patient turned her "good mother" therapist into a persecuting, depriving mother. It was the setting of the limit about the fee that allowed the transference to flow, although both patient and therapist then experienced the loss of ego boundaries that so often threatened the patient, just as they had characterized the patient's experience with her primitive mother and later with her previous, boundary-violating therapist. Because Sandor was so uncomfortable with the patient's anger, she began to placate it, but what had been more effective was her quiet and steady acceptance of the anger. I suggested that instead of tying the anger directly to the patient's mother she might begin by saying something like, "You feel I am torturing you and you're having to pay me for doing it, while you feel you are doing enough by paying me anything at all." I said that constant attention to the boundaries and frame of the therapy was of prime importance in safeguarding the work. I predicted, with humorous irony, that if the therapy went well, there would be more sessions in which the patient could express her hate. That would be an achievement made possible by Sandor's growing capacity for containment and understanding. Easy for me to say from the safety of being two thousand miles away. The group laughed, and Sandor relaxed considerably.

What I found remarkable in this session, as in so many of the meetings with this group, was how closely it resembled supervisory experiences with a group physically in the same room with me. The emotional responsiveness of the group, the differentiated activity of various members, and the capacity for thoughtfulness and for humour were all familiar, as was the obvious growth of the members in their cognitive understanding of the therapeutic process and their capacity for emotional attunement and facilitation. Each patient–therapist pair had a different pattern, and the group would have a differentiated emotional flavour when discussing each case, as when another therapist in the group presented a delightful, inventive 6-year-old girl, whose corrections of the therapist and whose discovery that "You know, I can be a lot like Flora sometimes!" (the somewhat obnoxious girl doll of the play therapy) made the patient an exciting object for the group, a girl we all looked forward to hearing about.

In her paper, Sandor (2014) wrote about her group supervision experience:

> The internal supervision group [which she carried away from experience with the group and with me] served as my benevolent "internal gang" and held me during this moment. Their support allowed me to recover from a stalemate . . . Then when we met in supervision after the session, their responses helped me to understand that the patient had felt threatened in the therapy process, had regressed, and had a difficult time distinguishing me from her mother.
>
> (p. 112)

This kind of internalization of the supervisory experience is what we always hope for. In this case, the internalization of the supervision happened in a way and at a pace that was indistinguishable from in-person supervision. These supervisions also began a path that led to the development of candidates for our psychoanalytic programme by 2005. Sandor and the therapist of the "exciting girl" patient both eventually became analytic trainees and have since qualified as analysts. Because they are also faculty members at Westminster College, our partner institution in Salt Lake City, through them the college has established a clinical graduate programme with an analytic focus that allowed other students to benefit from our distance learning programmes. In turn, several students from this next generation enrolled in our analytic psychotherapy and psychoanalytic programmes, which include residential experiences in Washington.

Having offered distance supervision, both individual and group, by videoconference, we have found that an effective group can also be convened on the telephone, provided the participants already know each other from face-to-face contact and have written material to focus on. We regularly employ written transcripts when doing group distance supervision, especially, as is now common, when the participants are spread among several sites, and especially because English is not always the first language of all members. Members of our telephone groups call into a conference number from their offices, the transcript having been distributed ahead of time so that everyone, including the supervisor, looks at the material simultaneously. (These transcripts are encrypted and password-protected before being emailed to members of the group.) This is now also the preferred method for the conduct of our infant observation training.

Multiple video connections are now possible using platforms such as Zoom, Webex, VSee and Skype, and up to 50 or more connections using other commercially available programmes. There are three reasons we do not use Skype itself. First, the reliability of the connection is better on other platforms or on the phone. Second, there are concerns about the security of Skype, which is not certified as HIPAA-competent, whereas VSee, Zoom and Webex offer upgrades to HIPAA-competent versions that include a Business Associate Agreement that the clinician signs as a further protection beyond the usual encryption. Third, members are essentially focused on the discussion of transcripts in any event, and because they know each other from intensive meetings, the importance of meeting face-to-face diminishes. Nevertheless, the lack of visual contact does pose some difficulty, as people have to talk over each other to be heard. It requires more attentiveness from the teacher to regulate discussion. On the benefit side, the situation simulates the process of sitting behind an analytic patient and listening carefully without benefit of full face-to-face contact. Reliability, quality, security, and cost of video technology have improved, and it is now less expensive than telephone conference. Consequently we have moved almost all our seminars, group supervisions, and most individual supervisions onto secure Internet platforms.

Technical problems and disruptions in distance learning

Our consideration of distance learning would not be complete without some mention of the technical difficulties encountered. Writers have noted regularly that dropped calls disrupt tele-psychoanalysis and telepsychotherapy, and even with the telephone there can be occasional problems. Similar problems attend videoconferencing, even at the advanced technical level we now employ. In the beginning, there were frequent disruptions, along with the anxiety attendant on correcting them. Although less frequent today, such problems are still with us. We are more likely to have repeated difficulty with certain sites or with a member attempting to connect from a personal computer or iPad. Often these problems are due to inadequate bandwidth at that site. Some sites have had difficulty so often that they expect it and have telephone backup at the ready. In the past, these issues made it almost imperative to have an audiovisual technician in attendance or at least on standby, but this is no longer necessary. The telephone is generally more reliable, but telephone conferencing systems too are subject to occasional problems. We might liken these to problems of weather or traffic for students who attend courses in person: no arrangement, even local gatherings, can be guaranteed to be problem-free on all occasions.

Nevertheless, what has struck my colleagues and me from the beginning 20 years ago is *how much it is possible to learn*, despite the glitches and the anxiety that attends them. Beginning with our early infant observation and seminar programmes, and with the early group supervisions, teaching and learning of an ordinary sort have been possible through thick and thin. The basic fact that distance can be conquered to let us offer high-quality learning has always held.

Legal issues

From the beginning of our venture into this realm, faculty and members of our board of trustees considered the legal risks of discussing clinical material via videoconference and telephone. Legal consultation has helped us move forward with confidence. Unlike the situation where treatment is conducted electronically across state lines, the issue of licensure does not arise where teaching is concerned. When we offer teaching sessions that include continuous case conferences, we are clear that the teaching analyst or analytic psychotherapist is acting in a purely didactic capacity, not as a supervisor responsible for the conduct of a case.

Different considerations apply, however, for supervision or consultation to cases by an analytic supervisor. First, ethical concerns apply. Because ethical codes regarding tele-supervision are specific to each discipline, clinicians must observe the rules governing the discipline in which they are qualified (Wanlass, 2015). Another concern is the variation in regulations from state to state. Since each state's regulations are different, it is the responsibility of supervisors to determine the rules that apply in their home state and in the state of their supervisees. Wanlass (2015) reports that McAdams and Wyatt (2010), in an investigation into state regulatory practices, found that regulations had been promulgated for telephonic supervision and consultation in only 13 per cent of states, with another 30 per cent considering such action. While few state boards forbade telephonic supervision, most suggested informed consent, restricted use by unlicensed professionals, and promoted the development of graduate coursework in the ethical, competent practice of telemental health with HIPAA-compliant service delivery. They also recommended the identification of local supervisors to assist with emergencies. Wanlass suggests that supervisors who plan to offer supervision across state lines may want to obtain permission from the licensing boards of both states before doing so. It is not uncommon for a supervisor to decide not to abide by particularly restrictive or onerous regulations, but this of course carries legal risks, even if they seem remote.

Recent developments

Ten years ago, IPI established a twice-monthly course in couple psychoanalysis, using the electronic bridge at Westminster College, in partnership with Tavistock Relationships in London, the oldest, most established training and research institution centred on couples and marriage in the English-speaking psychoanalytic sphere. That partnership enabled us to reach students globally, offering twice-monthly live seminars and distance telephone supervision to trainees around the world. Senior analysts from the International Psychoanalytical Association's Committee on Family and Couple Psychoanalysis (COFAP) have also taught from sites around the world. COFAP's most recent course featured psychoanalysts teaching from five countries outside the United States. In the current version of the course, the screen has been filled with more than 50 participants, joining from across the United States, as well as from Panama, Honduras, Israel, Turkey, Greece, Iran, China, Lithuania, Latvia, Poland, Taiwan, Hong Kong, England, and South Africa – all connected in live time. On the screen, the boxes showing participants are large enough to show recognizable faces, but in some platforms they may be too small for sharing the written materials that often accompany presentations. So instead of showing PowerPoint slides or illustrations like children's drawings when using those platforms, we distribute them electronically ahead of time so that participants can follow along with the presenter. In addition, for those wishing to engage in a more complete training, we offer individual and group supervision by phone, mentoring, and the option of attendance in person at seminars in Washington, DC or at our summer institutes, held over the last few years in Salt Lake City, Panama; London; and Rhodes, Greece.

Progress in distance supervision and group teaching

In other recent developments, I have offered group supervision by video connection to a group in Moscow, and another faculty member and I give live group supervision to students in China, as does one of my colleagues. I use the programme Zoom, which allows for up to fifty participants to be seen onscreen and provides adequate space for a document or PowerPoint slide. Participants are connected from their own computers, each person appearing in a separate small screen in which they are clearly recognizable. Additionally, because most of our Chinese and Russian supervisees do not have adequate English, we use a translator for the presentations and group discussion. Whenever possible, I prefer the presentation to be translated ahead of time for the sake of efficiency, leaving more time for discussion of a case. The Chinese supervisees for the most part come from a training programme in couple and family psychoanalysis that we now offer in Beijing to therapists from across China and Taiwan who come to Beijing twice yearly for six-day courses. Russian students connect from around the country and travel once a year to meet us in person for an immersion training in Moscow. In this way we can offer regular group supervision from a distance to the most advanced trainees. This establishes the kind of continuity essential to substantial clinical growth. Our hope is to train a cadre of Chinese and Russian clinicians who will eventually be able to conduct the training themselves. Over the years, we have experienced increased use of distance supervision and class teaching. Much of this was originally done via telephone. Since our psychotherapy and psychoanalytic trainees come from all around the United States, from Panama, and from as far away as Europe, individual and group supervision is now done equally easily on a secure Internet platform. Students in our programmes – psychoanalytic training, or beginning and advanced psychotherapy training – typically come together in person five times a year (seven days in the summer and four three-day weekends), usually in Washington. In the weekend programmes, there is often a well-known guest analyst with whom the students and faculty engage over the three days. In between these in-person seminars, we offer monthly or weekly seminars and/or group supervision by Zoom, Webex or telephone to give continuity to the training.

Establishment of a distance psychoanalytic training programme

In 2003 we established a psychoanalytic training programme, the practicalities of which are based on the distance learning principles we learned earlier in teaching analytic psychotherapy. Although some candidates come from the Washington area, most commute to us from distant places, many from outside the United States, because analytic training is not available where they live, they are drawn to our particular orientation in psychoanalytic object relations theory, or they value the group affective learning model. In the programme, candidates meet together with faculty in person for five days each summer and for four three-day weekend teaching programmes each year for the four years of the training. These seventeen days annually in which they are together in person with faculty provide time for close study and clinical examination, as well as for daily small affective learning groups that integrate theoretical learning, clinical work, and personal experience (Scharff & Scharff, 2000, 2014, 2017). To maintain continuity in the educational experience when candidates are back home, they attend weekly seminars conducted via Internet conferencing. These seminars alternate between clinical case conferences and theoretical material. The number of didactic and clinical teaching hours each year is equivalent to programmes at institutes of the American Psychoanalytic and International Psychoanalytical Associations. Weekly supervision of analytic cases is done in person, whenever possible, or by telephone or Internet communication, preferably one of the new, HIPAA-compliant ones, depending on the preference of the supervisory pair. While my own preference, whether on the phone or using a video connection, is to use the candidate's written process notes so that we are looking at the same material, other supervisors have varying requirements. (The notes, of course, are transmitted in encrypted form.) Meetings of the analytic and supervisory faculty (including planning sessions and committee meetings, such as meetings to discuss candidate progress) take place both when faculty members are together for summer or weekend teaching and by Internet or telephone conference call in the intervals.

An analytic continuous case conference via telephone

Some years ago, I taught a continuous case conference for a cohort of analytic candidates. The point I wish to illustrate in presenting this example is that ordinary teaching, usually indistinguishable from in-person teaching, is possible at a distance. These case conferences aim to explore candidates' ways of working and to illustrate theory being taught during the same period. We do not aim to conduct supervision, since candidates have their own supervisors. As we move through the sessions that are presented, we encourage the group to think of what the presenting analyst might have in mind, and to explore the ongoing process of the analysis, while not presuming to "know better than" the presenter.

The following example occurred on teleconference call, years before we moved to an Internet platform. The candidates dialled the conference call number (they paid only for their own long-distance call; if from a cell phone, there was no charge). They were calling from cities such as Manchester (New Hampshire), Burlington (Vermont), Indianapolis, Tampa, Salt Lake City, Panama City (Panama), and London. I called in one or two minutes before our starting time, with the presenting candidate's electronically pre-circulated transcript in front of me. As the candidates announced themselves one by one, I took roll, and then, at the appointed time, the presenter began to read the transcript aloud.

On the first day of this continuous case, Sandra, who was reporting in from Manchester, New Hampshire, where she lives and works, read a two-page summary of her analysand's history. Even though the five other candidates and I had the history in front of us, her reading allowed us to stop when any member of the group had a question or comment, and it gave the group a shared experience. (The following case material has been thoroughly disguised and is summarized here with Sandra's permission. Manchester is a city similar in size to Sandra's, but is not the actual city.) The analysand was in her late thirties, married with a preadolescent child. Sandra's brief history included a summary of the two years of preliminary psychotherapy. During this time, the patient had realized she had always felt neglected and overlooked. She had begun to see her ongoing affair with her rabbi as an attempt to fill a void. The patient has doted on her only child in compensation, while pronouncing her marriage dead. She tends to take on needy, helpless people in ways that often swamp her own needs. (The group had already had several sessions discussing a different case with another IPI faculty member, so they were used to a mode of thinking collaboratively, rather than of "one-upping" the presenter. This attitude was demonstrated in the thoughtful attitude of the discussion right from the beginning. They now entered into a brief discussion of the history, wondering what form the neediness and "acting out" of affairs might take in the transference.)

As I asked her to, Sandra listened silently, taking in the ideas and speculation. At the end of the group's discussion, she said their ideas had reminded her that once during the two years of psychotherapy, before the patient had herself asked to increase the frequency – essentially asking for analysis – the patient had suddenly hugged Sandra at the end of a session. Sandra had been stunned, unable to think about the meaning of this. Now she wondered if this brief physical contact would ruin the prospects for analysis, despite her feeling that the patient was moving towards being more thoughtful and reflective.

(The group now discussed the situation, empathizing not only with Sandra's discomfort but also with her fears that she had done something wrong that might compromise or ruin the analysis. They decided that this fear was a countertransference internalization of the patient's own sense of having done something wrong; something that she had said had "ruined everything in [her] life".)

I had asked Sandra to present the first analytic session with her patient, because I have found that the content, form, and transference right at the beginning of analysis often presage later developments.

Sandra recounted the first session. The patient, lying down on the couch for the first time, began by noting how "ready" the room and couch were for her and complimenting Sandra on this readiness. The patient had talked with her husband about her doubts, and he had told her, "Go ahead and start." She said to Sandra, "I mean, you're training. You're a candidate. I mean have you done this before? I mean you are picking me and I am, too." The patient's speech seemed choppy, ambiguous, and more disconnected than Sandra was used to.

(We interrupted the presentation again for group discussion. The group considered the way this reference to the husband was a variant of the theme of the affair he might unconsciously be giving the patient permission for. The patient's choppy speech showed her anxiety and perhaps some early developmental disorganization that was being demonstrated in these beginning moments. Group members wondered if this had something to do with the patient's being on the couch for the first time, despite her complimenting Sandra. But the patient had also emphasized the mutuality and partnership she was counting on.)

Sandra picked up the presentation with the next part of the session: the patient went on to talk about the frame and expectations regarding payment and cancellations. The patient wondered if Sandra had done this work before. Sandra told her she had been working in similar ways for several years but was now formalizing her training. The patient continued and said she was working on catching what came across her mind. Sandra encouraged this. The patient seemed to be trembling. She adjusted her position on the couch and soon said, "That fly is trapped in your window. I hate flies. There's no way out for him." Sandra asked what thoughts followed. The patient said, "I'm trapped without a way out . . . in my marriage. . . . Trapped inside myself, a little girl inside me." And a little later: "In every picture from my childhood, I look lost. My mother didn't notice me. I just wanted someone to notice." Sandra said, "Maybe you want to be noticed here so you won't feel trapped like the fly in my window." At the end of the session, the patient said, "Well, I did it! See you tomorrow."

The group now noted the early transference of alternating trust and fear of being trapped. They appreciated that Sandra had seen and commented on the fear that the analysis might feel like it was going to trap the patient, who was seeing the window that had the fly trapped in it from a new angle, since she was lying on the couch for the first time. I said that her comment here was an important early transference interpretation, precisely because it picked up fear about analysis and was likely to give the patient the reassurance of having her fear of the analysis understood. I noted that this point referred to previous didactic teaching on the importance of paying attention to issues of mistrust from the beginning of analytic work. I also noted that it might also refer to Sandra's own background fear that, in presenting to the group, she could be trapped in the web of the group's thinking, having her work so closely scrutinized through the "window" of the group's observation. Sandra confirmed that she had worries about presenting to the group and to me in this forum. Her colleagues reassured her that they were learning and had appreciated her efforts and her clarity, and that they could easily put themselves in her shoes.

In this vignette, with students each participating from their own office (some in distant countries), telephone technology and use of the Internet to circulate encrypted clinical material offered high-quality teaching and continuity of learning to candidates who could not meet together in person once a week. This continuous case discussion has a feel that will be familiar to teachers and candidates in a similar situation. Although the telephone was a satisfactory vehicle for connection, we have now moved to videoconference face-to-face communication, which gives an added sense of connectedness.

To complete the profile of our distance-learning psychoanalytic training I note also that, as a central part of training, candidates' personal analyses may be conducted by a combination of in-person and distance meetings if there is no suitable analyst available locally for the candidate. In such distance meetings for analysis, analysand and analyst meet through video connection or telephone, depending on their preference. This use of distance technology for clinical psychoanalysis is the subject of wide interest and debate in the analytic community (see Carlino, 2011; Lemma & Caparrotta, 2013; J. Scharff, 2012, 2013a, 2013b, 2015; Zalusky, 2005).

Candidates' personal analyses are central in our training programme, as in traditional, locally based programmes and in "geographic" programmes that have employed "shuttle analysis" to deal with the problem of providing training in areas lacking a local psychoanalytic faculty (Fonda, 2011). Recent training psychoanalyses for the implementation of psychoanalytic training in China have relied on the use of Skype and other platforms after (in some cases) an extensive initial in-person period of analysis (Dettbarn, 2013). Some institutes of the American Psychoanalytic Association now employ distance analysis for candidates in cases where special circumstances and geography require it (Richard Zeitner, personal communication), and the International Psychoanalytical Association has recently developed a position statement on the use of technology in remote analysis in the training of candidates in combination with in-person analysis. We have also put together continuing education seminars by Internet to support the graduate analysts of our programme as we begin developing an analytic society for faculty and graduate analysts separated by the same distances that face our trainees.

Concluding remarks

Increasingly we live and work in a connected global community. Developments in technology over the last thirty years offer an unparalleled opportunity for the spread of knowledge in all fields, including psychoanalysis and psychotherapy. In this wired and interconnected world, we cannot afford to ignore opportunities that are only now available for the spread of knowledge and training in psychoanalysis and psychoanalytic psychotherapy. I believe that what is central to psychoanalysis is the process attained by patient and analyst. Similarly, what is central to analytic education is the actual teaching and learning achieved by students and candidates, as developed by the teacher–student pair and the teacher–candidate group. Thus, whenever the use of video and telephone technology can enhance educational opportunities, it should be employed, with due attention of course to the processes and dynamics of the distance-learning situation.

References

Alexander-Guerra, L. (2015). Not so lost in translation: Supervising psychoanalytic psychotherapy candidates in China. *Psychoanalysis & Psychotherapy in China*, 1: 150–157.

Alvarez, A. (1992). *Live Company*. Hove: Routledge.

Alvarez, A. (2012). *The Thinking Heart*. Hove: Routledge.

Bick, E. (1964). Notes on infant observation in psycho-analytic training. *International Journal of Psychoanalysis*, 45: 558–566.

Carlino, R. (2011). *Distance Psychoanalysis: The Theory and Practice of Using Communication Technology in the Clinic*. London: Karnac.

Dettbarn, I. (2013). Skype as the uncanny third. In: J. S. Scharff (Ed.), *Psychoanalysis Online: Mental Health, Therapy, and Training* (pp. 15–25). London: Karnac.

Fishkin, R., Fishkin, L., Leu, U., Katz, B., & Snyder, E. (2011). Psychodynamic treatment, training, and supervision using internet-based technologies. *Journal of the American Academy of Psychoanalysis & Dynamic Psychiatry*, 39: 155–168.

Fonda, P. (2011). A virtual training institute in Eastern Europe. *International Journal of Psychoanalysis*, 92: 695–713.

Horwitz, L. (2014). *Listening with the Fourth Ear: Unconscious Dynamics in Analytic Group Therapy*. London: Karnac.

Lemma, A., & Caparrotta, L. (2013). *Psychoanalysis in the Technoculture Era*. London: Karnac.

McAdams, C. R., & Wyatt, K. L. (2010). The regulation of technology-assisted distance counseling and supervision in the United States: An analysis of current extent, trends, and implications. *Counselor Education & Supervision*, 49: 179–192.

Miller, L., Rustin, M. E., Rustin, M. J., & Shuttleworth, J. (Eds.). (1989). *Closely Observed Infants*. London: Duckworth.

Sandor, C. (2014). The group supervision model. In: J. S. Scharff (Ed.), *Clinical Supervision of Psychoanalytic Psychotherapy* (pp. 105–124). London: Karnac.

Scharff, D. E. (2005a). Conquering geographic space: Teaching psychoanalytic psychotherapy and infant observation by video link. In M. Stadter & D. E. Scharff (Eds.), *Dimensions of Psychotherapy, Dimensions of Experience: Time, Space, Number and State of Mind* (pp. 115–125). Hove: Routledge.

Scharff, D. E. (2005b). Infant observation augmented by the affective learning experience. In: J. Magagna, N. Bakalar, H. Cooper, J. Levy, C. Norman, & C. Shank (Eds.), *Intimate Transformations: Babies with Their Families* (pp. 198–211). London: Karnac.

Scharff, J. S. (2012). Clinical issues in analysis over the telephone and the internet. *International Journal of Psychoanalysis*, 93: 81–95.

Scharff, J. S. (2013a). Technology-assisted psychoanalysis. *Journal of the American Psychoanalytic Association*, 61: 491–509.

Scharff, J. S. (Ed.). (2013b). *Psychoanalysis Online*. London: Karnac.

Scharff, J. S. (Ed.). (2015). *Psychoanalysis Online 2*. London: Karnac.

Scharff, J. S., & Scharff, D. E. (2000). *Tuning the Therapeutic Instrument*. Northvale, NJ: Aronson.

Scharff, J. S., & Scharff, D. E. (2014). Das affektbasierte Ausbildungsmodell fur die Ausbildung in psychoanalytischer Theorie und klinischer Praxis der psychoanalytischen Psychotherapie und Psychoanalyse [The Group Affective Model of learning psychoanalytic theory and clinical practice of psychoanalytic psychotherapy and psychoanalysis]. *Psyche 11*: 1132–1163.

Scharff, J. S. & Scharff, D. E. (2017). Group affective learning in training for psychotherapy and psychoanalysis. *International Journal of Psychoanalysis*, 98(6): 1619–1639.

Wanlass, J. (2015). The use of technology in clinical supervision and consultation. In: J. S. Scharff (Ed.), *Psychoanalysis Online 2* (pp. 123–132). London: Karnac.

Zalusky, S. (2005). Telephone psychotherapy and the 21st century. In: M. Stadter & D. E. Scharff (Eds.), *Dimensions of Psychotherapy, Dimensions of Experience: Time, Space, Number and State of Mind* (pp. 107–114). London: Routledge.

Index

For Product Safety Concerns and Information please contact our EU
representative GPSR@taylorandfrancis.com
Taylor & Francis Verlag GmbH, Kaufingerstraße 24, 80331 München, Germany

9 781138 312425